T0212919

Communications in Computer and Information Science 1603

Editorial Board Members

Joaquim Filipe ⓘ
Polytechnic Institute of Setúbal, Setúbal, Portugal

Ashish Ghosh
Indian Statistical Institute, Kolkata, India

Raquel Oliveira Prates ⓘ
Federal University of Minas Gerais (UFMG), Belo Horizonte, Brazil

Lizhu Zhou
Tsinghua University, Beijing, China

More information about this series at https://link.springer.com/bookseries/7899

Johanna Barzen · Frank Leymann ·
Schahram Dustdar (Eds.)

Service-Oriented Computing

16th Symposium and Summer School, SummerSOC 2022
Hersonissos, Crete, Greece, July 3–9, 2022
Revised Selected Papers

Springer

Editors
Johanna Barzen (ID)
University of Stuttgart
Stuttgart, Germany

Frank Leymann (ID)
University of Stuttgart
Stuttgart, Germany

Schahram Dustdar (ID)
TU Wien
Vienna, Austria

ISSN 1865-0929   ISSN 1865-0937 (electronic)
Communications in Computer and Information Science
ISBN 978-3-031-18303-4   ISBN 978-3-031-18304-1 (eBook)
https://doi.org/10.1007/978-3-031-18304-1

© The Editor(s) (if applicable) and The Author(s), under exclusive license
to Springer Nature Switzerland AG 2022
This work is subject to copyright. All rights are reserved by the Publisher, whether the whole or part of the material is concerned, specifically the rights of translation, reprinting, reuse of illustrations, recitation, broadcasting, reproduction on microfilms or in any other physical way, and transmission or information storage and retrieval, electronic adaptation, computer software, or by similar or dissimilar methodology now known or hereafter developed.
The use of general descriptive names, registered names, trademarks, service marks, etc. in this publication does not imply, even in the absence of a specific statement, that such names are exempt from the relevant protective laws and regulations and therefore free for general use.
The publisher, the authors, and the editors are safe to assume that the advice and information in this book are believed to be true and accurate at the date of publication. Neither the publisher nor the authors or the editors give a warranty, expressed or implied, with respect to the material contained herein or for any errors or omissions that may have been made. The publisher remains neutral with regard to jurisdictional claims in published maps and institutional affiliations.

This Springer imprint is published by the registered company Springer Nature Switzerland AG
The registered company address is: Gewerbestrasse 11, 6330 Cham, Switzerland

Preface

The 16th Symposium and Summer School on Service-Oriented Computing (Summer-SOC 2022) continued a successful series of summer schools that started in 2007. SummerSOC regularly attracts world-class experts in service-oriented computing (SOC) to present state-of-the-art research during a week-long program organized in several thematic tracks: IoT, formal methods for SOC, cloud computing, data science, advanced manufacturing, software architecture, digital humanities, quantum computing, and emerging topics. The advanced summer school is regularly attended by top researchers from academia and industry as well as by PhD and graduate students.

During the SummerSOC symposium original research contributions in the areas mentioned above were presented. All accepted contributions were submitted in advance and were peer-reviewed in a single-blind review process. All papers received three reviews. Based on the reviews the program chairs accepted or rejected contributions. Out of 25 submitted contributions, only nine were accepted with an acceptance rate of less than 40%. The contributions were extensively discussed after their presentation during the paper session. In addition to the reviewer's comments, the feedback from these discussions was folded into the final version published in this special issue.

The volume is structured into three parts focusing on (i) advanced application architecture, (ii) data science and applications, and (iii) quantum computing. The first article in the section on advanced application architecture introduces a new plugin architecture combining microservices and micro frontends, which is followed by an article on enhancing IoT platforms for autonomous device discovery and selection; this second contribution received the SummerSOC Young Researcher Award sponsored by ICSOC. The next article provides answers to the question of serverless or serverful architectures based on a pattern-based approach for exploring hosting alternatives. The final article of the first part focuses on approaching immediate feedback for security relevant code in development environments. The section on data science and applications contains four contributions which propose a detection approach and its evaluation on unsupervised labor intelligence systems, provide an empirical investigation on MicroStream vs. JPA, enlighten the role of the data provider in the enterprise data marketplace supporting the process from data asset to data product, and offer data-aware service placement in the Cloud-IoT continuum. The final section on quantum computing provides an article focusing on optimizing the prioritization of compiled quantum circuits based on machine learning approaches.

August 2022

Johanna Barzen
Schahram Dustdar
Frank Leymann

Organization

General Chairs

Schahram Dustdar   Technische Universität Wien, Austria
Frank Leymann   Universität Stuttgart, Germany

Organization Committee

Johanna Barzen   Universität Stuttgart, Germany
George Koutras   OpenIT, Greece
Themis Kutsuras   OpenIT, Greece

Steering Committee

Marco Aiello   Universität Stuttgart, Germany
Schahram Dustdar   Technische Universität Wien, Austria
Christoph Gröger   Bosch, Germany
Frank Hentschel   Universität zu Köln, Germany
Willem-Jan van Heuvel   Eindhoven University of Technology, The Netherlands
Rania Khalaf   Inari, USA
Frank Leymann   Universität Stuttgart, Germany
Andreas Liebing   StoneOne AG, Germany
Kostas Magoutis   University of Crete, Greece
Bernhard Mitschang   Universität Stuttgart, Germany
Dimitris Plexousakis   University of Crete, Greece
Wolfgang Reisig   Humboldt-Universität zu Berlin, Germany
Norbert Ritter   Universität Hamburg, Germany
Jakka Sairamesh   CapsicoHealth Inc., USA
Sanjiva Weerawarana   WSO2, Sri Lanka
Guido Wirtz   Universität Bamberg, Germany
Alfred Zimmermann   Hochschule Reutlingen, Germany

Program Committee

Marco Aiello   Universität Stuttgart, Germany
Johanna Barzen   Universität Stuttgart, Germany
Steffen Becker   Universität Stuttgart, Germany

Wolfgang Blochinger   Hochschule Reutlingen, Germany
Uwe Breitenbücher   Universität Stuttgart, Germany
Antonio Brogi   Università di Pisa, Italy
Guiliano Casale   Imperial College London, UK
Christian Decker   Hochschule Reutlingen, Germany
Stefan Dessloch   TU Kaiserslautern, Germany
Schahram Dustdar   TU Wien, Austria
Sebastian Feld   TU Delft, The Netherlands
Frank Hentschel   Universität zu Köln, Germany
Melanie Herschel   Universität Stuttgart, Germany
Willem-Jan van Heuvel   Eindhoven University of Technology,
                                 The Netherlands
Eva Kühn   TU Wien, Austria
Ralf Küsters   Universität Stuttgart, Germany
Winfried Lamersdorf   Universität Hamburg, Germany
Frank Leymann   Universität Stuttgart, Germany
Claudia Linnhoff-Popien   Ludwig-Maximilians-Universität München,
                                 Germany
Kostas Magoutis   University of Crete, Greece
Bernhard Mitschang   Universität Stuttgart, Germany
Eric Newcomer   WSO2, Sri Lanka
Daniela Nicklas   Universität Bamberg, Germany
Maria Papadopouli   University of Crete, Greece
Adrian Paschke   Freie Universität Berlin, Germany
Cesare Pautasso   University of Lugano, Switzerland
Srinath Perera   WSO2, Sri Lanka
René Reiners   Fraunhofer FIT, Germany
Wolfgang Reisig   Humboldt-Universität zu Berlin, Germany
Norbert Ritter   Universität Hamburg, Germany
Jakka Sairamesh   CapsicoHealth Inc., USA
Ulf Schreier   Hochschule Furtwangen, Germany
Heiko Schuldt   Universität Basel, Switzerland
Stefan Schulte   TU Wien, Austria
Holger Schwarz   Universität Stuttgart, Germany
Craig Sheridan   University of Edinburgh, UK
Stefan Tai   TU Berlin, Germany
Damian Tamburri   Eindhoven University of Technology,
                                 The Netherlands
Massimo Villari   Università degli Studi di Messina, Italy
Stefan Wagner   Universität Stuttgart, Germany
Sanjiva Weerawarana   WSO2, Sri Lanka
Manuel Wimmer   Johannes Kepler University Linz, Austria

Guido Wirtz	Universität Bamberg, Germany
Uwe Zdun	Universität Wien, Austria
Alfred Zimmermann	Hochschule Reutlingen, Germany
Olaf Zimmermann	Hochschule für Technik Rapperswil, Switzerland

Additional Reviewers

Benjamin Weder
Felix Truger

Contents

Quantum Computing

Advanced Application Architecture

Combining the Best of Two Worlds: Microservices and Micro Frontends as Basis for a New Plugin Architecture

Fabian Bühler$^{(\boxtimes)}$, Johanna Barzen , Lukas Harzenetter ,
Frank Leymann , and Philipp Wundrack

University of Stuttgart, Institute of Architecture of Application Systems,
Universitätsstraße 38, 70569 Stuttgart, Germany
{fabian.buehler,johanna.barzen,lukas.harzenetter,frank.leymann,
philipp.wundrack}@iaas.uni-stuttgart.de

Abstract. Plugins can be used to extend applications with new functionality without requiring expensive code changes for the application. To enable users to interact with the new functionality, plugins must be able to contribute new elements to the user interface of the application. However, as plugins are built for specific applications, they are not reusable in other applications. Microservices on the other hand are built with reusability in mind: Applications can invoke microservices to utilize their functionality. However, a developer has to write code and create the corresponding UI for the application to interact with the microservice. To address the shortcomings of both plugins and microservices, we propose a reference architecture that blends concepts of plugins and microservices to allow microservices to provide code and user interfaces to existing applications. Our reference architecture allows the creation of microservices that can be used as plugins and as usual microservices at the same time. To demonstrate the practical feasibility, we also present a prototypical implementation of the architecture and evaluate the approach for a specific use-case.

Keywords: Micro frontend · Microservice · Plugin architecture · Software reuse · Quantum computing · Digital humanities

1 Introduction

Plugins are a way to extend an application dynamically by plugging in new components that provide additional features [25]. To enable users to interact with the new feature, plugins can extend the user interface (UI) of an application [7]. Thereby, plugins must conform to the application's plugin contract which defines, e.g., the invocation of plugins [25]. Therefore, plugins are purpose-built for the application. While this is a strength of plugins, it becomes a weakness when it comes to reusability. Plugins are tightly bound to the application they are developed for and, thus, cannot be used in other contexts or applications.

© The Author(s), under exclusive license to Springer Nature Switzerland AG 2022
J. Barzen et al. (Eds.): SummerSOC 2022, CCIS 1603, pp. 3–23, 2022.
https://doi.org/10.1007/978-3-031-18304-1_1

Microservices on the other hand facilitate their reuse by providing their functionality through an application programming interface (API). Their APIs can be invoked via common standard access mechanisms like HTTP, which makes it easy to use the API [22]. A single microservice may be used by multiple applications at the same time [11]. However, for an application to use a microservice with an unknown API, a developer first has to extend the application manually for it to interact with the new API. If the new functionality should be exposed to a user through the UI, then the developer also has to extend the UI of the application. Applications can be extended to use new microservices, but it needs a developer to adapt the application code to do so. In contrast to microservices, plugins can be used automatically and without developer intervention, but they are not as reusable [26].

Reusing existing software is an effective means to reduce costs for development and maintenance [19]. However, integrating a reusable software component into the existing software also requires development and maintenance effort. With plugins, this development effort is only required for implementing and maintaining the plugin interface that can be reused by multiple plugins. Plugins that can be used in multiple applications in parallel would benefit from both, the reuse of the plugins itself and the reuse of the plugin interface. Therefore, the research question we are tackling in this paper is:

RQ *How can microservice-based applications be enriched at runtime with additional functionalities that are bundled with their own user interfaces and can be reused in different applications in parallel?*

To solve this, we introduce the concept of *Reusable Microservice-based Plugins (RAMPs)* that allows microservices to be used as plugins by compatible applications. Additionally, we present a reference architecture that is capable of dynamically integrating and using RAMPs. The architecture adapts plugin techniques for their use with microservices. Microservices built for this architecture can still be used as normal microservices by other applications. However, the enhanced microservices can also extend compatible applications automatically to provide new functionality. They can contribute UI elements to enable users of these applications to interact with the new functionality. The UI elements are provided as micro frontends [34] that can be styled by the application to blend in with the rest of the application's UI. This allows the microservice plugins to be used in different applications without compromising their visual appearance.

The remainder of this paper is structured as follows: Sect. 2 contains a short explanation of the necessary background and terms of plugins, microservices and micro frontends as well as our motivating scenario. The reference architecture is introduced in detail in Sect. 3. Our prototypical implementation of the reference architecture for our use-case is discussed in Sect. 4, which is followed by a brief discussion of the reference architecture in general in Sect. 5, followed by related work in Sect. 6 and a conclusion in Sect. 7.

2 Fundamentals and Motivating Scenario

This section describes the fundamentals about plugins, microservices, micro frontends. Additionally, our motivating scenario and use-case QHAna [5] is described. QHAna is used as a motivating scenario, use case for the reference architecture, and as a prototypical implementation of the architecture.

2.1 Plugins

Plugins are a well-established concept in the software engineering domain. Patterns for plugins document their existence since at least 1999 [25, 26]. Plugins are used to allow a software to load new functionality on demand. This enables the development of new features independent of the main application, which reduces the complexity of the application itself.

To allow plugins to extend an application, it must define an interface for plugins, also referred to as *plugin contract* [25]. Plugins that provide new functionality for an application must comply with its plugin contract. Otherwise, they cannot be recognized and used by the application. In general, applications are unaware of existing plugins at build time. An application is only depending on the plugin contract instead of depending on the plugins. In fact, plugins can be developed after the application is completed.

In the plugin architecture described by Marquardt [25], an application can use multiple plugins but the architecture does not allow for dependencies between plugins. Newer plugin-based applications are built completely from plugins [14]. These plugins can depend on other plugins that must be loaded in advance. Birsan [7] calls this type of application a *pure plugin system*. In contrast, plugins as described by Marquardt [25] extend a host application that can function without plugins and cannot have dependencies to other plugins. However, both plugin systems require a component that can find and load the required plugins. Since many plugin systems are based on loading new code into the current process, the plugin discovery mechanisms often rely on the local file system [14,46]. In object-oriented languages, plugins typically implement the plugin interface provided by the application [46].

2.2 Microservices and SOA

Microservices [11,29] are applications only providing a single business capability, e.g., to get the current stock list of a warehouse [29]. An application that uses a microservice architecture is composed of multiple microservices working together [11]. The microservices are loosely coupled and provide lightweight communication mechanisms like an HTTP API to interact with each other [29]. A microservice is usually an independent unit to facilitate individual deployment which enables the microservices to have their own development and deployment lifecycle [8]. Microservices are often used to break up big monoliths into smaller and more maintainable components to reduce complexity, avoid "dependency hell" [27], improve scalability, etc. [11].

Service oriented architecture (SOA) is an architectural style and a way to use and organize distributed capabilities over the network [20]. These capabilities are available as services that can be used to solve business problems. To enable interoperability, the communication between components uses standardized protocols. One implementation of SOA is Web Services [20].

2.3 Micro Frontends

Frontend development for the web often faces the problem of a monolithic code base for the user interface [34]. The tight coupling of frontend components within a frontend-monolith and the overall complexity of a large application has a negative impact on the development process: small changes in single components require a full redeployment of the whole application, which can take a significant amount of time depending on the complexity of the application. Micro frontends apply the idea of small, single-purpose and individually deployable components to frontend development [33]. Thus, the benefits they offer are similar to microservices. The limited complexity of the micro frontends together with an independent development and release cycle of the independently developed components are benefits driving the adoption of micro frontends [34]. However, a consistent user experience over all micro frontends is one of the challenges of using micro frontends [34].

Micro frontends can be implemented in different ways: It can be differentiated between *server-side* and *client-side* integration [36]. With the server-side integration approach, micro frontends can be integrated during the building process of the application, which reintroduces tight coupling between the micro frontends, or using server-side template composition, where micro frontends are composed into a single user interface by the server [17].

For client-side integration three methods can be differentiated [45]: The first method, *route distribution*, assigns each micro frontend its own URL. Since the micro frontend controls the whole page, other micro frontends can only be accessed through a full page transition, e.g., by clicking a link. While being straight-forward, this approach is very limited, as it only allows one micro frontend to be displayed at the same time.

The second method for client-side integration is using client-side code to load and embed the micro frontend. This method is the most powerful one as the micro frontends can execute arbitrary code in the application context. Sharing the same execution context allows for shared dependencies and straight-forward communication mechanisms. Web Components [47] are a special form of using code to embed the micro frontend. Web Components are a set of standardized APIs that can be used to create building blocks for Web UIs [38]. If there are security concerns, e.g., when the micro frontend comes from a potentially untrusted source, then this method of micro frontend integration should not be used, as it allows arbitrary code execution in the context of the application.

The third method for client-side integration uses *iframes* to embed a micro frontend into a page. This method is unique to HTML and allows embedding full webpages that are displayed in the bounds of the iframe element. Iframes can isolate their content and code from the embedding page. This "sandbox" property of iframes enables embedding untrusted sources within a secure sandbox environment. However, the iframe embedding approach also has disadvantages in certain contexts, as they limit the communication between the embedded content and the host application. Nesting iframes can further complicate this situation, as the communication of the nested iframe has to be passed through all iframe layers to reach the application.

Micro frontends are similar to portlets that predate the term micro frontend. Portlets are user interface components that are composed by a portal server into an application UI. There are two standards for building and interacting with portlets, the Java specific JSR 362 [30] and the language agnostic WSRP [1] for remote portlets. Portlets and the portal servers composing them are server-side technologies, i.e., the application logic of a portlet is implemented in the portlet server and the portlet UI is sent to the portal server as static markup [10]. Communication between portlets is coordinated by the portal server and events that lead to state changes of a portlet, e.g., new user inputs, can require the whole page to be rebuilt [1,2]. This is in contrast to micro frontends where the UI specific application logic can be implemented in the micro frontend itself which is executed by the client. Communication between micro frontends can happen in the client without involving a server. Interactions with micro frontends can be implemented without requiring page reloads as the micro frontends can asynchronously request and display the new state.

2.4 Motivating Scenario: QHAna

The Quantum Humanities Analysis tool (QHAna) [5] is an application developed in the domain of the Digital Humanities (DH). It enables its users to experiment with different machine learning algorithms to examine a specified dataset [6]. With the availability of quantum computers in the cloud, it became viable to evaluate the possible advantages of quantum algorithms for the DH community [5]. Because of their unique computation model, quantum algorithms may outperform classical algorithms in speed [40] or accuracy [15]. As the current quantum computers are new, evaluating these algorithms is needed to determine relevant use-cases and to compare classical and quantum algorithms. Hence, QHAna can be used to experiment with quantum machine learning algorithms and compare them to classical ones on a given dataset. The current version consists of a user interface that allows users to define all parameters relevant for the current experiment. The prototype is built specifically for one dataset and it is not feasible to extend it to work with different datasets and new algorithms. Hence, an extensible plugin architecture that allows the integration of new data sources and quantum algorithms as plugins is needed. However, in this scenario reusing the algorithms in other applications is not possible, as the plugins need to be built specifically for QHAna.

2.5 Problem Statement

Creating and maintaining software often requires huge implementation costs. Such costs can be offset by reusing existing software where possible [19]. This is especially true for quantum algorithms as they require completely different skills than required for classical programming [16]. However, even if the desired functionality is already implemented in a reusable piece of software, e.g., as a microservice, there is often the need to create a small adapter, e.g., an API client, to use the packaged functionality through the provided interface.

Plugins can be automatically integrated into applications without the need for such an adapter. This enables also users without software development skills to customize applications using plugins. However, plugins are developed for specific applications and cannot be reused in other applications. Thus, choosing a plugin architecture allows automated integration of new features at the cost of limiting reusability.

Moreover, plugins for one application must all be implemented in the same programming language mandated by the plugin contract of that application. This means that reusable software artifacts implemented in a different programming language cannot be used in a plugin, which further limits the possibility for code reuse. For QHAna, for example, we would need a separate plugin system for all quantum programming languages we want to support, e.g., Q#[1], OpenQASM[2], QUIL[3] or Silq[4] to name just a few [44]. Conflicting plugin dependencies, e.g., with two plugins depending on incompatible versions of a library, will produce errors without careful handling of plugin dependencies. Plugin systems that can work with different programming languages and conflicting plugin dependencies are hard to develop and maintain.

Even if the plugin itself can be reused in different applications, we need to consider its graphical user interface as well. Different applications can have vastly different UI styles. The plugin UIs have to adapt their look to blend in with the application UI. Otherwise, users may fail to recognize important interactive elements in the user interface.

As outlined above, plugins that can be reused in multiple applications can reduce development costs. To achieve this, we need a solution that allows building plugins in a way that makes them reusable. Therefore, the current challenges are:

- Defining a plugin system that facilitates the reuse of plugins.
- Creating a plugin system that allows plugins to use different programming languages and otherwise conflicting dependencies.
- Enable UIs to be reusable with adaptable styles.

---

[1] https://docs.microsoft.com/azure/quantum/overview-what-is-qsharp-and-qdk.
[2] https://qiskit.github.io/openqasm.
[3] https://github.com/quil-lang/quil.
[4] https://silq.ethz.ch.

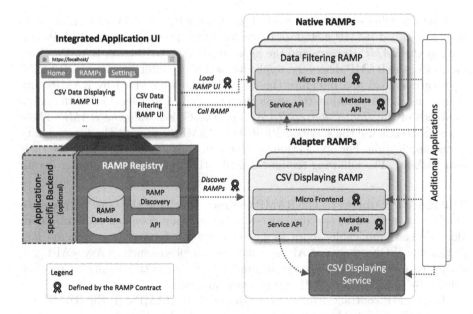

Fig. 1. An overview of the RAMP-architecture.

3 A Reference Architecture for Reusable Microservice-Based Plugins

This section presents the reference architecture that allows microservices with an integrated UI to be used as reusable plugins by multiple applications in parallel. The section starts with a general description of the architecture followed by more detailed descriptions of its components.

3.1 Overview

To solve the problems identified in Sect. 2.5, we propose the concept of *Reusable Microservice-based Plugins* (RAMPs). Therefore, we present a reference architecture, the RAMP-architecture, to build applications that can use RAMPs. The RAMP-architecture, as shown in Fig. 1, consists of three main components: different *RAMPs*, the *RAMP Registry* and the *applications* using the RAMPs. The centrepiece of the reference architecture is the *RAMP contract*. It ensures that all components can work together. The RAMP contract defines the common interface between applications and the RAMPs, it is a plugin contract for RAMPs. RAMPs implement the API defined in the plugin contract. If the contract is flexible enough, the whole application can be built only from RAMPs, similar to the pure plugin systems mentioned by Birsan [7]. The contract can also be used to restrict the extension points for RAMPs. Both kinds of plugin contracts are supported by the RAMP-architecture. Additionally, the plugin contract describes everything required to discover RAMPs. This includes *meta-data*, also called RAMP metadata in the following, provided by the RAMPs and used by the *RAMP Registry* and the *applications*, e.g., to discover RAMPs. However, after the RAMP discovery, applications directly interact with the RAMPs. Applications load and integrate the micro frontends provided by RAMPs into their own UI. For example, the application shown in Fig. 1 has loaded the micro frontends of the *Data Filtering RAMP* and the *CSV Displaying RAMP*. These micro frontends use the service API of their RAMP to provide the functionality to the application. For application specific functions applications may use their own backend. The following sections describe the architecture in greater detail.

The RAMP Contract. The RAMP contract, which has the same purpose as a plugin contract, can be specified as part of an existing documentation or standalone. Where applicable, more formal specification formats, e.g., schema languages like JSON schema or API specification languages such as AsyncAPI [28], should be used. This can prevent misunderstandings as the semantics are then defined by the schema or API specification language.

The RAMP contract defines three aspects of the RAMPs: (i) the RAMP discovery mechanism, (ii) how an application can load RAMPs, and (iii) the interface between the application UI and the RAMP UI once the RAMP is loaded. First, an application has to be aware of the available RAMPs through a discovery mechanism defined by the RAMP contract. This discovery mechanism is backed by the RAMP Registry that the application can use to find RAMPs. The application can use the metadata provided by the RAMPs to select which RAMP to load. What information the RAMP metadata contains is defined in the plugin contract. It must contain a description of the functionality provided by the RAMPs that can be displayed to a user who can decide whether to use that RAMP for a given task. Additional metadata can be used to automatically filter the list of RAMPs shown to the user, to only include the applicable RAMPs based on the current application state. For example, RAMPs can declare in their metadata what types of data they can operate on, e.g., JSON or CSV, and the application uses this data to only show JSON RAMPs for JSON data. Other relevant metadata can be pricing information or legal information, e.g., what is the cost per use, where is the RAMP's location, or who operates the RAMP. The RAMP Registry can cache this metadata for the applications and should provide a query mechanism that allows applications to search for RAMPs with specific metadata.

The RAMP metadata must contain the location of the micro frontend that provides the UI of the RAMP. Applications need this information to load and integrate the micro frontends into their UI. If the RAMP UI has dependencies, these must be declared in the metadata and used by the application to resolve and load the dependencies. Dependency resolution is done during the RAMP loading process of the application.

How the RAMP UI is loaded by an application is part of the plugin lifecycle that is defined by the plugin contract. However, because RAMPs are microservices that are already running, there is no need for lifecycle phases related to the installation of plugins. Hence, applications only need to discover the RAMPs and load their micro frontends as specified in the plugin contract. For RAMPs that have dependencies to other RAMPs, a dependency resolution step is required either before or after the RAMP UI is loaded and integrated into the application UI. The dependency resolution can be done after the RAMP UI is loaded, if the dependencies can be bound late. This can be the case for optional dependencies that provide additional functions for a RAMP UI that can be added even after the UI is loaded, e.g., as entries in a menu of the RAMP UI. Microservice dependencies, i.e., dependencies to other microservices, must be resolved without involving an application, e.g., by using a service registry, because RAMPs are isolated services that are running out of the scope of a specific application. However, a RAMP may expose its microservice dependencies as choices to a user allowing the user to decide which dependency to use. For example, a RAMP for creating navigating instructions can allow the user to select from different microservices to calculate the route.

When a RAMP micro frontend is loaded, the communication with the application uses an API defined in the plugin contract. At this point, the loaded micro frontend is executed or interpreted by the application. As the RAMPs can provide custom UIs to the application, the plugin contract must specify an interface that can be used by the applications to style these UIs to blend in with their UI. This *styling interface* allows different applications with their own design systems to use the same RAMPs and adapt their UI styling to fit visually into their design system. Additionally, the RAMP contract can specify when and how the micro frontend of a RAMP can be unloaded.

RAMPs. Microservices already provide a reusable API that plugins can be created from. Therefore, our implementation of reusable plugins is based on microservices. A *Reusable Microservice-based Plugin* (RAMP) is a microservice bundled with a micro frontend and a predefined metadata API that provides metadata about the RAMP. The micro frontend is the graphical user interface of the RAMP that can be used to interact with the service. To enable the use of existing microservices as a RAMP, an *Adapter RAMP* which provides the micro frontend and plugin metadata can be used as shown in Fig. 1. This allows integrating microservices controlled by a third party into the RAMP-architecture. The adapter RAMP uses the existing microservice by forwarding calls to its API.

RAMP metadata provided by the metadata API is used by applications and their users to decide if the RAMP UI should be loaded and to find the location of the micro frontend. This metadata can, for example, contain a description of the RAMP functions that can be displayed to a user who can then decide whether to use the RAMP. The RAMP contract defines what is part of the metadata.

Dependencies of RAMPs must also be declared in the metadata. The RAMP as a microservice can depend on other microservices. These dependencies need to be resolved by a different method than the dependency resolution used for RAMP UI dependencies. This is because the RAMP can be used as a microservice even without the other components of the RAMP architecture in place to support it. The micro frontend is usually not aware of these dependencies, however, it can also have dependencies to other micro frontends. While the microservice dependencies are managed by the service maintainers, the micro frontend dependencies must be resolved by the application by using the RAMP Registry.

A RAMP UI can expose the microservice dependencies of a RAMP to the user. For example, if there are multiple alternative microservices that can be used internally by the RAMP to provide the required functionality, the micro frontend can ask the user to select the specific microservice from the list of available microservices. A user could, for example, decide between a cheaper or a more accurate service based on the requirements of the current task. The RAMP UI can utilize the micro frontends of other RAMPs that are used as microservice dependencies, to provide the user with additional controls or features. For example, given a plugin service that manages a data transformation pipeline and depends on a number of transformation services that provide the actual data transformations, the RAMP UI of the pipeline service can utilize the RAMP UIs of the transformation services to allow the user to specify the data transformation parameters.

There are two possibilities for a RAMP UI to use another RAMP UI. The first method is for one RAMP UI to directly use the objects and functions defined by the other micro frontend. This only works if both RAMPs are in the same execution context to share code with another. The second method is for one RAMP UI to act as an application loading the other RAMP as defined by the plugin contract. This method can be used even if the RAMP UIs are sandboxed and, thus, cannot share their code. For this method the RAMP UI also needs access to the RAMP Registry to resolve its own dependency. The styling interface for micro frontends must also take this into account, to allow the styles to be passed through to nested RAMP UIs.

RAMP Registry. The RAMP Registry maintains a list of available RAMPs in a database. It checks the current availability of RAMPs periodically by querying the metadata API or a specific health check API of the RAMPs. They can be registered through different means, e.g., service discovery mechanisms, manual registration or self-registration of the RAMPs.

The registry allows the applications to query its database for the available RAMPs. It is aware of the RAMP metadata to allow filtering based on the metadata. This allows applications to search for specific RAMPs based on the metadata. It can, for example, be used to find all RAMPs that can work with data in a specific format, e.g., CSV or JSON. A RAMP to display CSV files does not need to be loaded if the data is encoded as JSON. Filtering RAMPs based on their metadata allows the applications to display a smaller list of more relevant RAMPs for users to choose from. If the metadata is more verbose it can even be used for completely automatic decisions by the applications. For example, if data is only available as JSON but there is only a CSV RAMP in the registry, then an application may search for a RAMP that can convert JSON to CSV in the registry and recommend the data conversion RAMP to the user when he selects the CSV RAMP.

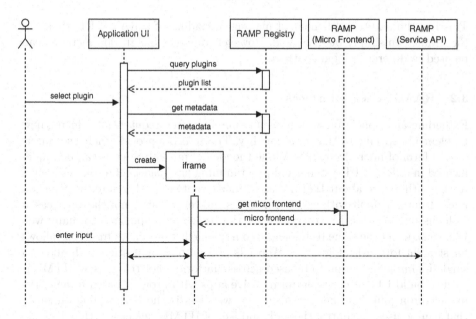

Fig. 2. A sequence diagram showing the process of loading a RAMP.

Integrated Application User Interface. In the proposed reference architecture, we refer to the web UI that is able to integrate the RAMP UIs into a single UI as *application*. Applications can have their own UI into which the RAMP UIs are integrated, or they can be built completely with RAMP UIs, similar to the pure plugin systems described by Birsan [7]. RAMPs are discovered by an application through the RAMP Registry. Applications optionally can use their own backend for application specific functionalities.

The RAMP UIs are integrated visually into the application UI. To achieve this, the application changes the appearance of the RAMP UIs to blend in with its own UI through the styling interface defined in the plugin contract. This allows multiple applications to load the same RAMP UI, as they can all change the RAMP UI appearance to match their own UI. This is fundamentally important to achieve reusability of the RAMP UIs.

Applications can load RAMPs based on their metadata or on request from a user. To load a RAMP UI, the application first has to know the location of the micro frontend which is specified in the RAMP metadata. Then the RAMP UI is integrated into the application UI through one of the client-side integration methods of micro frontends as discussed in Sect. 2.3. Figure 2 shows the process of loading a RAMP UI without dependencies using the iframe embedding method. First the application lets the user select a plugin, then it uses the plugin metadata to locate the micro frontend of the selected RAMP that is loaded in a newly created iframe. At this point the user can interact with the RAMP UI and the RAMP UI can communicate with the application and the service API of the RAMP. With this method the RAMP UI runs in a secure sandbox environment.

This has the additional benefit of making unloading of a RAMP UI trivial, as the iframe can simply be discarded. However, different integration methods can be used in different plugin contracts.

3.2   RAMP User Interfaces

Extending an application with new functionality often requires introducing new UI elements specific to that functionality. The RAMPs provide their user interface in form of micro frontends. While the idea of micro frontends can be implemented in different UI systems and programming languages, all resources known to the authors are about HTML-based micro frontends. Therefore, we focus on micro frontends built with web technologies. However, this is not the only reason to focus on web UIs. Microservices are the backend components to many web UIs, thus, using the same technologies to implement their micro frontends allows for straight-forward integration. Web UIs are platform-agnostic which allows a single UI implementation to be used across platforms. For this reason, HTML is used to build UIs for cross-platform native apps with browser-based frameworks like electron [39]. Another reason to use web UIs is the CSS styling language that can be used to control the look and feel of HTML elements if they have no local styles applied. While HTML provides the general structure and semantic meaning of the UI elements, CSS defines the visual appearance. The same web UI can have different looks using different style sheets.

HTML-based micro frontends can be implemented using different methods [34] which were already discussed in Sect. 2.3. The server delivering the web UI can insert the micro frontend into the web UI before it is delivered to the user. The micro frontend can also be integrated client-side by using JavaScript to load the micro frontend dynamically. Both, server-side inclusion and client-side inclusion using JavaScript, directly include the micro frontend into the web UI of the application, including any JavaScript code that is part of the micro frontend. This can be problematic when the RAMP may not be fully trusted because it is not open-source or the plugin microservice is controlled by an external party. To address security concerns with running untrusted code in the application context, the micro frontend can be isolated in a sandbox by an iframe.

Security. The decision on how micro frontends are integrated into the main UI has an impact on security. Because this decision is part of the plugin contract and cannot be changed once the plugin contract is in use, the potential security implications must be considered before committing to a plugin contract.

The current driving forces to build micro frontends are related to splitting up larger UIs into smaller and easier to maintain micro frontends [34]. Micro frontends that are the result of splitting up larger applications are still developed by the same developers, thus, they do not pose a security risk. However, loading a potentially untrusted micro frontend, especially if it is allowed to execute JavaScript, can compromise the security of the application. Even static forms can become an attack vector by abusing the autofill function of the browser [23].

If the micro frontend cannot be distinguished from the application by users, they may even willingly enter their credentials into a legitimate looking input of the plugin UI. Software architects and application developers should be aware of the risks of loading untrusted plugins.

An iframe element can be used to sandbox a micro frontend from the application. The iframe can be configured to isolate the plugin from the application UI, while still allowing the execution of arbitrary JavaScript inside the sandbox. However, communication with the host of the iframe is limited to a passing messages and requires JavaScript on both ends. Applications may allow trusted RAMPs to use other, more powerful, extension methods including the execution of JavaScript in the application context. As a precaution, micro frontends of trusted RAMPs should be verified cryptographically before they are loaded. A cryptographic validation can be performed through checking the certificate of the RAMP or comparing the micro frontend payload against a signed hash. Both methods can be used simultaneously.

Styling. The RAMP UI must expose an interface for changing its appearance to match the application UI. This interface has to be part of the plugin contract to ensure that every RAMP UI can be styled in the same manner to achieve a consistent user experience between the application and the plugins. However, not all design decisions can be compensated later by such a styling interface. Thus, to ensure consistency and accessibility, a higher level design guideline for user interfaces should be mandated by the RAMP contract.

CSS can apply styling rules to HTML elements based on the element itself or the CSS classes of that element. Inline CSS styles on the HTML elements will not be covered here, as they cannot be set by applying a CSS stylesheet. A baseline style can be applied by directly styling HTML elements, e.g., the different heading elements h1 to h6 or buttons and form elements.

The styling interface can consist of a set of CSS classes that can be applied to HTML elements. The values of the classes are then provided by the application. In some cases, it may be required to specify which classes can be used together or how classes and the elements they are applied to may be nested to achieve certain effects, e.g., showing certain child nodes only when the parent node is hovered. Portlet UIs also have to be styled to blend with the application style. WSRP defines a number of CSS names that portlets can use and for which the portal server must provide the actual values [1].

A different approach to implement a styling interface is to use CSS variables [4]. The micro frontend can use its own CSS classes as long as all their properties are derived from the specified CSS variables. This allows the micro frontend more styling freedom while still maintaining the visual coherence. For example, the application may define a colour palette using CSS variables, but the micro frontend can decide which elements of its UI uses the colours. Both approaches can be mixed, e.g., using CSS variables for the colour theme and CSS classes for layout elements that require a specific nesting of multiple elements.

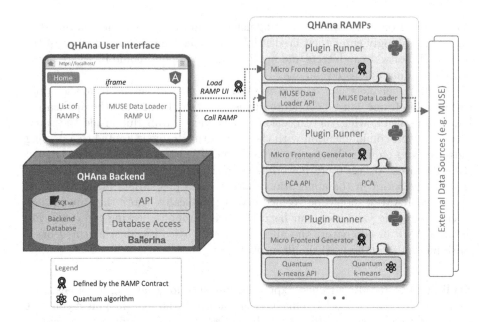

Fig. 3. The architecture of QHAna.

4 Prototypical Evaluation

To evaluate the feasibility of our proposed architecture, we used it to redesign QHAna [5]. The generic requirements outlined in Sect. 2.5 can be fulfilled by the proposed reference architecture. This section starts with an overview of the architecture of the QHAna prototype and the specific design choices for implementing the proposed architecture. The overview is followed by two sections describing specific implementation details.

4.1 The QHAna Prototype

Figure 3 shows the architecture of the revised QHAna prototype. The components can be mapped directly to the RAMP-architecture. The QHAna UI is an Angular application implemented in TypeScript and corresponds to the application in our RAMP-architecture. The QHAna backend is implemented in Ballerina[5] and provides a REST API for the user interface. It is managing a persistent storage for all data related to an experiment in the QHAna tool. Data is stored in the backend database and in the local filesystem. The backend also manages a list of plugins acting as a RAMP Registry. The algorithms implemented for QHAna are packaged as RAMPs. To ease the development of RAMPs, we created the *Plugin Runner* python framework that handles all generic RAMP tasks, e.g., reading config values, setting up background tasks for long-running jobs,

---

[5] https://ballerina.io.

and contains helper functions. The plugin runner also contains a generator for creating simple micro frontends out of API models. To create a new RAMP, only the algorithm implementation and the algorithm specific API, which is also responsible for the RAMP metadata, have to be provided.

The QHAna UI presents the user with a list of available plugins to choose from. We are experimenting with different ways to present the plugin list, e.g., by grouping plugins, as the number of implemented plugins keeps on growing, with the current plugins already counting 26. If the user selects a plugin in the UI, then the UI loads the micro frontend of the selected plugin inside an iframe. We chose the iframe embedding method for our micro frontends, because QHAna will have to handle API tokens for quantum computing resources in the cloud that are associated with a significant amount of money. The sandboxing properties of the iframe are used to prevent plugins from accessing these tokens without the user's consent. The QHAna UI tells the micro frontend loaded in the iframe what CSS styles should be loaded through the messaging channel provided by the iframe. QHAna RAMPs use a styling interface that uses both, CSS classes and variables. The prototype is developed as an open-source application and can be found on GitHub[6].

Plugin Interactions. In our prototypical implementation, the QHAna backend is also a RAMP Registry. RAMPs in QHAna typically implement a single function that has input data, can be configured by hyper-parameters, and produces output data. The root resource of a QHAna RAMP is the metadata API. It contains the location of the micro frontend and also the corresponding service API endpoint used internally by the micro frontend. This allows applications that do not need a graphical frontend to directly use the service API. Loading RAMPs in QHAna follows the process described in Fig. 2. The RAMP UI is loaded inside an iframe configured to isolate its content from the QHAna UI. A channel to pass messages based on events is the only interface between the micro frontend and the QHAna UI. The messages allowed on this channel are specified using an AsyncAPI [28] specification that is part of the plugin contract. This channel is, for example, used by the application to tell the micro frontend which CSS files to load. Users can directly interact with the iframe content through the browser. Once the user starts the algorithm implemented by the plugin via the RAMP UI, it calls the corresponding resource of the microservice and then reports to the QHAna UI. The QHAna UI then instructs the backend to watch for the finished result of the algorithm.

Data Handling. QHAna RAMPs consume data and produce new data. They act similar to filters of a pipes-and-filters architecture. The different algorithms implemented for QHAna require different types of input data. To simplify the development of plugins, we decided to only pass data by reference as a URL. This simplifies the logic to work with data, as RAMPs only need to support reading data from URLs. It also allows for streaming or batch-processing of large datasets that don't fit into memory.

---

[6] https://github.com/UST-QuAntiL.

To help users selecting compatible data for a RAMP, QHAna stores a content type and a data type tag as metadata for all data. The content type describes how the data is serialized while the data type describes what kind of data is serialized. As different plugins require different data formats, there is a need for data transformers that can translate data from one format into another. Data from external sources is loaded via data loading RAMPs that import the data in a common format such as CSV. In the future, we plan to implement RAMPs that can translate between data formats and are used automatically if required.

5   Discussion

Our prototypical implementation proves that the RAMP-architecture can be used to create applications that can be enriched with additional functionalities through RAMPs. The RAMPs can be used by multiple applications in parallel. RAMPs bring their own UI with them in form of a micro frontend that can be embedded into the application UI. Through a styling interface, RAMP UIs can be adjusted to match the style of the application UI they are used in.

If an application attempts to load many RAMPs at startup, this may slow down the application significantly. Applications loading large amounts of plugins also exhibit this behaviour [7]. The same countermeasures, e.g., only loading plugins when they are used, can be applied to RAMP-based applications. Additionally, RAMPs can offload some of their computation tasks from the micro frontend into the microservice.

RAMPs are still fully functioning microservices as all plugin specific functionalities are built on top of the microservice API. They can be used as a normal microservice by any application. For an application to benefit from the plugin functionalities of a RAMP, it needs to implement the API defined in the plugin contract. To enrich multiple applications with RAMPs, all applications must use the same plugin contract. On a small scale, this can be solved by defining a plugin contract that takes the requirements of every application into consideration. However, conflicting requirements may require incompatible plugin contracts. The plugin contract should be designed in a way to maximize the potential reuse of RAMPs in different applications. We plan on further researching how to design such a plugin contract in the future.

Security must be considered before loading a RAMP. In this paper, we have addressed the basic security concerns of loading untrusted RAMPs by using the iframe sandbox. However, we do not claim that this solves all potential security issues. Further research on the security of loading external micro frontends is needed to fill this gap.

6   Related Work

Several case studies have been done where micro frontends were used for the reimplementation of an existing monolithic frontend application [35,45]. Other case studies have implemented new frontend applications from scratch using micro frontends [33,42,48]. All of these case studies used a microservice-based backend. However, none of the mentioned case studies considered the reusability of the micro frontends in other applications.

Portlets are built to be reused in different applications. As one of the two major standards for Portlets is Java specific, many portlet implementations and tools require Java [2,3]. Portlets require a portal server that composes the portlet markup and handles inter-portlet communication [2]. They cannot take advantage of the client side integration techniques available for micro frontends and frequently require the whole page to be refreshed to render new portlet state [10]. This makes portlets difficult to integrate into applications that are implemented with frameworks that render the page and updates to the page on the client. Our approach uses micro frontends and, thus, supports client side integration.

Patterns for plugins are described in several works [25,26]. Whereas Mayer et al. [26], Birsan [7] and Wolfinger et al. [46] describe how plugins can use other plugins and how to build whole applications out of plugins, Marquardt [25] does not mention plugins depending on other plugins. The extension of the user interface with plugins is explicitly considered in most of these works [7,26,46]. Birsan [7] uses the term *pure plug-in architecture* to describe applications that are entirely made out of plugins and only contain a small runtime engine for executing the plugins. While some works are language agnostic [25,26], Wolfinger et al. [46] introduce a plugin architecture for the .NET platform. Asqium [43] is plugin based framework for web application development that allows building applications from plugins that can extend server and client side code at the same time. However, these plugins can only be implemented in JavaScript. None of these works describe how plugins that were developed for one application could be reused by another application.

Pahl and Jamshidi [31] did a mapping study comparing existing research about microservices. From the 21 studies they considered, only two of them mentioned reusability which is an important aspect of our work. Dragoni et al. [11] reviewed the history of software architecture and the state-of-the-art of microservices. They briefly mentioned reusability of microservices in their results. A systematic mapping study was conducted by Cerny et al. [8] related to microservices. They found that the most commonly mentioned challenges regarding microservice were communication, integration, deployment operations, performance, and fault tolerance. Reusability was considered as part of communication/integration. Garriga [13] created a taxonomy and used it to analyse state-of-the-art approaches regarding microservices. A key finding of the analysis was that microservices are being used in-house and that they are not reused for new tasks and use cases, instead new microservices get developed. This is in contrast to our work which promotes software reuse.

A discovery mechanism for services is a centralized registry of services as described by Curbera et al. [9]. Service discovery mechanisms like this can be used to implement the RAMP discovery mechanism of the RAMP Registry. Dustdar and Papazoglou [12] give an introduction to services and service composition. Service composition is the development of a service that invokes other services as part of the business logic [21,37]. A web service composition middleware that allows users to compose web services in a graphical user interface, such as Triana [24] or the older BioOpera Flow Language [32], require precise descriptions of the services' functionalities, interfaces and supported protocols. Service composition is analogous to RAMPs that call other RAMPs as part of their execution. However, the result of a service composition is just another service without a user interface [18,41]. RAMPs that are aware of and can use the RAMP UIs of their dependencies can even compose the UIs to present them to a user.

7   Conclusion and Future Work

A plugin architecture provides a way to extend existing applications with new functionality using plugins. Plugins can be loaded by users of an application allowing them to customize the application. Because the plugins are developed specifically for one application, they cannot be reused for other purposes. On the other hand, microservices are built for reusability. They can be easily integrated into multiple applications, but this integration must be done by a developer. The microservices cannot directly contribute new functionality to an application, as the user interface often needs additional elements to support the new functions. Microservices have no way of extending the user interface of existing applications.

In this paper, we presented the concept of RAMPs that can be used as plugins and microservices at the same time. This is achieved by bundling a microservice API together with a micro frontend and allows RAMPs to be reused by multiple applications in parallel. As the APIs of the microservices are not changed, RAMPs can always be used as microservices. They can also be used like plugins and do not require a developer for the integration in an application supporting RAMPs. Just like plugins, they can be integrated by users. Users only need to select available RAMPs from the RAMP Registry to integrate their functionality into an application. Unlike plugins, the user interfaces provided by RAMPs can be integrated into multiple applications with different styles through a styling interface. This opens up new possibilities for plugins and microservices.

The implementation of the RAMP-architecture in the redesigned prototype of our research tool QHAna shows the potential value of the RAMP-architecture. In future work, we plan on orchestrating the QHAna RAMPs with workflows. While the workflows will mostly interact directly with the microservice API, the RAMP UI can be used in human tasks. The insights gathered from these experiments will help to form an intuition of how a plugin contract for RAMPs should be designed to maximize the reusability of RAMPs. Additionally, we plan to implement data transformation RAMPs for automatic data format translations and expand our first prototype for micro frontend generation in the plugin runner component to generate more complex UIs.

Acknowledgements. The work was partially funded by the *Federal Ministry for Economic Affairs and Climate Action* project PlanQK (01MK20005N).

References

1. Web services for remote portlets specification v2.0 (2008). https://docs.oasis-open. org/wsrp/v2/wsrp-2.0-spec.html
2. Akram, A., Chohan, D., Wang, X.D., Yang, X., Allan, R.: A service oriented architecture for portals using portlets. In: Uk e-Science All Hands Conference 2005. CCLRC (2005)
3. Allan, R., Awre, C., Baker, M., Fish, A.: Portals and portlets 2003. In: Proceedings of the NeSC Workshop, pp. 14–17. CCLRC (2004)
4. Attardi, J.: Basic CSS concepts. In: Modern CSS: Master the Key Concepts of CSS for Modern Web Development, pp. 33–59. Apress (2020). https://doi.org/10.1007/ 978-1-4842-6294-8_3
5. Barzen, J.: From digital humanities to quantum humanities: potentials and applications. In: An Introduction to Core Concepts, Theory and Applications, Springer, Cham (2021). https://doi.org/10.1007/978-3-030-95538-0_1
6. Barzen, J., Leymann, F.: Quantencomputing in den digital humanities: innovativ oder übertrieben? ZfdG - Zeitschrift für digitale Geisteswissenschaften. Fabrikation von Erkenntnis: Experimente in den Digital Humanities, pp. 1–22 (2021). https:// doi.org/10.26298/melusina.8f8w-y749-qidd
7. Birsan, D.: On plug-ins and extensible architectures. Queue **3**(2), 40–46 (2005). https://doi.org/10.1145/1053331.1053345
8. Cerny, T., Donahoo, M.J., Trnka, M.: Contextual understanding of microservice architecture: Current and future directions. SIGAPP Appl. Comput. Rev. **17**(4), 29–45 (2018). https://doi.org/10.1145/3183628.3183631
9. Curbera, F., Duftler, M., Khalaf, R., Nagy, W., Mukhi, N., Weerawarana, S.: Unraveling the web services web: an introduction to SOAP, WSDL, and UDDI. IEEE Internet Comput. **6**(2), 86–93 (2002). https://doi.org/10.1109/4236.991449
10. Dıaz, O., Rodrıguez, J.: Portlets as web components: an introduction. J. Univ. Comput. Sci. **10**(4), 454–472 (2004). https://doi.org/10.3217/jucs-010-04-0454
11. Dragoni, N., et al.: Microservices: yesterday, today, and tomorrow. In: Present and Ulterior Software Engineering, pp. 195–216. Springer, Cham (2017). https://doi. org/10.1007/978-3-319-67425-4_12
12. Dustdar, S., Papazoglou, M.P.: Services and service composition-an introduction. IT-Inf. Technol. **50**(2), 86–92 (2008)
13. Garriga, M.: Towards a taxonomy of microservices architectures. In: Cerone, A., Roveri, M. (eds.) SEFM 2017. LNCS, vol. 10729, pp. 203–218. Springer, Cham (2018). https://doi.org/10.1007/978-3-319-74781-1_15
14. Geer, D.: Eclipse becomes the dominant java IDE. Computer **38**(7), 16–18 (2005). https://doi.org/10.1109/MC.2005.228
15. Havenstein, C., Thomas, D., Chandrasekaran, S.: Comparisons of performance between quantum and classical machine learning. SMU Data Sci. Rev. **1**(4), 30 (2018)
16. Abhijith, J., et al.: Quantum algorithm implementations for beginners (2020). version: 2
17. Jackson, C.: Micro frontends (2019). https://martinfowler.com/articles/microfrontends.html#IntegrationApproaches
18. Jula, A., Sundararajan, E., Othman, Z.: Cloud computing service composition: a systematic literature review. Expert Syst. Appl. **41**(8), 3809–3824 (2014). https:// doi.org/10.1016/j.eswa.2013.12.017

19. Krueger, C.W.: Software reuse. ACM Comput. Surv. **24**(2), 131–183 (1992). https://doi.org/10.1145/130844.130856
20. Laskey, K.B., Laskey, K.: Service oriented architecture. Wiley Interdiscipl. Rev. Computat. Stat. **1**(1), 101–105 (2009)
21. Lemos, A.L., Daniel, F., Benatallah, B.: Web service composition: a survey of techniques and tools. ACM Comput. Surv. **48**(3), 33:1–33:41. https://doi.org/10.1145/2831270
22. Lewis, J., Fowler, M.: Microservices: a definition of this new architectural term (2014). https://martinfowler.com/articles/microservices.html
23. Lin, X., Ilia, P., Polakis, J.: Fill in the Blanks: Empirical Analysis of the Privacy Threats of Browser Form Autofill, pp. 507–519. ACM, New York, NY, USA (2020). https://doi.org/10.1145/3372297.3417271
24. Majithia, S., Shields, M., Taylor, I., Wang, I.: Triana: a graphical web service composition and execution toolkit. In: Proceedings. IEEE International Conference on Web Services, 2004, pp. 514–521. IEEE (2004). https://doi.org/10.1109/ICWS.2004.1314777
25. Marquardt, K.: Patterns for plug-ins. In: Proceedings of the Fourth European Conference on Pattern Languages of Programming and Computing (1999)
26. Mayer, J., Melzer, I., Schweiggert, F.: Lightweight plug-in-based application development. In: Aksit, M., Mezini, M., Unland, R. (eds.) NODe 2002. LNCS, vol. 2591, pp. 87–102. Springer, Heidelberg (2003). https://doi.org/10.1007/3-540-36557-5_9
27. Merkel, D., et al.: Docker: lightweight linux containers for consistent development and deployment. Linux J. **239**, 2 (2014)
28. Méndez, F., et al.: AsyncAPI specification. AsyncAPI, https://www.asyncapi.com/docs/specifications/v2.3.0
29. Newman, S.: Building Microservices. O'Reilly Media, Inc., Sebastopol (2021)
30. Nicklous, M.: Jsr 362: Portlet specification 3.0 (2017). https://www.jcp.org/en/jsr/detail?id=362
31. Pahl, C., Jamshidi, P.: Microservices: A systematic mapping study. In: Proceedings of the 6th International Conference on Cloud Computing and Services Science, pp. 137–146. SCITEPRESS (2016). https://doi.org/10.5220/0005785501370146
32. Pautasso, C., Alonso, G.: Visual composition of web services. In: 2003 IEEE Symposium on Human Centric Computing Languages and Environments (HCC 2003), 28–31 October 2003, Auckland, New Zealand, pp. 92–99. IEEE Computer Society (2003). https://doi.org/10.1109/HCC.2003.1260208
33. Pavlenko, A., Askarbekuly, N., Megha, S., Mazzara, M.: Micro-frontends: application of microservices to web front-ends. J. Internet Serv. Inf. Secur. (JISIS) **10**(2), 49–66 (2020). https://doi.org/10.22667/JISIS.2020.05.31.049
34. Peltonen, S., Mezzalira, L., Taibi, D.: Motivations, benefits, and issues for adopting micro-frontends: a multivocal literature review. Inf. Softw. Technol. **136**, 106571 (2021). https://doi.org/10.1016/j.infsof.2021.106571
35. Pölöskei, I., Bub, U.: Enterprise-level migration to micro frontends in a multi-vendor environment. Acta Polytechnica Hungarica **18**(8), 7–25 (2021)
36. Prajwal, Y., Parekh, J.V., Shettar, R.: A brief review of micro-frontends. United Int. J. Res. Technol. **2**, 123–126 (2021)
37. Rao, J., Su, X.: A survey of automated web service composition methods. In: Cardoso, J., Sheth, A. (eds.) SWSWPC 2004. LNCS, vol. 3387, pp. 43–54. Springer, Heidelberg (2005). https://doi.org/10.1007/978-3-540-30581-1_5
38. Rojas, C.: Building Native Web Components: Front-End Development with Polymer and Vue.js. Apress (2021). https://doi.org/10.1007/978-1-4842-5905-4

39. Scoccia, G.L., Autili, M.: Web frameworks for desktop apps: an exploratory study. In: Proceedings of the 14th ACM / IEEE International Symposium on Empirical Software Engineering and Measurement (ESEM). ESEM 2020, ACM, New York, NY, USA (2020). https://doi.org/10.1145/3382494.3422171

40. Shor, P.: Algorithms for quantum computation: discrete logarithms and factoring. In: Proceedings 35th Annual Symposium on Foundations of Computer Science, pp. 124–134. IEEE (1994). https://doi.org/10.1109/SFCS.1994.365700

41. Strunk, A.: QoS-aware service composition: A survey. In: Eighth IEEE European Conference on Web Services, pp. 67–74 (2010). https://doi.org/10.1109/ECOWS.2010.16

42. Tilak, P.Y., Yadav, V., Dharmendra, S.D., Bolloju, N.: A platform for enhancing application developer productivity using microservices and micro-frontends. In: IEEE-HYDCON, pp. 1–4. IEEE (2020). https://doi.org/10.1109/HYDCON48903.2020.9242913

43. Triglianos, V., Pautasso, C.: Asqium: a javascript plugin framework for extensible client and server-side components. In: Cimiano, P., Frasincar, F., Houben, G.-J., Schwabe, D. (eds.) ICWE 2015. LNCS, vol. 9114, pp. 81–98. Springer, Cham (2015). https://doi.org/10.1007/978-3-319-19890-3_7

44. Vietz, D., Barzen, J., Leymann, F., Wild, K.: On decision support for quantum application developers: categorization, comparison, and analysis of existing technologies. In: Paszynski, M., Kranzlmüller, D., Krzhizhanovskaya, V.V., Dongarra, J.J., Sloot, P.M.A. (eds.) ICCS 2021. LNCS, vol. 12747, pp. 127–141. Springer, Cham (2021). https://doi.org/10.1007/978-3-030-77980-1_10

45. Wang, D., et al.: A novel application of educational management information system based on micro frontends. Procedia Comput. Sci. **176**, 1567–1576 (2020). https://doi.org/10.1016/j.procs.2020.09.168

46. Wolfinger, R., Dhungana, D., Prähofer, H., Mössenböck, H.: A component plug-in architecture for the .net platform. In: Lightfoot, D.E., Szyperski, C. (eds.) JMLC 2006. LNCS, vol. 4228, pp. 287–305. Springer, Heidelberg (2006). https://doi.org/10.1007/11860990_18

47. Wusteman, J.: The potential of web components for libraries. Library Hi Tech. **37**, 713–720 (2019). https://doi.org/10.1108/LHT-06-2019-0125

48. Yang, C., Liu, C., Su, Z.: Research and application of micro frontends. In: IOP Conference Series: Materials Science and Engineering, p. 490 (2019). https://doi.org/10.1088/1757-899x/490/6/062082

Enhancing IoT Platforms for Autonomous Device Discovery and Selection

Jan Schneider$^{(\boxtimes)}$ and Pascal Hirmer

Institute for Parallel and Distributed Systems, University of Stuttgart,
Universitätsstraße 38, 70569 Stuttgart, Germany
{jan.schneider,pascal.hirmer}@ipvs.uni-stuttgart.de

Abstract. The Internet of Things (IoT) encompasses a variety of technologies that enable the formation of adaptive and flexible networks from heterogeneous devices. Along with the rising number of applications, the amount of devices within IoT ecosystems is constantly increasing. In order to cope with this inherent complexity and to enable efficient administration and orchestration of devices, IoT platforms have emerged in recent years. While many IoT platforms empower users to define application logic for use cases and execute it within an ecosystem, they typically rely on static device references, leading to huge manual maintenance efforts and low robustness. In this paper, we present an approach that allows IoT platforms to autonomously and reliably execute pre-defined use cases by automatically discovering and selecting the most suitable devices. It establishes loose coupling and hence does not impose major technical constraints on the ecosystems in which it is operated.

Keywords: Internet of Things · IoT platforms · Device discovery

1 Introduction

In the world of tomorrow, digital ecosystems will be able to autonomously create synergies between so-called smart devices and let them jointly perform tasks for the benefit of the people in their environment. This way, a smart home may autonomously detect the presence of an internet-enabled heating system and a smart phone and use them to control the room temperature depending on the current location of its owner. Turning such scenarios into reality is one of the visions of the Internet of Things (IoT) [51]. It encompasses various technologies that enable the interconnection of virtual or physical internet-enabled devices ("things") and to constitute advanced services from them [24]. These devices typically comprise different capabilities and interfaces and are equipped with sensors and/or actuators, providing them the ability to perceive their environment and to interact with it [20]. Typical examples of IoT devices include micro-controllers, smart phones and other objects of the everyday life, as long as they possess basic computing and communication capabilities [35] that allow them to exchange data within a shared IP network.

© The Author(s), under exclusive license to Springer Nature Switzerland AG 2022
J. Barzen et al. (Eds.): SummerSOC 2022, CCIS 1603, pp. 24–44, 2022.
https://doi.org/10.1007/978-3-031-18304-1_2

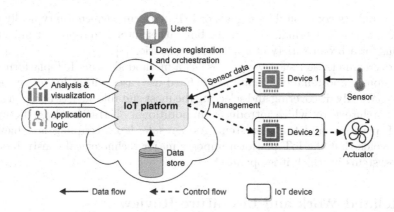

Fig. 1. Exemplary IoT ecoystem with integrated IoT platform and two devices.

Along with the rapidly growing number of world-wide available IoT devices [50] and their increasing affordability, also the individual IoT ecosystems become more and more complex: They can now comprise several thousands of heterogeneous devices [44], reaching from low-end micro-controllers to powerful backend services in the cloud. The high dynamics of IoT ecosystems, to which new devices may be added and from which existing devices may be removed at runtime, impose further challenges [11]. In order to cope with the resulting complexity, so-called IoT platforms [22] have emerged in recent years, offering tools for the administration and orchestration of IoT devices. As depicted in Fig. 1, they may also provide means for the definition of application logic, enabling the implementation of custom use cases within an ecosystem. However, these IoT platforms typically require their users[1] *a)* to manually select suitable devices for realizing the desired use cases and *b)* to register them at the IoT platform using IP addresses or other static references. This leads to huge maintenance efforts, since the employed devices may become less preferable or even unavailable during runtime and hence demand human intervention for reconfiguring and adjusting the IoT platform accordingly.

To address this shortcoming and progress towards the previously described vision of self-controlled and autonomously operating IoT ecosystems, dynamic approaches for the automatic discovery of devices can be employed [11]. Device and service discovery are broad and well-established fields in literature, suggesting hundreds of different methods for the discovery of resources within networks [41]. However, they typically exploit very particular protocols and formats and hence can only be applied to ecosystems that support exactly these technologies. Due the high heterogeneity of the IoT and its devices, IoT platforms implementing such specialised approaches become severely limited in their scope of application and thus more difficult to integrate into existing ecosystems.

---

[1] For the scope of this paper, we differentiate between a) non-expert users, who want to implement their use cases within IoT ecosystems by leveraging an IoT platform and b) administrators, who are responsible for maintaining the technical setup.

This contradicts common design goals of IoT platforms, which are typically not tailored towards individual ecosystems, but rather intend to represent universal solutions for a broad variety of application scenarios [8].

To overcome these issues, we propose *a)* a method allowing IoT platforms to autonomously and reliably execute pre-defined use cases within IoT ecosystems by automatically discovering and selecting the most suitable devices and *b)* a supporting architecture, which introduces an additional abstraction layer between the IoT platform and the ecosystem. As a result, loose coupling is achieved, which avoids that the IoT platform imposes major technological constraints on the ecosystems in which it is operated.

2   Related Work and Literature Review

We conducted a comprehensive literature research in which we investigated many papers proposing various approaches for discovery within IoT ecosystems.

2.1   Method

Most relevant work in literature is available under the keyword *IoT discovery*. We searched for papers by using the online search engines of *Google Scholar*, *The Collection of Computer Science Bibliographies*, *ACM Digital Library*, *IEEE Xplore Digital Library* and *dblp* and refined our queries by adding the terms *device, sensor, platform, selection, query, directory* and *ranking* both individually and in various combinations. In addition, the references of the publications were followed up recursively. We selected the papers on the basis of *a)* their assumed relation to our work, *b)* their recency, *c)* their reputation within the scientific community, but *d)* also in a manner to cover a broad thematic and technological spectrum to do justice to the variety of concepts in this field. Publications that are not directly related to the IoT or do not address local, self-contained IoT ecosystems, are out of the scope of our work due the different problem dimensions and were thus only marginally considered. The same applies to proposals that are fundamentally unsuited for integration in cloud-operated IoT platforms, including solutions specifically designed for proximity-based technologies.

2.2   Literature Overview

Table 1 provides an detailed overview about the different reviewed discovery approaches and their characteristics that we were able to identify. These concepts can generally be divided into three overlapping categories, comprising *a)* proposals based on the paradigm of Service-oriented computing (SoC) [37], which pursue to apply holistic concepts, technologies and standards of Service-oriented Architecture (SoA) [30] to the IoT, *b)* suggestions for centralized solutions, in which one or multiple central repositories are used to store and query formal descriptions of devices and *c)* decentralized approaches, where the IoT devices directly communicate with each other in order to accomplish discovery, comparable to searches in graph data structures. Accordingly, the second column of Table 1 states if and how many central repositories are used within the approaches, while the third and fourth column indicate whether the devices decentrally interact with each other and whether they are based on SoA, respectively.

Some of the suggested solutions are able to discover new IoT devices joining the ecosystem automatically, while others require administrators to manually deposit device descriptions in corresponding repositories. Still others combine both approaches into one system. Therefore, the sixth column of Table 1 lists the entity which is responsible for initiating the first contact when a new device joins the ecosystem. In most cases, this is the device itself, i.e. it has to actively declare its presence against other components. The subsequent three columns indicate whether the approaches support a) keyword-based (free-text) queries for finding devices that are suitable for a certain use case, b) criteria-based queries which allow to specify mandatory capabilities for devices or c) automatic ranking of the search results according to the relevance of the devices to the query. As pointed out by Gomes et al. [19], the supported types of queries can be further classified as either synchronous or asynchronous. While synchronous queries are processed immediately by the discovery service and answered with a list of device descriptions matching the query, asynchronous requests allow other components to register subscriptions at the discovery service and be notified as soon as a change occurs in the result set of the issued query. Thus, asynchronous requests are particularly useful for IoT ecosystems that need to adapt themselves to changes at runtime, such as when a new device is added to the ecosystem or when an existing device is removed from it. In Table 1, the tenth column indicates the support for both types of queries. Finally, the last two columns provide information about a) the technology stacks on which the proposed solutions rely for the discovery of devices and the processing of queries, as well as b) the description languages that are used for formally modelling the IoT devices.

Two of the approaches listed in Table 1 are particularly related to our work: Papp et al. [38] propose a protocol which pursues to achieve interoperability among heterogeneous devices within a common ecosystem. For this purpose, it provides means for device abstraction and establishes an overlay on top of the Message Queuing Telemetry Transport (MQTT) protocol, which enforces a prescribed interaction model and, among other features, affords access to device capabilities. According to the protocol, the network and its devices have to follow a star topology with a so-called *IoT hub* in the center. Since this hub acts as a central controller and may implement application logic for the ecosystem, it can be considered as a kind of IoT platform. The concept includes a mechanism for the automatic detection of new devices joining the network based on Simple Service Discovery Protocol (SSDP), as well as a HTTP interface for manual registration. However, since the protocol relies on MQTT and prescribes a certain topic structure as well as message orders and formats, it can only be used with devices that actively support the particular protocol. As a result, IoT platforms that solely rely on this or another discovery approach from Table 1 inevitably dictate their communication technologies to the entire ecosystem, which renders them unusable for all other scenarios that are based on different technology stacks. In our work, we propose an abstraction layer between the IoT platform and the ecosystem in order to overcome this issue.

Gomes et al. [18] suggest a centralized approach for a discovery service that involves multiple federated repositories. By using a web interface, administrators are able to insert semantic descriptions of devices into the available repositories and then register the latter at the service. Subsequently, applications may use to service to retrieve descriptions of devices showing certain characteristics by issuing criteria-based queries. To process such a query, the discovery service creates a corresponding request and forwards it to the endpoints of all registered repositories. Upon completion, the service consolidates their responses into a common result set, which is then returned to the application. Both synchronous and asynchronous queries are supported. Due to its centralized architecture with federated repositories, the proposed discovery service is suitable for integration into IoT platforms. Furthermore, the asynchronous queries allow the IoT platform to be notified when previously used devices become unavailable or when new, potentially more suitable devices, join the ecosystem. However, there are still shortcomings: a) The discovery service does not evaluate and rank the search results obtained from the different repositories and instead returns an unsorted result set, from which suitable devices must be selected manually, b) the endpoints of all repositories need to be manually registered at the discovery service, leading to additional maintenance efforts, c) administrators are required to manually manage the device descriptions within the repositories, as these basically act as databases, d) as no concepts for the handling of duplicates in search results are mentioned, it has to be assumed that redundant storage of device descriptions in multiple repositories is not allowed, which possibly leads to a loss of information in case of failures and e) working with semantic descriptions of devices may overwhelm users of IoT platforms who often lack sufficient technical expertise [8]. We adapt some of the concepts of Gomes et al. for the scope of IoT platforms and enhance them in order to overcome the mentioned issues and enable the autonomous execution of use cases within IoT ecosystems.

Achieving interoperability between different IoT resources is also a key objective of the Web of Things (WoT) [29], which pursues to transfer concepts of the web to the IoT. With WoT Discovery [6], it includes a flexible discovery approach, in which directories or the devices itself provide so-called *Thing Descriptions* in response to synchronous or asynchronous queries. However, the specification is currently still in draft state and thus subject to frequent changes. Despite this, some of the underlying web technologies may not be available or unreliable in certain scenarios due to resource restrictions, while concepts for failure-tolerant storage of device descriptions are not available yet. Furthermore, it is left open which entities are responsible for inserting device descriptions into the directories, as well as how based on the descriptions the most suitable devices can be selected for the use cases at hand. We address these open aspects for the scope of IoT platforms by proposing a corresponding architecture and method.

In prior work [15,36], we investigated the modeling of complex context information that was managed in a world-wide scalable infrastructure through hierarchical registers and extensible ontologies. In contrast, the concepts proposed in this paper provide a lightweight approach with reduced expressiveness to cater the specific requirements of IoT platforms and resource-limited ecosystems.

Table 1. Overview about the reviewed literature, sorted by year of publication. CR: *Reliance on central repositories;* D: *Decentralized discovery between devices possible;* S: *Exploitation of SOA-related concepts and technologies;* M: *Usage of semantic technologies;* IN: *Entity initiating first contact;* K: *Support for keyword-based queries;* C: *Support for criteria-based queries;* R: *Ranking of query results;* Q: *Query type, either synchronous (s), asynchronous (as) or both (b)*

	CR	D	S	M	IN	K	C	R	Q	Technologies	Device description
[42]	Single	✗	✗	✓	Unspec.	✓	✗	✗	s	REST	SensorML
[52]	Single	✗	✓	✗	Device	✗	✓	✓	s	SOA stack	WSDL, QoS readings
[2]	Single	✗	✗	✗	Device	✗	✗	✗	-	CoAP, CoRE-RD	Comm. behaviour
[17]	Federated	✗	✗	✓	Device	✓	✓	✗	s	DNS-SD	DNS names, TXT-RRs
[32]	Per ecosys.	✓	✗	✗	Device	✗	✓	✗	s	CoAP, CoRE-RD, P2P	(Range) attributes
[12]	None	✓	✗	✗	Device/P2P	✗	✓	✓	s	Unstructured P2P	QoS attributes
[38]	Single	✗	✗	✗	Device or IoT hub	✗	✗	✗	-	SSDP/UPNP, HTTP, MQTT	JSON
[34]	Single	✗	✓	✓	User	✓	✗	✓	s	REST	JSON-LD
[4]	Per gateway	✗	✗	✗	Device	✓	✗	✗	s	DNS-SD, mDNS, CoAP, 6LoWPAN	Resource records
[6]	Arbitrary	✓	✗	✓	Device	✓	✓	✗	b	DNS-SD, mDNS, CoAP, server-sent events	WoT Thing Description
[10]	Blockchain	✗	✗	✓	Provider	✗	✓	✗	s	SPARQL	SSN/SOSA extension
[18]	Federated	✗	✗	✓	User	✗	✓	✗	b	MQTT, SPARQL	SSN, SAN, OWL-S
[43]	None	✗	✗	✗	Scanner	✗	✗	✗	-	Network/port scanner	Open network ports
[40]	Per sniffer	✓	✗	✗	Device	✗	✗	✗	b	MQTT, multicast	JSON
[48]	None	✓	✗	✗	Device	✗	✓	✗	s	Unspecified	Feature list
[13]	Arbitrary	✓	✗	✗	Device	✓	✓	✗	s	CoAP, CoRE-RD, P2P	e.g. CoRE Link Format
[39]	Single	✗	✗	✗	Device	✗	✗	✗	-	HTTP proxy	XML, JSON
[49]	Per gatew.	✓	✗	✗	Device	✓	✗	✗	b	CoAP, CoRE-RD, P2P	CoRE Link Format
[1]	Federated	✗	✗	✗	Device	✓	✗	✗	s	CoAP, CoRE-RD	JSON
[14]	Per router	✓	✗	✗	Device	✓	✗	✗	s	ICN, CoAP	CoRE Link Format
[27]	Single	✗	✓	✗	Device	✗	✗	✗	-	DPWS, multicast, MQTT	JSON
[5]	Single	✗	✗	✓	User	✗	✓	✗	s	SPARQL	Custom ontology
[26]	Sngle	✗	✗	✗	Device	✓	✓	✗	s	REST, Bluetooth, ZigBee, Wi-Fi	JSON
[19]	Federated	✗	✗	✓	User	✗	✓	✗	b	SPARQL	SSN, SAN, OWL-S
[33]	Single	✗	✓	✗	User/MW	✓	✗	✓	s	SOA middleware	XML
[46]	Single	✗	✗	✓	Device	?	✓	?	s	X-GSN, SPARQL	SSN extension
[9]	Single	✗	✗	✗	Device	✓	✗	✓	s	REST, LWM2M, CoAP	CoRE Link Format
[31]	None	✓	✗	✓	n.a	✓	✓	✓	s	P2P Skipnet	Context ontologies
[7]	Per gateway	✓	✗	✗	Device or gateway	✓	✗	✗	s	DNS-SD, mDNS, P2P, CoAP	CoRE Link Format or JSON-WSP
[28]	Arbitrary	✓	✗	✗	device	✓	✗	✗	b	DNS-SD, mDNS, Bonjour	TXT-RR
[21] [3]	Single	✗	✓	✗	Device or disc. unit	✓	✓	✓	s	WS-Discovery, DPWS, multicast	WSDL
[47]	Federated	✗	✗	✓	Device	✓	✓	✗	s	AtomPub, mDNS	Atom Syndic. Format

2.3   Conclusion and Challenges

Based on the literature review, we conclude that our work needs to address the following core challenges:

Limited Resources. Devices and networks of IoT ecosystems are often severely resource-constrained and hence possess only few computing and hardware capabilities, as well as low bandwidth [51]. Accordingly, when designing a discovery mechanism for IoT platforms, it must be ensured that the additional computional load for the devices is as low as possible. With respect to the network, the interaction model between the IoT platform and the devices should also minimize the exchange and size of messages and be robust against connection failures. Furthermore, it must be taken into consideration that the ecosystem might support only a small selection of technologies. For instance, many of the approaches listed in Table 1 rely on UDP multicast, which however may be unavailable in the underlying networks of certain ecosystems.

Need for Fault-Tolerance. Many of the reviewed approaches are based on a single central repository (cf. Table 1), in which the formal descriptions of all devices are stored. However, such architectures are often unreliable, as the repositories represent single point of failures. Furthermore, they typically scale poorly with an increasing number of devices [16] and become a bottleneck as the system grows. For this reason, an architecture with federated repositories is to be preferred. In addition, it should allow to redundantly store the descriptions of devices in several repositories at the same time in order to avoid loss of information in case of failures of individual repositories.

High Dynamics. Most IoT ecosystems are highly dynamic, as devices can continuously join or leave them during runtime. Accordingly, devices that previously participated in a use case may be modified or become unavailable. In this case, the discovery component of the IoT platform must be able to detect these kind of changes and compensate for them, e.g. by transferring the affected tasks to other suitable devices of the ecosystem. In order to enable the efficient and timely detection of such events, the discovery mechanism should support asynchronous requests, as already offered by some of the approaches listed in Table 1. In addition, the high dynamics require that as many tasks as possible are performed automatically by the IoT platform and without human intervention, so that huge manual maintenance efforts are avoided. Thus, in contrast to some of the proposals in literature, the discovery approach should not necessarily require administrators to manually write, register and maintain descriptions of devices.

High Flexibility. IoT platforms are typically not tailored towards individual IoT systems and domains, but rather represent universal solutions that are supposed to be applicable in as many different contexts and ecosystems as possible. For this reason, they either employ technology-agnostic concepts or support a variety of different technologies. In contrast, the literature proposes a vast number of discovery approaches, which rely on different technology stacks and also vary strongly in their individual characteristics [25]. Furthermore, in the areas of enterprise systems, industry and home automation, numerous other discovery protocols are available that are individually optimized for their respective domains, but mostly unsuited for constrained IoT environments [40]. Due to the interoperability issue discussed earlier for the proposal of Papp et al. [38], it does not suffice to just integrate a single discovery approach into an IoT platform. On the other hand, the parallel integration of multiple different discovery approaches involves unreasonable implementation and maintenance efforts and still renders the IoT platform useless for ecosystems relying on other technologies. For this reason, a more flexible approach is needed that can be easily adapted to the characteristics and requirements of individual IoT ecosystems.

3   Method for Autonomous Execution of Use Cases

In order to enhance IoT platforms for the autonomous execution of pre-defined use cases within IoT ecosystems, we propose the method depicted in Fig. 2. It assumes an ecosystem into which a discovery-enabled IoT platform has already been integrated. The process can be divided into two main parts: The first one is called *User Process* and is carried out only once by the users of the IoT platform. With the beginning of the *Discovery Process*, the IoT platform then takes over and autonomously performs various discovery-related tasks.

In step ① of this method, the users of the IoT platform define use cases that are supposed to be executed within their ecosystem. Such use cases typically involve the sensing of the environment, the recognition of situations and the intended reactions to those. The description "when a fire is detected in the factory building, the extinguishing system should be activated." could be considered as a simple example. While the use cases may be described either formally or informally at this point, they are always device-independent, meaning that they do not explicitly specify which devices of the ecosystem are supposed to be used for their implementation. As depicted in Fig. 2, the designed use cases represent the resulting artifact of this method step.

Based on the first step, the users translate the use cases into corresponding application logic for the IoT platform in step ②. As described in Sect. 1, IoT platforms typically support the definition of application logic either in a model-based manner or in the form of "if-then" rules. However, in this method, the application logic remains device-independent and does not refer to specific devices of the IoT ecosystem. Hence, the users do not need to manually register devices at the IoT platform by providing distinct identifiers, such as IP addresses, and link them with the application logic. Instead, they define the application logic with placeholders, which the IoT platform will automatically replace at runtime with those devices of the ecosystem that appear to be the most suitable ones for realizing the use cases. Ultimately, the specified application logic with the device placeholders forms the resulting artifact of this step.

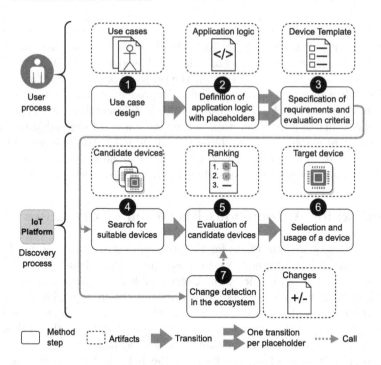

Fig. 2. The proposed method for the autonomous execution of use cases in IoT ecosystems by employing automatic device discovery and selection.

While the first two steps are performed only once within an iteration of the method, the following steps are executed for each device placeholder that is part of the previously specified application logic. In step ③, the users define criteria for each placeholder by describing the characteristics a device of the IoT ecosystem must possess to be considered a possible fill-in. In order to support this in a modular manner and to allow the reuse of criteria for multiple placeholders, the users register so-called *Device Templates* at the IoT platform and attach them to one or multiple placeholders of the application logic. Device templates can be considered as blueprints for the devices that are supposed to be discovered by the IoT platform within the ecosystem and selected as fill-ins for the placeholders. Each device template consists of *a)* a set of requirements, which correspond to search criteria and describe the hardware and software characteristics that a device must possess in order to become a possible fill-in for the respective placeholder, as well as *a)* a set of evaluation criteria specifying a scheme by which the devices meeting all requirements are supposed to be evaluated in order to determine the device that appears to be the most suitable fill-in. For example, a device template may prescribe that the devices must necessarily be located in a specific room and must be equipped with a temperature sensor in order to qualify as fill-in for a certain placeholder. On the other hand, the evaluation criteria of the device template may define that among all the devices fulfilling these requirements always the device with the highest measurement accuracy should be selected as substitute for the placeholder. The user-defined device template for each placeholder forms the resulting artifact of this step.

With step ④, the method transitions to the discovery process. Here, the IoT platform searches the IoT ecosystem for devices that fulfill the requirements of the device templates. While in principle one or multiple of the discovery approaches discussed in Sect. 2 could be used for this purpose, we introduce a loosely-coupled architecture in Sect. 4 that allows to do this in a more flexible and technology-agnostic manner. During this procedure, the IoT platform verifies each device template that has been attached to a placeholder and retrieves the formal descriptions of all devices of the ecosystem that fulfill the specified requirements. Since these devices are potentially suitable candidates for filling in a specific placeholder, they are called *candidate devices*. If no candidate devices can be found for a placeholder, it will currently not be possible to implement the corresponding use case and hence the process terminates at this point. However, it can be resumed as soon as suitable devices become available (cf. step ⑦). The descriptions of the candidate devices form the artifact of this step.

In step ⑤, the IoT platform assesses the previously retrieved candidate devices for each device template. For this purpose, a score is calculated and assigned to the candidate devices by applying the evaluation criteria of the device template to the device descriptions. The resulting score reflects how well the respective device suits as fill-in for the placeholder in comparison to the other candidate devices. After all candidate devices for the device template have been evaluated, they are ranked based on their scores in descending order, such that the device with the highest score is listed at the top. This ranking can be considered as a recommendation in terms of which devices should preferably be used as fill-in for the placeholder and represents the resulting artifact of this step.

Based on the ranking, the IoT platform in step ⑥ selects a so-called *target device* among the associated candidate devices for each placeholder. Ideally, the decision is made in favor of the first device in the ranking, but the IoT platform must also ensure that this device is currently available in the IoT ecosystem and thus can actually be used as a fill-in. In case the device is unavailable, e.g., due to a technical issue, the next device in the ranking is selected and checked for its readiness. The finally selected target device is the output of this step.

After the start of the discovery process, step ⑦ becomes active in parallel to step ④. It makes use of asynchronous queries as introduced in Sect. 2, so that the IoT platform is notified about changes within the ecosystem. This way, the IoT platform is able to quickly detect *a)* when a new device that also satisfies the requirements of a user-defined device template joins the ecosystem, *b)* when an existing device satisfying the requirements of a device template becomes unavailable within the ecosystem, or *c)* when an existing device satisfying the requirements of a device template is modified, such that its capabilities change. Each of these three cases might have an impact on the candidate and target devices that were previously determined for a device template. For example, it could turn out that a new device joining the ecosystem receives a higher score in step ⑤ than the devices that were formerly evaluated and thus represents a more suitable fill-in for the placeholder in the application logic. On the other side, a device that was selected in step ⑥ might become unavailable or change its capabilities over time, such that it does not fulfill the requirements of its device template anymore and hence can no longer be considered a candidate device. In order to cope with these situations, step ⑦ re-initiates the execution of the steps ⑤ and ⑥ as soon as it is notified about a modification in the ecosystem that actually affects the candidate devices of at least one placeholder. As part of the invocation of step ⑤, a formal description of the observed changes is passed, such that the set of candidate devices can be updated and the ranking re-calculated accordingly. As a result, step ⑦ allows the IoT platform to adapt to changes within highly dynamic ecosystems at runtime by re-evaluating the candidate devices and, if necessary, switching the fill-in devices for placeholders.

4   Architecture Supporting Discovery for IoT Platforms

To accommodate the application of the previously presented method in IoT ecosystems, we propose the architecture illustrated in Fig. 3. According to it, an IoT ecosystem consists of at least three different types of components: *a)* an IoT platform, *b)* an arbitrary number of devices and *c)* at least one so-called *discovery repository (DR)*. The device entities in this architecture do not solely refer to physical IoT devices, but may also encapsulate possibly necessary IoT gateways [53] for mediating between different networks and communication technologies. DRs are self-contained software components that collect formal descriptions of the devices within an ecosystem and provide them to the IoT platform on request via a prescribed interface. Since they serve as an additional abstraction layer between the IoT platform in a cloud environment and the devices at the edge, loose coupling can be achieved.

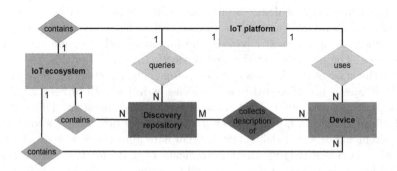

Fig. 3. ER model of the components that are involved in the architecture.

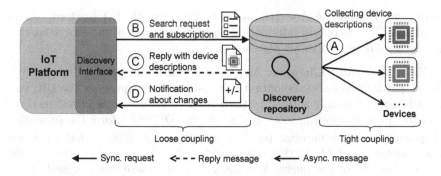

Fig. 4. Interactions between an IoT platform and a discovery repository.

4.1 Discovery Repositories

Discovery repositories (DRs) are explicitly developed and deployed for an IoT ecosystem by its administrators. They are similar to the repositories proposed by Gomes et al. [18], but more flexible and independent in their design and they undertake a broader field of responsibilities. They basically pursue three tasks:

Collection of Device Descriptions: The main task of a DR is to search, collect and manage the formal descriptions of the devices that are available within the IoT ecosystem, as depicted in Fig. 4 (A). This includes the storage of new descriptions when devices join the IoT ecosystem, the deletion of descriptions when devices leave or become unavailable, and the updating of descriptions in case device characteristics change over time. The selection of technologies and approaches that are employed for carrying out this task is however left to the individual implementation of the DRs. In the simplest case, the administrators of an IoT ecosystem can manually manage a DR by adding, deleting and updating the descriptions of their devices as needed. Here, the DR can be considered a simple database. In more complex systems though, the DRs may implement one or even multiple of the discovery approaches that are proposed in literature (cf. Sect. 2), which then enable the automatic discovery of devices and the collection of their descriptions. Since individual requirements tend to change from ecosystem to ecosystem, the administrators are encouraged to decide which approaches they consider most suitable for the DRs in their present scenario. In case they plan to employ several DRs, these may also implement different techniques.

Retrieval of Device Descriptions: As shown in Fig. 4 (B), each DR provides an interface through which the IoT platform is able to issue search queries for devices. This interface is prescribed by the IoT platform implementing the method as introduced in Sect. 3, such that the DRs can be developed against this interface. The queries contain the requirements that were previously defined by a user at the IoT platform as part of a device template. When a DR receives such a request, it is expected to search its collected device descriptions and eventually return a response to the IoT platform (cf. (C)) that contains the set of all device descriptions meeting the given requirements. This way, the IoT platform can use the DRs in order to obtain information about the devices of the ecosystem that embody candidate devices for placeholders.

Notification About Changes: As part of a search query for devices (cf. Ⓑ), the IoT platform has also the option to register a subscription at the DR, such that it is asynchronously notified by the DR about changes that affect the result set of the query during runtime. As a result, the DR will inform the subscribed IoT platform with a message (cf. Ⓓ) as soon as it detects that *a)* a new device became available in the IoT ecosystem whose description also satisfies the requirements of the query, *b)* a device whose description originally satisfied the requirements of the query became unavailable in the IoT ecosystem, or that *c)* the description of a device that either previously or now satisfies the requirements of the query was modified with respect to its capabilities.

Optionally, a DR may also be used to transform already existing descriptions of devices, e.g. as provided by the device manufacturers, into formats that are supported by the IoT platform. In this case, the DR additionally acts as a message translator [23] that allows the reuse of device descriptions and thus eases the integration of the IoT platform into existing IoT ecosystems.

The DRs do not necessarily need to be realized as stand-alone applications; instead, they can also be implemented on top of existing components, such as IoT gateways [53]. This applies in particular to ecosystems in which the gateways wrap larger groups of devices and even perform discovery tasks themselves.

In summary, the DRs encapsulate all ecosystem-specific aspects and hide them from the IoT platform, which can then use the DRs through a prescribed interface. As a result, the DRs become tightly coupled with the ecosystem and its contained devices, but potentially loosely coupled with the IoT platform.

4.2   Request-Reply Interactions

In our proposed architecture, publish-subscribe-based messaging [23] via a message broker facilitates the communication between the IoT platform and the DRs. Accordingly, we assume that the DRs subscribe to so-called *request topics* at this message broker, under which they expect to receive query messages from the IoT platform. Similar to the concept of Gomes et al. [18], the administrators need to register the endpoints of the available DRs at the IoT platform. However, in our approach, they do this by specifying the request topics instead of network addresses. As a result, a one-to-many relationship between topic registrations and DRs is achieved, because an arbitrary number of DRs may be accessible under the same request topic due to the publish-subscribe paradigm. This is an important step towards loose coupling. Furthermore, in order to avoid the generation of individual request messages for each DR, our approach employs the *scatter gather* messaging pattern [23], which allows to broadcast a single request message to multiple DRs at once and to subsequently collect and combine their responses. Figure 5 illustrates how this pattern is applied to search queries: In

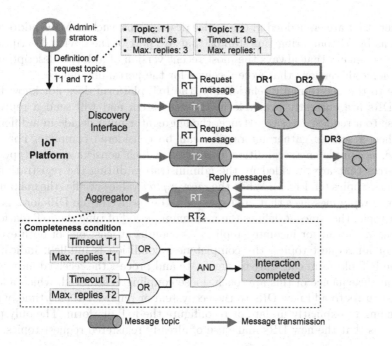

Fig. 5. Application of the scatter gather messaging pattern for achieving loose coupling between the IoT platform and the discovery repositories.

the given ecosystem, three DRs are available, of which DR1 and DR2 are subscribed to the same request topic T1, while DR3 is subscribed to T2. Both request topics have already been registered at the IoT platform by the administrators. In case a search query for device descriptions is supposed to be issued against all DRs according to (B) in Fig. 4, the IoT platform creates a corresponding request message and publishes it under the request topics T1 and T2 at the message broker. This way, the request message is broadcasted to all available DRs and processed by them. It is worth noting that for the delivery of the request message the IoT platform does not need to know how many DRs are actually subscribed to each request topic. Next to the requirements of a device template, the request message also contains a so-called *reply topic* RT, which was previously generated by the IoT platform and subscribed by it at the message broker. It serves as a return address [23] for the DRs. Accordingly, after the individual DRs processed the request message, they publish their reply messages under this topic, so that the message broker can deliver them back to the IoT platform. Here, a software component called *aggregator* [23] receives the replies and aggregates them into a common data structure, which can then be further processed in correspondence with the method steps presented in Sect. 3. Since all device descriptions are allowed to be redundantly available in multiple DRs at the same time and even in different versions, the aggregator is also responsible for eliminating duplicated device descriptions from the result set. This is done by *a)* verifying unique device identifiers that are embedded in the device descriptions, such as MAC addresses, as well as by *b)* comparing timestamps that are part of the device descriptions in order to ensure that always the most recent version of a device description is used among all versions that were received for the pertaining device.

Due to the one-to-many relationship, the IoT platform does not know how many DRs are currently available in the ecosystem and will send a reply in response to a request message. Hence, the aggregator must decide in a different way when a scatter gather interaction can be considered complete. For this purpose, a completeness condition is applied, which consists of two types of parameters that are provided by the administrators during the registration of the request topics (cf. Fig. 5): While the *max. replies* value specifies the maximum number of reply messages that are expected to be received from DRs for a given request topic, the *timeout* defines the maximum period of time the IoT platform is supposed to wait for incoming replies. As soon as at least one of both events occur for all request topics, the completeness condition is fulfilled, indicating that the IoT platform can start to aggregate and process the received messages.

As a consequence of this approach, loose coupling is achieved, which allows administrators to add new DRs to the ecosystem or remove DRs anytime, without needing to explicitly update or reconfigure the IoT platform. The only prerequisite is that the new DRs make use of already registered request topics.

5 Prototype and Discussion

As proof of concept, we integrated the method as presented in Sect. 3 into the Multi-purpose Binding and Provisioning Platform (MBP)[2] [45], an open source IoT platform that allows the definition of rule-based application logics. For testing purposes, we developed an exemplary DR[3] that implements the tasks as described in Sect. 4 and is able to communicate with the MBP via MQTT in accordance with the proposed interaction scheme. The software architecture of this DR is depicted in Fig. 6. At its core, it consists of a Spring Boot application with a REST interface that allows administrators to manually manage the descriptions of the devices that are available within the IoT ecosystem. Accordingly, they can add descriptions of devices joining the ecosystem, remove descriptions of leaving devices and update descriptions of modified devices. The application does not store the device descriptions itself, but instead uses an instance of Elasticsearch for this purpose, which treats and indexes the device descriptions as documents. This way, the DR is able to efficiently process incoming search requests of the IoT platform by translating them into corresponding queries for Elasticsearch. Furthermore, the DR supports subscriptions and is thus able to asynchronously notify the IoT platform about changes that affect the result sets of preceding search requests. By using the discovery-enabled MBP and running multiple instances of this DR in parallel, we were able to practically test and evaluate our concepts.

---

[2] MBP on GitHub: https://github.com/IPVS-AS/MBP.
[3] DR on GitHub: https://github.com/IPVS-AS/MBP-DiscoveryRepository.

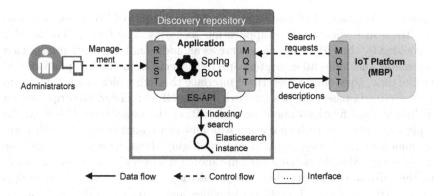

Fig. 6. Architecture of our discovery repository that serves as proof of concept.

The proposed method and its underlying architecture can support IoT ecosystems that involve such an IoT platform at improving their **availability**: Since the DRs might be able to monitor the devices within the ecosystem and notify the IoT platform asynchronously about detected changes, the IoT platform can quickly react to device failures at runtime by re-evaluating the candidate devices and selecting the next most suitable device for the affected placeholder. On the other hand, the use of multiple, federated, but potentially also differently implemented DRs avoids the establishment of single point of failures. Furthermore, the aggregator component (cf. Fig. 5) is able to deal with duplicates, which allows the redundant storage of device descriptions within multiple DRs and hence leads to higher robustness. The federated architecture gives also rise to **scalability**, because an increasing number of devices can be countered by the deployment of additional DRs. The prerequisite for this is that the DRs share their responsibilities of discovering and monitoring the devices, such that not all DRs need to assess all available devices. This can be achieved e.g. by the usage of subnets. Due to the loose coupling, new DRs can be flexibly added to or removed from the ecosystem without needing to reconfigure the IoT platform, which eases horizontal scaling. With this approach, almost arbitrary numbers of devices and DRs can be inserted into an IoT ecosystem, until the IoT platform, which is a centralized component by nature, becomes a bottleneck itself. The proposed concepts can also be considered as **efficient** in terms of resource consumption, as they *a)* do not necessarily put additional tasks or load onto the typically resource-constrained devices, albeit this also depends on the specific implementation of the DRs, *b)* apply the scatter gather messaging pattern for the interaction between the IoT platform and the DRs, which can also be used on top of lightweight messaging protocols such as MQTT and avoids overhead in the generation of request messages and *c)* allow the developers of the DRs to select the most suitable and most efficient technologies for the discovery of devices within their ecosystem, based on the application scenario at hand and by considering the actually available resources. In contrast to the proposals in literature (cf. Sect. 2), the main benefit of our approach is its **flexibility**. It allows to integrate the enhanced IoT platforms into different kinds of IoT ecosystems and to use them in a wide range of application scenarios. The foundations for this are provided by the DRs, since they serve as an additional abstraction layer that encapsulates and hides all ecosystem-specific aspects from the IoT platform. At the same time, they offer a prescribed interface through which the IoT platform can issue criteria-based queries for devices, as well as register subscriptions for asynchronous notifications about changes within the ecosystem. This way, the IoT platform remains technology-agnostic and can co-operate with both manually managed IoT ecosystems, as well as highly dynamic ones that need to make use of specific, potentially custom-tailored discovery technologies. In addition, the DRs also support the reuse of already existing device descriptions. Consequently, such an IoT platform provides high interoperability and can be integrated in various kinds of IoT ecosystems without having to adapt the IoT platform itself. On the downside, the additional abstraction layer may cause overhead in terms of development efforts, latency and resource consumption. However, this highly depends on the individual implementations of the DR.

6   Conclusion

In this paper, we presented a method that allows IoT platforms *a)* to assist their users in the specification of device-independent application logic for use cases by employing placeholders, *b)* to let their users define device templates, which prescribe requirements and evaluation criteria for devices that should be selected as fill-ins for the placeholders, *c)* to autonomously discover and search for devices within an IoT ecosystem that fulfill the user-defined requirements and thus constitute candidate devices for the placeholders, *d)* to score and rank candidate devices with respect to the user-defined evaluation criteria, *e)* to select the most suitable candidate devices as fill-ins for the placeholders and *f)* to detect changes in highly dynamic IoT ecosystems at runtime and to cope with them by re-evaluating the candidate devices of the affected placeholders. To ease the application of this method, we also introduced a supporting architecture for IoT ecosystems. It comprises so-called discovery repositories, which are tailored towards the specific needs of the application scenario at hand and serve as an additional abstraction layer between the IoT platform and the ecosystem to establish loose coupling. As a result, IoT platforms implementing our method can remain technology-agnostic and thus be applied to a wide range of different scenarios without needing to adapt the IoT platform itself. Furthermore, also the availability and scalability of the encompassing IoT systems can be improved.

In future work, we pursue to conduct tests in larger IoT ecosystems in order to empirically verify our assumptions. Moreover, we plan to consider options for the automatic selection of suitable criteria for device templates as well as for including availability predictions into the evaluation of candidate devices.

References

1. Barreto, F.M., Duarte, P.A.d.S., Maia, M.E., et al.: Coap-ctx: a context-aware CoAP extension for smart objects discovery in internet of things. In: 2017 IEEE 41st Annual Computer Software and Applications Conference, vol. 1, pp. 575–584 (2017)
2. Baykara, C., Şafak, I., Kalkan, K.: SHAPEIoT: secure handshake protocol for autonomous IoT device discovery and blacklisting using physical unclonable functions and machine learning. In: 13th International Conference on Network and Communications Security (NCS 2021), September 2021
3. Chirila, S., Lemnaru, C., Dinsoreanu, M.: Semantic-based IoT device discovery and recommendation mechanism. In: 2016 IEEE 12th International Conference on Intelligent Computer Communication and Processing (ICCP), pp. 111–116 (2016)
4. Chiu, Y.H., Liao, C.F., Chen, K.: Transparent web of things discovery in constrained networks based on mDNS/DNS-SD. In: 2021 International Conference on Platform Technology and Service (PlatCon), pp. 1–6. IEEE (2021)
5. Chun, S., Seo, S., Oh, B., et al.: Semantic description, discovery and integration for the internet of things. In: Proceedings of the 2015 IEEE 9th International Conference on Semantic Computing (IEEE ICSC 2015), pp. 272–275. IEEE (2015)
6. Cimmino, A., McCool, M., Tavakolizadeh, F., et al.: Web of Things (WoT) Discovery. W3C working draft. In: World Wide Web Consortium (W3C), July 2022
7. Cirani, S., Davoli, L., Ferrari, G., et al.: A scalable and self-configuring architecture for service discovery in the internet of things. IEEE Internet Things J. 1(5), 508–521 (2014)
8. da Cruz, M.A.A., Rodrigues, J.J.P.C., et al.: A reference model for internet of things middleware. IEEE Internet Things J. 5(2), 871–883 (2018)
9. Datta, S.K., Bonnet, C., Nikaein, N.: An IoT gateway centric architecture to provide novel m2m services. In: 2014 IEEE World Forum on Internet of Things (WF-IoT), pp. 514–519. IEEE (2014)
10. Dawod, A., Georgakopoulos, D., Jayaraman, P.P., et al.: An IoT-owned service for global IoT device discovery, integration and (re) use. In: 2020 IEEE International Conference on Services Computing (SCC), pp. 312–320. IEEE (2020)
11. Del Gaudio, D., Hirmer, P.: Fulfilling the IoT Vision: Are We There Yet? In: IoTBDS, pp. 367–374 (2020)
12. Demir, K.: A QOS-aware service discovery and selection mechanism for IoT environments. Sādhanā 46(4), 1–13 (2021)
13. Djamaa, B., Kouda, M.A., Yachir, A., et al.: FetchioT: efficient resource fetching for the internet of things. In: 2018 Federated Conference on Computer Science and Information Systems (FedCSIS), pp. 637–643. IEEE (2018)
14. Dong, L., Ravindran, R., Wang, G.: ICN based distributed IoT resource discovery and routing. In: 2016 23rd International Conference on Telecommunications (ICT), pp. 1–7. IEEE (2016)
15. Dürr, F., Hönle, N., Nicklas, D., Becker, C., Rothermel, K.: Nexus - a platform for context-aware applications. Roth, Jörg, editor 1, 15–18 (2004)
16. Evdokimov, S., Fabian, B., Kunz, S., et al.: Comparison of discovery service architectures for the Internet of Things. In: 2010 IEEE International Conference on Sensor Networks, Ubiquitous, and Trustworthy Computing, pp. 237–244 (2010)
17. Fernandez, S., Amoretti, M., Restori, F., et al.: Semantic identifiers and DNS names for IoT. In: 2021 International Conference on Computer Communications and Networks (ICCCN), pp. 1–9. IEEE (2021)

18. Gomes, P., Cavalcante, E., Batista, T., et al.: A semantic-based discovery service for the internet of things. J. Internet Serv. Appl. **10**(1) (2019)

19. Gomes, P., Cavalcante, E., Rodrigues, T., et al.: A federated discovery service for the internet of things. In: Proceedings of the 2nd Workshop on Middleware for Context-Aware Applications in the IoT, pp. 25–30 (2015)

20. Gubbi, J., Buyya, R., Marusic, S., et al.: Internet of things (IoT): A vision, architectural elements, and future directions. Fut. Gene. Comput. Syst. **29**(7), 1645–1660 (2013)

21. Guinard, D., Trifa, V., Karnouskos, S., et al.: Interacting with the SOA-based internet of things: discovery, query, selection, and on-demand provisioning of web services. IEEE Trans. Serv. Comput. **3**(3), 223–235 (2010)

22. Guth, J., Breitenbücher, U., Falkenthal, M., et al.: Comparison of IoT platform architectures: a field study based on a reference architecture. In: 2016 Cloudification of the Internet of Things (CIoT), pp. 1–6. IEEE (2016)

23. Hohpe, G., Woolf, B.: Enterprise Integration Patterns: Designing, Building, and Deploying Messaging Solutions. Addison-Wesley Professional, Boston (2004)

24. ITU: ITU-T Recommendation Y.2060: Overview of the Internet of things. Tech. rep., International Telecommunication Union, June 2012

25. Khaled, A.E., Helal, S.: Interoperable communication framework for bridging restful and topic-based communication in IoT. Futur. Gener. Comput. Syst. **92**, 628–643 (2019)

26. Khodadadi, F., Dastjerdi, A.V., Buyya, R.: Simurgh: a framework for effective discovery, programming, and integration of services exposed in IoT. In: 2015 Internat. Conference on Recent Advances in Internet of Things, pp. 1–6. IEEE (2015)

27. Kim, S.M., Choi, H.S., Rhee, W.S.: IoT home gateway for auto-configuration and management of MQTT devices. In: 2015 IEEE Conference on Wireless Sensors (ICWiSe), pp. 12–17. IEEE (2015)

28. Klauck, R., Kirsche, M.: Bonjour contiki: a case study of a DNS-based discovery service for the internet of things. In: Li, X.-Y., Papavassiliou, S., Ruehrup, S. (eds.) ADHOC-NOW 2012. LNCS, vol. 7363, pp. 316–329. Springer, Heidelberg (2012). https://doi.org/10.1007/978-3-642-31638-8_24

29. Kovatsch, M., Matsukura, R., Lagally, M., et al.: Web of Things (WoT) Architecture. In: W3c recommendation, World Wide Web Consortium (W3C), April 2020

30. Krafzig, D., Banke, K., Slama, D.: Enterprise SOA: Service-Oriented Architecture Best Practices. Prentice Hall, Hoboken (2005)

31. Li, J., Zaman, N., Li, H.: A decentralized locality-preserving context-aware service discovery framework for internet of things. In: 2015 IEEE International Conference on Services Computing, pp. 317–323. IEEE (2015)

32. Li, Z., Yao, J., Huang, H.: A CoAP-based decentralized resource discovery for IoT network. In: 2021 6th International Conference on Communication, Image and Signal Processing (CCISP), pp. 398–402. IEEE (2021)

33. Lunardi, W.T., de Matos, E., Tiburski, R., et al.: Context-based search engine for industrial IoT: discovery, search, selection, and usage of devices. In: 2015 IEEE 20th Conference on Emerging Technologies & Factory Automation, pp. 1–8 (2015)

34. Madjarov, I., Slaimi, F.: A graph-based web services discovery framework for IoT ecosystem. Open J. Internet of Things **7**(1), 1–17 (2021)

35. Miorandi, D., Sicari, S., De Pellegrini, F., et al.: Internet of things: vision, applications and research challenges. Ad Hoc Netw. **10**(7), 1497–1516 (2012)
36. Nicklas, D., Mitschang, B.: On building location aware applications using an open platform based on the nexus augmented world model. Softw. Syst. Model. **3**(4), 303–313 (2004)
37. Papazoglou, M.P., Georgakopoulos, D.: Introduction: service-oriented computing. Commun. ACM **46**(10), 24–28 (2003)
38. Papp, I., Pavlovic, R., Antic, M.: WISE: MQTT-based protocol for IP device provisioning and abstraction in IoT solutions. Elektronika ir Elektrotechnika **27**(2), 86–95 (2021)
39. Pêgo, P.R., Nunes, L.: Automatic discovery and classifications of IoT devices. In: 12th Iberian Conference on Information Systems and Technol. pp. 1–10. IEEE (2017)
40. Pereira, E.M., Pinto, R., dos Reis, J.P.C., Gonçalves, G.: MQTT-RD: a MQTT based resource discovery for machine to machine communication. In: IoTBDS, pp. 115–124 (2019)
41. Pourghebleh, B., Hayyolalam, V., Aghaei Anvigh, A.: Service discovery in the internet of things: review of current trends and research challenges. Wireless Netw. **26**(7), 5371–5391 (2020)
42. Raghu Nandan, R., Nalini, N., Hamsavath, P.N.: IoT-CBSE: a search engine for semantic Internet of Things. In: Shetty, N.R., Patnaik, L.M., Nagaraj, H.C., Hamsavath, P.N., Nalini, N. (eds.) Emerging Research in Computing, Information, Communication and Applications. LNEE, vol. 789, pp. 265–271. Springer, Singapore (2022). https://doi.org/10.1007/978-981-16-1338-8_23
43. Riggs, C., Patel, J., Gagneja, K.: IoT device discovery for incidence response. In: 2019 Fifth Conference on Mobile and Secure Services, pp. 1–8. IEEE (2019)
44. Sharma, M., Pant, S., Kumar Sharma, D., et al.: Enabling security for the industrial internet of things using deep learning, blockchain, and coalitions. Trans. Emerg. Telecommun. Technol. **32**(7), e4137 (2021)
45. Franco da Silva, A.C., Hirmer, P., Schneider, J., et al.: MBP: Not just an IoT platform. In: 2020 IEEE International Conference on Pervasive Computing and Communications Workshops (PerCom Workshops), pp. 1–3. IEEE (2020)
46. Soldatos, J., et al.: OpenIoT: open source internet-of-things in the cloud. In: Podnar Žarko, I., Pripužić, K., Serrano, M. (eds.) Interoperability and Open-Source Solutions for the Internet of Things. LNCS, vol. 9001, pp. 13–25. Springer, Cham (2015). https://doi.org/10.1007/978-3-319-16546-2_3
47. Stirbu, V.: Towards a restful plug and play experience in the web of things. In: 2008 IEEE International Conference on Semantic Computing, pp. 512–517 (2008)
48. Sunthonlap, J., Nguyen, P., Wang, H., et al.: SAND: a social-aware and distributed scheme for device discovery in the internet of things. In: 2018 Internat. Conference on Computing, Networking and Communications (ICNC), pp. 38–42. IEEE (2018)
49. Tanganelli, G., Vallati, C., Mingozzi, E.: Edge-centric distributed discovery and access in the internet of things. IEEE IoT J. **5**(1), 425–438 (2017)
50. Transforma Insights: Global IoT market to grow to 24.1 billion devices in 2030, generating $1.5 trillion annual revenue, May 2020. https://transformainsights.com/news/iot-market-24-billion-usd15-trillion-revenue-2030. Accessed 2 July 2022
51. Vermesan, O., Friess, P.: Internet of Things: Converging Technologies For Smart Environments and Integrated Ecosystems. River Publishers, Aalborg (2013)

52. Wang, R., Lu, J.: Qos-aware service discovery and selection management for cloud-edge computing using a hybrid meta-heuristic algorithm in IoT. Wirel. Person. Commun. pp. 1–14 (2021)

53. Zhu, Q., Wang, R., Chen, Q., Liu, Y., Qin, W.: IoT gateway: bridging wireless sensor networks into internet of things. In: 2010 IEEE/IFIP International Conference on Embedded and Ubiquitous Computing, pp. 347–352 (2010)

Serverless or Serverful? A Pattern-Based Approach for Exploring Hosting Alternatives

Vladimir Yussupov[1(✉)], Uwe Breitenbücher[1], Antonio Brogi[2], Lukas Harzenetter[1], Frank Leymann[1], and Jacopo Soldani[2]

[1] Institute of Architecture of Application Systems, University of Stuttgart, Stuttgart, Germany
{yussupov,breitenbuecher,harzenetter,leymann}@iaas.uni-stuttgart.de
[2] Department of Computer Science, University of Pisa, Pisa, Italy
{antonio.brogi,jacopo.soldani}@unipi.it

Abstract. Various cloud service models with different management requirements can be used for hosting a certain application component. For instance, more consumer-managed serverful options can be preferred if a component has special requirements related to deployment stack or scaling configuration management, whereas more provider-managed serverless alternatives can be used if no customization is needed. However, finding a suitable hosting variant based on the deployment stack or scaling configuration management requirements is cumbersome without clear guidelines. In our previous work, we introduced a set of Component Hosting Patterns that represent different management trade-offs and can help finding suitable hosting options for a component to be deployed. However, selecting the most appropriate pattern and exploring which concrete deployment alternatives can be used to technically realize the selected pattern was up to developers, thus, requiring considerable expertise in provider-specific offerings. Therefore, in this work, we (i) introduce four new complementary patterns representing abstract deployment stack customization and scaling configuration management decisions, which we (ii) combine with our Component Hosting Patterns in a new pattern language. Moreover, we (iii) introduce a method that supports application developers using the introduced pattern language as well as refining selected patterns to concrete technical deployment stacks. Finally, we (iv) show how the TOSCA modeling tool Eclipse Winery can be used to support our new method.

Keywords: Application deployment · Hosting · Patterns · Pattern language · Pattern refinement · Serverful · Serverless · Cloud computing

1 Introduction

Modern IT systems consist of various components, such as applications, databases, or message queues, that can be hosted using different cloud services that impose different management responsibilities on cloud consumers and

© The Author(s), under exclusive license to Springer Nature Switzerland AG 2022
J. Barzen et al. (Eds.): SummerSOC 2022, CCIS 1603, pp. 45–67, 2022.
https://doi.org/10.1007/978-3-031-18304-1_3

provide diverse scaling configuration opportunities [37]. This variety of options enables cloud consumers to select a certain hosting variant based on preferred management trade-offs. For example, it is easier to customize the environment for application components hosted on Infrastructure-as-a-Service (IaaS) offerings than for components hosted on provider-managed Function-as-a-Service (FaaS) platforms as special dependencies can be installed on virtual machines, but not on FaaS platforms. At the same time, cloud consumers become responsible for more management tasks, e.g., updating language runtimes, etc. Therefore, when no customization is required for hosting and scaling a given component, choosing a less consumer-managed offering can be preferable, i.e., hosting a small code snippet on IaaS would incur unnecessary management and scaling configuration overhead if simply a FaaS offering could be used for hosting and executing the code. Here, this FaaS-based hosting is one example for *serverless computing*, which focuses on developing applications hosted on provider-managed offerings to simplify operational aspects and enable more fine-grained, utilization-based billing [25]. As a result, the term *serverless* emphasizes a weaker role of processing, storage, and network resources for cloud consumers as providers are responsible for managing them, e.g., a provider-managed FaaS platform requires less management efforts from cloud consumers than more *serverful* IaaS offerings. However, answering our research question *"How to select the most appropriate hosting option for an application component to be deployed?"* requires technical expertise in the different variants, their benefits, and drawbacks.

To support decision making for finding a hosting variant based on desired management responsibilities, in our previous work [37], we introduced the *Component Hosting Patterns*, which provide solutions for frequently recurring problems regarding management trade-offs ranging from provider- to consumer-managed aspects. The introduced patterns provide solutions for hosting application components based on two management aspects: deployment stack and scaling configuration management. The former aspect distinguishes hosting options based on how much customization of the hosting environment is required, e.g., whether a general-purpose FaaS offering can be used to run a software component or if a special runtime needs to be used, which typically results in using virtual machines on IaaS. The latter aspect distinguishes hosting options based on who is responsible for the scaling configuration of the hosting. For example, the SERVERLESS HOSTING pattern describes that a component that requires no special management customization and scaling configuration should be hosted on a provider-defined deployment stack, e.g., a FaaS offering [37]. However, the available cloud offerings are heterogeneous and often enable implementing various hosting patterns, e.g., using different pricing modes in AWS offerings. Further, there is currently no support for choosing a suitable hosting pattern based on higher-level management decisions. Another issue is that selected patterns need to be refined manually to concrete technical deployment stacks, which is time-consuming and requires technical expertise.

In this paper we further expand on the topic of hosting patterns. Firstly, we (i) introduce *four new complementary patterns* that represent decisions related to customizability of deployment stacks and scaling configuration management.

Different combinations of these new patterns lead to specific hosting alternatives represented as Component Hosting Patterns [37]. We also (ii) introduce the *Component Hosting and Management Pattern Language* that intertwines the new and previous patterns [37] together. Moreover, we (iii) present the *Pattern-based Deployment Stack Exploration Method*, which guides developers in using our pattern language, i.e., selecting a suitable pattern to host a certain component. In addition, the method supports refining the selected pattern to a concrete technical deployment stack, which can be used for deploying the component in practice. Finally, we (iv) show (also including a video demonstration) how the TOSCA modeling tool Eclipse Winery [24] can be configured and used to support the method.

2 The Component Hosting and Management Pattern Language

This section presents the new *Component Hosting and Management Pattern Language*, which combines the Component Hosting Patterns introduced in our previous work [37] with four new complementary patterns related to deployment stack and scaling configuration management, namely the FIXED DEPLOYMENT STACK, CUSTOMIZABLE DEPLOYMENT STACK, CONSUMER-MANAGED SCALING CONFIGURATION, and PROVIDER-MANAGED SCALING CONFIGURATION patterns. All the presented patterns were captured by following the pattern identification and authoring process by Fehling et al. [13].

2.1 Pattern Basics and Terminology

This subsection discusses the pattern basics and briefly recapitulates on the fundamental terminology presented in more details in our previous work [37]. *Patterns* document proven solutions for problems reoccurring in specific contexts [1]. They are documented abstractly following a well-defined structure to enable solving multiple distinct problem instances. *Pattern languages*, e.g., Enterprise Integration Patterns [19] or Microservice Patterns [33], often group patterns from a certain domain and enable navigating between them using semantic links to also help solving potentially interconnected problems [12]. In this work, the patterns are structured following the best practices employed by researchers and practitioners [1,5,6,9,14,33,35]. Each pattern has a name and an icon to facilitate its memorability. Each pattern documents the *problem* it solves and the initial *context* in the eponymous paragraphs. The *forces* paragraph describes factors characterizing the problem and the *solution* paragraph presents an abstract solution with a graphical solution sketch. One or more simple examples of the pattern are presented in the *example* paragraph, while the *result* paragraph discusses the resulting context after the pattern is applied. Finally, the *known uses* paragraph presents three or more real-world occurrences of the pattern [6]. Next, to establish a clear vocabulary for patterns, we discuss core terms related to application hosting based on our previous work [37]:

Application and Software Component: An *application* interconnects general-purpose and application-specific *software components* [7,26] to provide a specific business functionality [26]. While general-purpose components provide general functionalities, e.g., a web server, application-specific components implement the business logic, e.g., a Java-based e-commerce component. Software components are run on certain *infrastructure*, i.e., processing, storage, and network resources [28].

Hosting Requirements and Capabilities: To run a software component, certain *hosting requirements* must often be fulfilled, e.g., a compatible Java Runtime Environment (JRE) is needed for a Java application. *Hosting capability* represents an ability to host a component, e.g., an operating system can host a JRE, whereas a NoSQL database is not capable to do so. Components can be stacked on top of each other when respective hosting requirements and capabilities match.

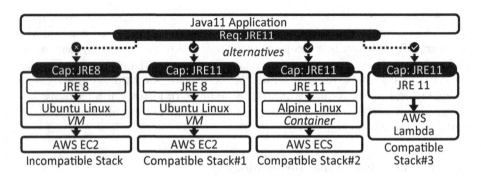

Fig. 1. Example deployment stacks for a Java 11 Application

Deployment Stack: A *deployment stack* is a combination of software components and infrastructure, i.e., processing, storage, and network resources, needed to run a given software component. Multiple deployment stacks can host the same software component, e.g., a Java application can be hosted on a FaaS platform or using IaaS offerings. Figure 1 shows one invalid and three valid deployment stacks for a *Java 11 Application* using Amazon services. The incompatible deployment stack only provides a *JRE 8* hosting capability, thus it cannot host a Java 11 application. The Compatible Stack #1 relies on AWS EC2 (IaaS) which enables installing the JRE 11 on the chosen virtual machine. Compatible Stack #2 enables installing the required JRE as a part of the container running on the provider-managed container engine. Compatible Stack #3 is mainly AWS-managed: cloud consumers select a compatible stack that supports Java 11. The management efforts needed to deploy the component vary since deployment stacks can comprise *provider-* or *consumer-managed* components.

Consumer-Managed Component: A component in a deployment stack is *consumer-managed* if cloud consumers are responsible for installing, configuring, and managing its dependencies. For example, the JRE in the Compatible Stack #2 in Fig. 1 is a part of container hosted on AWS ECS: while the underlying container engine is provider-managed, the JRE is installed and configured by the cloud consumer.

Provider-Managed Component: A component in a deployment stack is *provider-managed* if cloud providers are responsible for managing it. For instance, a JRE in Platform-as-a-Service (PaaS) is provider-managed since the provider is responsible for installing and configuring the deployment stack including the runtime itself.

Scaling Configuration: *Scaling configuration* is a combination of component's scaling rules (for horizontal and vertical scaling) and the amount of infrastructure resources required for hosting a software component. Scaling configuration can be consumer-managed or provider-managed, e.g., cloud consumers need to define the virtual machine size and scaling rules in the Compatible Stack #1 in Fig. 1, whereas in the Compatible Stack #3 the provider is responsible for allocating resources and scaling.

2.2 From the Component Hosting Patterns Catalog to a Pattern Language

The Component Hosting Patterns introduced in our previous work [37] aim to facilitate finding component hosting options based on preferred combinations of two management aspects: (i) who (cloud provider or cloud consumer) is responsible for *managing the deployment stack* and (ii) who is responsible for *managing the scaling configuration* as shown in Fig. 2. The SERVERFUL HOSTING and

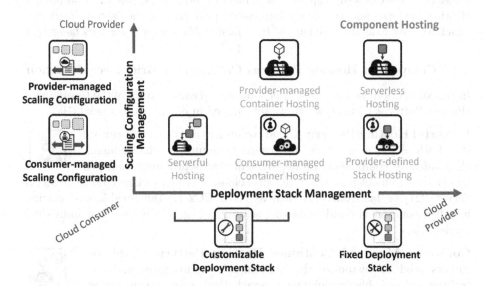

Fig. 2. Spectrum of component hosting patterns [37] (grey) and new patterns (black)

SERVERLESS HOSTING patterns [37] represent two extremes related to stronger or weaker control retained by cloud consumers, respectively. Hosting options in-between, therefore, represent different trade-offs based on the combination of aforementioned management aspects.

However, in our previous work, we did not treat the two high-level *management dimensions*, viz., (i) *deployment stack management* and (ii) *scaling configuration management*, independently. We instead combined them implicitly by each of the Component Hosting Patterns, although they actually exist separately from each other. For instance, in Fig. 2, it can also be observed that choosing a more consumer-managed deployment stack might be preferable if a component's environment needs to be customized, independently of who manages the scaling configuration. Therefore, in this work, we formulate these two independent management dimensions also as individual patterns which represent solutions *related to only one management dimension* and which are linked semantically with the existing Component Hosting Patterns that support them. As a result, selecting one pattern on each management dimension leads to a Component Hosting Pattern that supports both selected patterns. Please note that the combination of consumer-managed solutions in fact leads to two possible Component Hosting Patterns representing different kinds of virtualization, with container-based virtualization being a more lightweight option. The actual choice of the virtualization type may depend on various factors, such as virtualization and integration mechanisms employed for already existing components. For example, choosing a stack for new components in microservice-based applications running on a container orchestrator can shift the decision towards the container-based virtualization. Therefore, our new patterns have semantic links to the Component Hosting Patterns, which are typical qualities of a pattern language [12]. We explicitly capture these links by presenting how the Component Hosting Patterns and the newly-introduced patterns form a pattern language, which we refer to as the *Component Hosting and Management Pattern Language*.

2.3   Component Hosting Patterns Category: A Brief Recapitulation

In this subsection, we provide a brief summary of each pattern of the Component Hosting Patterns catalog, which we introduced in our previous work [37].

Serverful Hosting Pattern: Cloud consumers need to retain control over both, deployment stack and scaling configuration management. Host software components on deployment stacks primarily managed by cloud consumers, e.g., use bare metal cloud offerings such as IBM Bare Metal Servers [21] or IaaS offerings such as AWS EC2 [2] that enable customizing installed components and managing scaling configuration based on individual needs [37].

Consumer-Managed Container Hosting Pattern: Cloud consumers need to customize the component's environment and control the scaling configuration management. Host software components using provider-managed container engines or container orchestrators such as

Azure Kubernetes Service [29] that allow cloud consumers to customize the environment via container images and manage scaling configuration by defining the cluster size and configuring scaling rules [37].

Provider-Managed Container Hosting Pattern: Cloud consumers need to customize the component's environment without specific scaling configuration requirements. Host software components on a deployment stack with provider-managed container engines that do not require cloud consumers to manage scaling configuration, e.g., Google CloudRun [15] scales containers automatically [37].

Provider-Defined Stack Hosting Pattern: Cloud consumers need to host software components on any compatible deployment stack and control the scaling configuration management. Host software components on a provider-defined deployment stack that enables consumer-managed scaling configuration, e.g., a pre-defined Java runtime on AWS Beanstalk [2] with configurable auto-scaling rules [37].

Serverless Hosting Pattern: Cloud consumers need to host software components on any compatible deployment stack and without specific scaling configuration requirements. Host software components on a provider-defined deployment stack which is compatible with the given component and does not require cloud consumers to manage the scaling configuration, e.g., Python functions hosted on a predefined deployment stack on IBM Cloud Functions [21] and automatically scaled by the platform or a database table hosted on AWS DynamoDB [2,37].

2.4 Deployment Stack Management Category

In this section, we present the second category of our pattern language that contains two new patterns. The motivation for this category is distinguishing whether software components should be hosted on a combination of infrastructure and software components that need to be customized by executing custom configuration tasks. Thus, we introduce the FIXED DEPLOYMENT STACK and the CUSTOMIZABLE DEPLOYMENT STACK patterns that focus on the deployment stack customization: the former pattern is suitable for cases when no customization is needed and any compatible deployment stack can be employed, whereas the latter pattern can be applied in cases when a to-be-hosted component requires custom configuration of the underlying deployment stack.

The FIXED DEPLOYMENT STACK Pattern

 Problem: *"How to host a software component that requires no special underlying infrastructure or customization of the host environment it is running on?"*

Context: A software component needs to be hosted on a deployment stack, but there is no need for special customization of the stack by adding, removing, or changing components in it or configuring it in a special way.

Forces: Cloud service models require different management efforts for the under-lying deployment stack, e.g., hosting a component on a FaaS platform requires less management efforts than hosting it on a consumer-managed virtual machine on IaaS where the consumer has to take care of installing patches. Frequently, only the common dependencies are needed for to-be-deployed components, e.g., a Java application without specific customization requirements or a standard relational database.

Solution: Host a software component on a FIXED DEPLOYMENT STACK for which the cloud provider is responsible for setting up, configuring, and main-taining all infrastructure, execution environment, and middleware components needed to host and execute the given component. For instance, PaaS offerings can be used to host components on provider-defined deployment stacks, e.g., by providing a Java runtime of a specific version. Also serverless Database-as-a-Service (DBaaS) offerings are examples for this pattern since they can provide a specific version of the database without the need for the consumer to manage the underlying software dependencies. Hence, consumers can directly host software components on chosen provider-managed offerings without the need to config-ure or customize any components in the underlying stack. Figure 3a shows the solution sketch for this pattern that illustrates how a to-be-hosted software com-ponent is hosted on a compatible deployment stack defined by a cloud provider.

Examples: Fig. 3b and Fig. 3c show examples of the FIXED DEPLOYMENT STACK pattern for hosting different kinds of components. The component "My Java App" in Fig. 3b is hosted using a fixed, provider-defined stack: AWS Lambda is a serverless FaaS platform that enables choosing a specific Java runtime version to host the application. Another example is a NoSQL collec-tion created using AWS DynamoDB, a MongoDB-compatible DBaaS offering as shown in Fig. 3c. In both cases, instead of setting up all dependencies required for running the respective component, cloud consumers simply select the desired functionality from a list of provider-defined options.

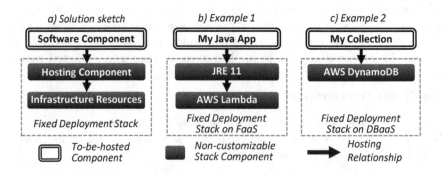

Fig. 3. Fixed deployment stack pattern: solution sketch and examples

Result: When applied, this pattern enables hosting components without any additional configuration since deployment stack customization is not required. This enables reducing the amount of deployment stack management efforts. However, changing such deployment stacks to other offerings could result in extra effort due to higher degree of lock-in with provider-specific services. For example, implementation and configuration of components becomes more provider-specific due to the usage of service-specific libraries, formats, packaging and configuration requirements [36].

Known Uses: The FIXED DEPLOYMENT STACK pattern is implemented by various provider-managed service offerings. For example, PaaS offerings such as AWS Beanstalk [2] or Azure App Service [29] can be used to host the business logic on provider-defined stacks. Further, serverless FaaS offerings such as AWS Lambda and Azure Functions [29], or serverless DBaaS offerings such as AWS S3 [2] and IBM Cloud Databases for Redis [21] enable hosting components on provider-defined stacks that require no management responsibilities for the cloud consumer.

The CUSTOMIZABLE DEPLOYMENT STACK Pattern

 Problem: *"How to host a software component when it requires customization of the underlying infrastructure or the host environment it is running on?"*

Context: A software component needs to be hosted such that cloud consumers are able to customize the underlying deployment stack with possibly nested software layers by adding, removing, or changing components in it or configuring the stack in a special way.

Forces: Cloud service models vary in modifiability of the underlying deployment stack, e.g., it is possible to install additional software on a virtual machine hosted using IaaS offerings, whereas FaaS offerings hide the underlying deployment stack to enable consumers deploying their applications without the need for technical expertise about underlying components. However, customization requirements

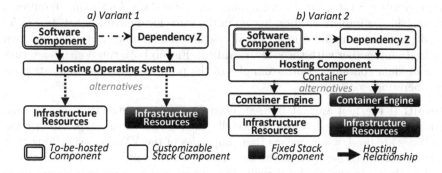

Fig. 4. Solution sketch for the Customizable Deployment Stack pattern

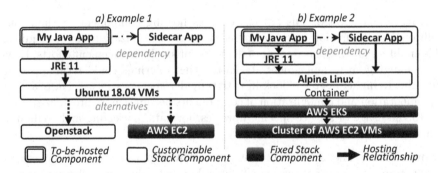

Fig. 5. Examples for the customizable deployment stack pattern

for hosting a component can arise due to various reasons, e.g., legacy applications that have special dependencies to other software components that need to run in the same operating system. Another example is a side car [4] that needs to be installed along with the component.

Solution: Host software components on a CUSTOMIZABLE DEPLOYMENT STACK in which the cloud consumer is responsible for setting up and configuring the infrastructure, execution environment, and middleware components needed to host the given software component. Hence, for a given software component, the cloud consumer can install and configure hosting components with required dependencies completely as required by the component to be deployed. The CUS-TOMIZABLE DEPLOYMENT STACK has two variants: Fig. 4a shows the first variant, which supports customizing the physical or virtual machine the component is running on. For example, software can be deployed on a physical machine, thus, enabling full customization of all infrastructure components. However, especially in the cloud, provisioning virtual machines and installing software on top of them with all required dependencies is a more common example for this variant. The second variant shown in Fig. 4b is based on containers, which can be customized regarding the software and its dependencies that must be installed.

Examples: Figure 5 shows concrete examples of applying the CUSTOMIZABLE DEPLOYMENT STACK for a Java application ("My Java App") that requires a custom sidecar implementation hosted in the same local environment. In Fig. 5a the deployment is realized in a virtual machine that enables installing the Java application together with the sidecar, while in Fig. 5b both components are running inside a container. Both examples of the pattern enable customization on the operating system level.

Result: If the first variant is used, even physical infrastructure can be customized if necessary—however, especially in a public cloud, typically virtual machines are used, which means that properties of the VM and everything that runs on the operating system can be customized. In contrast, if containers are used as shown in the second variant, the customization opportunities are more restricted.

Known Uses: The CUSTOMIZABLE DEPLOYMENT STACK pattern is implemented by various technologies and offerings, e.g., bare metal offerings such as IBM Cloud Bare Metal Servers [21], as well as virtualized IaaS offerings such as AWS EC2 [2] or Azure IaaS [29]. Further, the pattern is also implemented in container-centric services such as Azure Kubernetes Service [29] and AWS Fargate [2].

2.5   Scaling Configuration Management Category

Especially in cloud computing, automated scaling of software components is a key feature. However, components may also need to be hosted on deployment stacks requiring special scaling configuration. In this section, we introduce the PROVIDER-MANAGED SCALING CONFIGURATION and CONSUMER-MANAGED SCALING CONFIGURATION patterns that focus on scaling configuration management: the former pattern is relevant when no specific scaling configuration management is needed, whereas the latter can be used when a to-be-hosted component requires custom scaling configuration management.

The PROVIDER-MANAGED SCALING CONFIGURATION Pattern

 Problem: *"How to host a software component that needs to be scaled horizontally but requires no special scaling configuration?"*

Context: A software component needs to be hosted on a deployment stack for which cloud consumers do not have special requirements regarding the horizontal scaling behavior, i.e., they want to rely on the provider's default autoscaling mechanism.

Forces: Cloud offerings vary in degrees of control cloud consumers have over the underlying scaling configuration. For instance, many offerings only require specifying the underlying infrastructure resources in virtual memory and CPU values, without the need to know how many virtual machines are needed in advance, while other offerings may require managing scaling configuration explicitly. Often, more provider-managed services do not require manual specification of scaling configuration at all, e.g., AWS Lambda or AWS S3 are auto-scaled by default. Moreover, the underlying offerings often do not incur extra licensing costs, e.g., purchasing a number of licenses for a messaging middleware, which makes reduced scaling configuration management more favorable.

Solution: Host software components on a deployment stack that supports PROVIDER-MANAGED SCALING CONFIGURATION, which means that the cloud providers are mainly responsible for the specification of the underlying infrastructure resources and scaling rules. The solution sketch in Fig. 6a shows the high-level idea of the pattern: A software component is hosted on a deployment stack with blurred infrastructure boundaries represented using virtual resource values. Furthermore, horizontal scaling rules are mainly managed by providers and are not intended to be changed by cloud consumers, therefore, enabling only few or no customization at all.

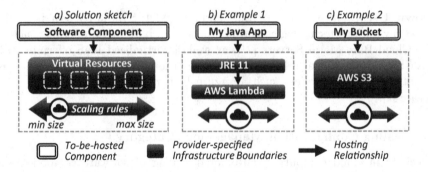

Fig. 6. Provider-managed acaling configuration pattern: solution sketch and examples

Examples: The examples shown in Fig. 6 depict two different kinds of components hosted on AWS-based deployment stacks that implemented the pattern. The examples deal with the required amounts of virtual resources for hosting a Java application (Fig. 6b) and an object storage bucket (Fig. 6c), while the corresponding horizontal scaling rules are managed completely by the provider: AWS Lambda functions are automatically scaled including scale to zero instances when the function execution completes, and on the other side, AWS S3 buckets also do not require specifying any scaling rules.

Result: When applied, this pattern simplifies the specification of infrastructure resource requirements and scaling rules. Hosting components on deployment stacks that support this pattern can be preferable when no specific scaling behavior is needed. This pattern can be combined with both the FIXED as well as with the CUSTOMIZABLE DEPLOYMENT STACK patterns to flexibly combine management decisions.

Known Uses: The PROVIDER-MANAGED SCALING CONFIGURATION pattern is supported by multiple offerings. For example, the pattern is supported by various FaaS offerings such as AWS Lambda [2] or Azure Functions [29]. Also provider-managed container offerings such as Google CloudRun [15] enable specifying virtual resources and automatically scale container instances based on the number of requests. Serverless storage offerings such as AWS DynamoDB [2] and Azure Blob Storage [29] also support the PROVIDER-MANAGED SCALING CONFIGURATION pattern as no explicit specification of the infrastructure resources and scaling rules are required.

The CONSUMER-MANAGED SCALING CONFIGURATION Pattern

 Problem: *"How to host a software component that needs to be scaled horizontally while also requiring a tailored scaling configuration?"*

Context: A software component needs to be hosted on a deployment stack for which cloud consumers can explicitly specify the underlying infrastructure

resources and retain a high level of control over the horizontal scaling rules, e.g., the size of virtual machine clusters and the desired autoscaling rules for it.

Forces: Cloud service offerings differ in how scaling configuration is managed. For instance, some services require specifying the infrastructure resources, i.e., decide on virtual machine images and number of instances, whereas more provider-managed services abstract away resources to memory and virtual CPU values. The configuration of horizontal scaling behavior also differs. More provider-managed services, e.g., AWS Lambda or AWS S3, are often auto-scaled and require no manual specification of scaling rules. In contrast, more consumer-managed services, e.g., AWS EC2 or Azure EKS, are more customizable. In addition, consumers may only have a limited number of available licenses for a software, hence requiring to manage that exact number of instances.

Solution: Host software components on a deployment stack that supports CONSUMER-MANAGED SCALING CONFIGURATION, which means that cloud consumers retain more control over the specification of the underlying infrastructure resources and horizontal scaling rules. The solution sketch in Fig. 7a shows a high-level view of the CONSUMER-MANAGED SCALING CONFIGURATION pattern: a software component is hosted on a deployment stack with explicitly defined infrastructure boundaries and consumer-managed horizontal scaling rules. If this pattern is applied, the corresponding deployment stacks provide more transparency for cloud consumers with regard to specific aspects of scaling configuration such as explicitly defining the desired infrastructure boundaries and having more control over the horizontal scaling rules.

Examples: The example shown in Fig. 7b depicts a deployment stack on AWS Beanstalk [2] that supports the CONSUMER-MANAGED SCALING CONFIGURATION pattern. Cloud consumers can select the desired virtual machine images for a given Java application component and specify the horizontal scaling rules. Other consumer-managed services, e.g., bare-metal, IaaS, or container orchestration offerings, often provide more fine-grained control over the scaling configuration since cloud consumers can explicitly decide on the type and amount of the underlying infrastructure resources.

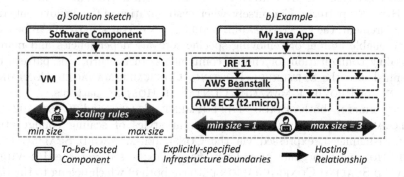

Fig. 7. Consumer-managed scaling configuration: solution sketch and example

Result: When applied, this pattern enables explicitly specifying the infrastructure resource boundaries for the underlying deployment stack in terms of the amount and flavor of the virtual machines as well as providing more control over the horizontal scaling rules customization. The actual scaling configuration is service-specific and depends on the specific service type, e.g., defining auto-scaling rules for container orchestration services such as the Azure Kubernetes Service differs from configuring autos-scaling rules for PaaS offerings such as AWS Beanstalk. This pattern can be combined with both the FIXED and the CUSTOMIZABLE DEPLOYMENT STACK patterns, which enables flexibly combining management decisions when choosing hosting options.

Known Uses: The CONSUMER-MANAGED SCALING CONFIGURATION pattern is supported by a variety of service offerings. For example, consumer-managed scaling configuration can be achieved using bare-metal and IaaS offerings such as IBM Cloud Bare Metal Servers [21], AWS EC2 [2], and Azure IaaS [29]. Container orchestration services such as Azure Kubernetes Service [29] or AWS Elastic Kubernetes Service [2] also enable explicitly defining the size of the cluster and the horizontal scaling rules for the to-be-hosted containers. Additionally, some existing PaaS offerings such as AWS Beanstalk support the CONSUMER-MANAGED SCALING CONFIGURATION pattern to some degree, e.g., by enabling cloud consumers to specify exact numbers of instances and providing finergrained control over horizontal scaling rules.

2.6   The Pattern Language Graph

Figure 8 shows the *Component Hosting and Management Pattern Language* that organizes the new and previously-introduced patterns into three categories and semantically connects them. Two patterns in the *Deployment Stack Management* category, i.e., FIXED DEPLOYMENT STACK and CUSTOMIZABLE DEPLOYMENT STACK, represent solutions to stack customization issues. The FIXED DEPLOYMENT STACK pattern represents a component hosting on a deployment stack that cannot be customized, e.g., to reduce the needed management efforts when no customizations are required. This pattern can be refined into two Component Hosting Patterns, namely PROVIDER-DEFINED STACK HOSTING and SERVERLESS HOSTING patterns. Conversely, when customization of the deployment stack is a requirement, the CUSTOMIZABLE DEPLOYMENT STACK pattern can be used, e.g., to enable adding or removing specific software dependencies and managing scaling configuration for chosen components. In its turn, this pattern can be refined into the SERVERFUL HOSTING, CONSUMER-MANAGED CONTAINER HOSTING, or PROVIDER-MANAGED CONTAINER HOSTING patterns.

Furthermore, both FIXED DEPLOYMENT STACK and CUSTOMIZABLE DEPLOYMENT STACK can support different styles of scaling configuration: consumer-managed, expressed via the CONSUMER-MANAGED SCALING CONFIGURATION pattern, and provider-managed, expressed via the PROVIDER-MANAGED SCALING CONFIGURATION pattern, both of which belong to the *Scaling Configuration Management* category. Thus, if patterns from the different

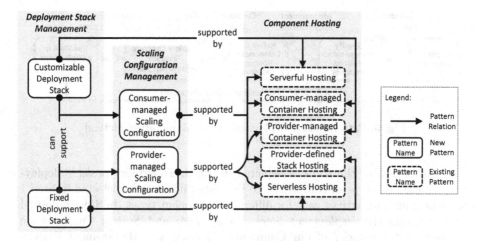

Fig. 8. Overview of the Component Hosting and Management Pattern Language

two new categories are combined, suitable deployment stack options from the Component Hosting Patterns category reduce in number, e.g., a combination of FIXED DEPLOYMENT STACK and PROVIDER-MANAGED SCALING CONFIGURATION leads to exactly one pattern, the SERVERLESS HOSTING pattern. As a result, pattern combinations from the Component Hosting and Management Pattern Language can help finding component hosting options based on both, the desired customizability of the deployment stack and preferred scaling trade-offs.

3 A Pattern-Based Deployment Stack Exploration Method

This section introduces the *Pattern-based Deployment Stack Exploration Method* to simplify the search for *concrete technical deployment stacks* to deploy a certain component using our pattern language from Sect. 2. Here, a *concrete technical deployment stack* means a detailed description of the stack that specifies (i) the technical components required, (ii) their dependencies, and (iii) their configurations. Thus, such a stack provides all technical details for a *declarative deployment model* [9] executable by a *deployment automation technology* such as AWS CloudFormation or TOSCA Orchestrators.

3.1 Overview of the Method

The basic idea of the method is to use our patterns when creating a deployment model: For each component, the developer selects appropriate patterns from our language, which are then semi-automatically refined by the method-enabling tooling to propose possible technical realizations of the patterns, i.e., concrete technologies, services offerings, and the corresponding configurations that form a concrete technical deployment stack.

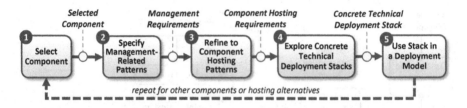

Fig. 9. Pattern-based Deployment Stack Exploration Method

An overview of the steps is depicted in Fig. 9. To explore possible deployment stacks, the type of component to be hosted needs to be selected in Step 1 since hosting alternatives vary for different component types. In Step 2, desired patterns from the *Deployment Stack Management* and *Scaling Configuration Management* categories of our Component Hosting and Management Pattern Language are used to specify the *Management Requirements* from these two management dimensions: The component to be hosted is combined with (i) either the CUSTOMIZABLE or FIXED DEPLOYMENT STACK pattern from the *Deployment Stack Management* category to represent stack customization requirements, and/or with (ii) either the PROVIDER- or CONSUMER-MANAGED SCALING CONFIGURATION pattern from the *Scaling Configuration Management* category to specify the desired scaling configuration requirements. In Step 3, the selected patterns are refined to *Component Hosting Requirements*, which are represented by the patterns from the *Component Hosting* category, e.g., to the SERVERLESS HOSTING pattern. This transition is achieved by refining the combination of component type and *Deployment Stack Management* as well as *Scaling Configuration Management* patterns into exactly one *Component Hosting* pattern by using the links in our pattern language shown in Fig. 8. The resulting *Component Hosting* pattern is refined in Step 4 to a concrete technical deployment stack options that realizes the semantics of the pattern for the specified component type to be deployed. As a result, developers can discover suitable options that fulfill the characteristics of selected patterns by iteratively refining their abstract requirements into technical deployment stacks. After a suitable hosting alternative is chosen, in Step 5 the technical deployment stack can be used in deployment modeling and the same process can be repeated for other components.

3.2   Application Examples of the Method

Figure 10 shows examples of our method applied to different component types. The transition for a component selected in Step 1 can happen between three different layers, namely (i) *Management Requirements Layer*, (ii) *Component Hosting Requirements Layer*, and (iii) *Technical Deployment Stack Alternatives Layer*. The Management Requirements Layer corresponds to Step 2 of our method and represents general requirements on customizability of the deployment stack and scaling configuration management for a given component: By hosting components on the CUSTOMIZABLE DEPLOYMENT STACK or FIXED

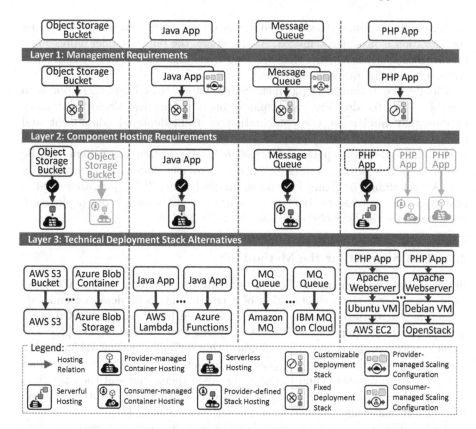

Fig. 10. Examples of Pattern-based Deployment Stack Exploration Method

DEPLOYMENT STACK patterns, modelers can express their stack customization preferences, while by annotating components with the PROVIDER-MANAGED SCALING CONFIGURATION or CONSUMER-MANAGED SCALING CONFIGURATION patterns, modelers can express scaling configuration management requirements. For example, Fig. 10 shows a *Java Application* component that requires no customization and the *PHP Application* component that requires a customizable deployment stack. Thus, in the Management Requirements Layer, these components are associated with different patterns, namely the FIXED DEPLOYMENT STACK and PROVIDER-MANAGED SCALING CONFIGURATION for the Java Application, and the CUSTOMIZABLE DEPLOYMENT STACK pattern for the PHP Application.

The Component Hosting Requirements Layer corresponds to Step 3. Here, modelers can explore hosting options with respect to their preferences. By using the pattern relations shown in Fig. 8, each previously-specified pattern or their combination can be refined into a more specific *Component Hosting Pattern*. For example, the FIXED DEPLOYMENT STACK pattern can be refined into the PROVIDER-DEFINED STACK HOSTING pattern that enables consumer-managed scaling configuration, or the SERVERLESS HOSTING pattern in which the scaling configuration is provider-managed. At this stage, the refined model represents a hosting solution that satisfies the expressed trade-offs between deployment stack and scaling configuration management.

Finally, the Technical Deployment Stack Alternatives Layer corresponds to Step 4 of Fig. 9. Modelers can explore concrete technical deployment stack options that implement the combination of to-be-deployed component and refined *Component Hosting* pattern from the previous layer. For example, the SERVERLESS HOSTING pattern for the *Java Application* component can be refined into a deployment stack based on a provider-managed FaaS platform, e.g., AWS Lambda or Azure Functions. Similarly, the *PHP Application* that is hosted on the SERVERFUL HOSTING pattern can be refined into a deployment stack based on the IaaS offerings, e.g., AWS EC2 [2].

3.3 Tool Support for the Method

In this section, we demonstrate how the exploration of concrete technical deployment stacks for a given combination of a component to be deployed and patterns from our pattern language can be automated based on the TOSCA standard [31] and the open source TOSCA modeling tool *Eclipse Winery* [24]. The TOSCA specification is an OASIS standard that defines a metamodel for *declarative deployment models*, i.e., graph-based models in which the vertices represent software components and the edges between them represent their relationships [9,31]. A goal of TOSCA is that such declarative deployment models can then be automatically executed by a *TOSCA Orchestrator* [31].

Eclipse Winery is an open-source TOSCA modeling tool that enables graphically creating declarative deployment models in TOSCA. In previous works, we extended Winery to support TOSCA-based *Pattern-based Deployment and Configuration Models* [16,17] that enable (i) using patterns as abstract components and (ii) annotating components with patterns to specify their behavior. Winery also supports the automatic refinement of such pattern-based models into concrete, executable deployment models using so-called *Pattern Refinement Models (PRM)* [16,17]. Each PRM defines (i) a *detector*, which is a small deployment model fragment that describes a combination of components and patterns that can be refined by the PRM, and (ii) a *refinement structure* that describes a concrete refinement into a technical deployment model fragment. PRMs can be used iteratively in Winery to find their detectors in pattern-based deployment models and to replace their parts matching the detectors with their corresponding refinement structures.

Therefore, Winery and its pattern-based modeling features can be used to enable our method in practice. For example, a pattern-based model on the left of Fig. 11 describes a *Java Application* that needs to be hosted on the FIXED DEPLOYMENT STACK pattern and its scaling behavior must follow the PROVIDER-MANAGED SCALING CONFIGURATION pattern. This could be the result of a developer's modeling using Winery. Winery can then be used to find

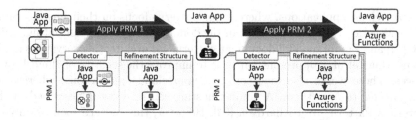

Fig. 11. Transitioning between the different modeling layers using Eclipse Winery [24] and the pattern refinement approaches introduced by Harzenetter et al. [16,17]

possible refinements of this model by automatically iterating over PRMs available in Winery's repository and finding matching detectors. PRM1 in Fig. 11 is applicable as it defines the modeled combination of *Java Application* and the two patterns as detector. This PRM1 enables refining the created model into a more concrete fragment, i.e., a *Java Application* hosted on the SERVER-LESS HOSTING pattern that exactly supports the semantics of the two patterns FIXED DEPLOYMENT STACK and PROVIDER-MANAGED SCALING CONFIGURA-TION used in the original model. The resulting model can be further refined using the PRM2 shown in Fig. 11 on the right: its detector matches exactly the fragment obtained after the application of PRM1 and can be refined to hosting the *Java Application* on *Azure Functions*. In practice, the refinement structure of PRM2 can provide more details for Azure, which are omitted for brevity. Moreover, PRM2 is just one example whose detector matches the resulting model and there could be more PRMs enabling other refinements, e.g., using AWS Lambda.

Thus, by leveraging this pattern refinement approach [16,17], we enable our method using two types of PRMs: The first type captures the refinements within the categories of our pattern language, which corresponds to the transition from the Management Requirements Layer to the Component Hosting Requirements Layer. The second type is PRMs that refine Component Hosting Patterns into concrete technical deployment stacks as described in Fig. 11 on the right, which corresponds to the transition from the Component Hosting Requirements Layer to the Technical Deployment Stack Alternatives Layer. To validate the tool support, we created all possible refinements for the first type of PRMs and hosted them on GitHub.[1] We also created several PRMs for the second type in the same repository. However, note that the PRMs for the second type can be further extended as more cloud offerings could be mapped to specific hosting patterns. To demonstrate how our method works in practice, we also created a video.[2]

4   Related Work

Multiple existing works [8,10,14,32] document patterns for structuring cloud-native applications. These works differ from ours as they propose patterns for

---

[1] https://github.com/OpenTOSCA/pattern-based-deployment-modeling.
[2] https://youtu.be/-GpGPS5Nc1Q.

designing cloud applications, whereas our patterns focus on their *hosting*. Similar considerations apply to patterns in the domain of serverless computing. Taibi et al. [34] and Zambrano [38] document patterns for architecting serverless applications. Hong et al. [20] present patterns to improve the security of cloud-hosted services. These works also focus on *designing* cloud applications, whereas we focus on *how to host* them. A similar hosting-centric view is described in the "Serverless Pattern" by Richardson [33]. However, this pattern focuses only on microservices and associates the term "serverless with FaaS platforms, hence, restricting its applicability. Instead, our patterns including the Serverless Hosting Pattern represent views on hosting options based on management trade-offs and are applicable to different kinds of application components.

Jamshidi et al. [22,23] propose a catalog of patterns for migrating on-premise applications to the cloud and a concrete method for enacting pattern-based migration. These patterns [22,23] differ from our patterns as they focus on adapting existing service-based applications to allow *migrating* them to the cloud, rather than on their *hosting*. Thus, these patterns can be combined with our patterns: developers may first exploit migration patterns to enable deploying applications in the cloud, and then implement our patterns for hosting application components. Morris [30] documents Infrastructure-as-Code patterns that focus on various aspects including the granularity of deployment stacks, build environments, configuration, and testing. Our patterns focus on the modeling and stack selection process and can be combined with the patterns by Morris, e.g., to enable manage changes in the selected deployment stack. Endres et al. [9] document two patterns for specifying application deployments – declarative and imperative, which are complementary and can be combined with our patterns.

Finally, several works focus on transitioning between patterns and solutions they document. Falkenthal et al. [11] show how pattern languages on different levels of abstractions can be refined to concrete solutions, i.e., implementation of a pattern using specific technologies. Leymann and Barzen [27] propose an approach and tool for navigating through pattern languages inspired by the analogy with cartography. Such approaches can help linking the patterns presented in this work with other pattern languages such as cloud computing patterns [14], and support the search for concrete solutions. Bibartiu et al. [3] introduce a modeling approach that depends on patterns to describe an application, which focuses on modeling of procedures and uses sequence diagrams to describe components interaction and refine patterns to concrete components. In our method, we rely on several existing pattern-based techniques in the domain of component hosting to automate the transitioning between abstract requirements and concrete solutions using our Component Hosting and Management Pattern Language.

5   Conclusion

In this work, we introduced four new patterns representing solutions to more general problems related to deployment stack and scaling configuration management that complement our previously-introduced Component Hosting Patterns [37].

The combined set of patterns forms the Component Hosting and Management Pattern Language, which can be used to identify suitable hosting options for application components and transition to the corresponding technical deployment stacks, as we have shown by presenting the Pattern-based Deployment Stack Exploration Method and the prototype supporting it.

In future work, we plan to further validate our method by applying it to multiple distinct serverless application models. We also aim to extend our toolchain to enable expressing other decisions for stack selection. Furthermore, using existing concepts [18] we plan to enable automatic refinement from concrete deployment models to pattern-based deployment models, hence, supporting the exploration of decisions related to a specific executable deployment stack.

Acknowledgments. This work was partially funded by the German Research Foundation (DFG) project IAC^2 (314720630).

References

1. Alexander, C.: A Pattern Language: Towns, Buildings, Construction. Oxford University Press, New York (1977)
2. Amazon Web Services: AWS Solutions Library (2022). https://aws.amazon.com/solutions/browse-all
3. Bibartiu, O., et al.: Clams: a cloud application modeling solution. In: Proceedings of the 2021 IEEE International Conference on Services Computing (SCC 2021), pp. 1–10 (2021)
4. Burns, B., Oppenheimer, D.: Design patterns for container-based distributed systems. In: 8th USENIX Workshop on Hot Topics in Cloud Computing (HotCloud 2016) (2016)
5. Buschmann, F., et al.: Pattern-Oriented Software Architecture: On Patterns and Pattern Language, vol. 5. Wiley, New York (2007)
6. Coplien, J.O.: Software patterns (1996)
7. Councill, B., Heineman, G.T.: Definition of a software component and its elements. In: Component-Based Software Engineering: Putting the Pieces Together, pp. 5–19. Addison-Wesley, San Francisco (2001)
8. Davis, C.: Cloud Native Patterns: Designing Change-Tolerant Software. Manning Publishing, New York (2019)
9. Endres, C., et al.: Declarative vs. imperative: two modeling patterns for the automated deployment of applications. In: Proceedings of the 9th International Conference on Pervasive Patterns and Applications (PATTERNS 2017), pp. 22–27. Xpert Publishing Services (2017)
10. Erl, T., et al.: Cloud Computing Design Patterns, 1st edn. Prentice Hall Press, Upper Saddle River (2015)
11. Falkenthal, M., et al.: Leveraging pattern application via pattern refinement. In: Proceedings of the International Conference on Pursuit of Pattern Languages for Societal Change (PURPLSOC 2015), pp. 38–61 (2015)
12. Falkenthal, M., et al.: The Nature of Pattern Languages. In: Pursuit of Pattern Languages for Societal Change, pp. 130–150. Tredition, October 2018

13. Fehling, C., Barzen, J., Breitenbücher, U., Leymann, F.: A Process for pattern identification, authoring, and application. In: Proceedings of the 19th European Conference on Pattern Languages of Programs (EuroPLoP 2014). ACM, January 2014

14. Fehling, C., et al.: Cloud Computing Patterns: Fundamentals to Design, Build, and Manage Cloud Applications. Springer, Vienna, January 2014. https://doi.org/10.1007/978-3-7091-1568-8

15. Google: Google Cloud products (2022). https://cloud.google.com/products/

16. Harzenetter, L., et al.: Pattern-based deployment models and their automatic execution. In: 11th IEEE/ACM International Conference on Utility and Cloud Computing (UCC 2018), pp. 41–52. IEEE Computer Society, Dec 2018

17. Harzenetter, L., et al.: Pattern-based deployment models revisited: automated pattern-driven deployment configuration. In: Proceedings of the Twelfth International Conference on Pervasive Patterns and Applications (PATTERNS 2020), pp. 40–49. Xpert Publishing Services, October 2020

18. Harzenetter, L., et al.: Automated detection of design patterns in declarative deployment models. In: Proceedings of the 2021 IEEE/ACM 14th International Conference on Utility Cloud Computing (UCC 2021), pp. 36–45. ACM, December 2021

19. Hohpe, G., Woolf, B.: Enterprise Integration Patterns: Designing, Building, and Deploying Messaging Solutions. Addison-Wesley, New York (2004)

20. Hong, S., et al.: Go serverless: securing cloud via serverless design patterns. In: 10th USENIX Workshop on Hot Topics in Cloud Computing (HotCloud 2018) (2018)

21. IBM: IBM Cloud Solutions (2021). https://www.ibm.com/cloud/solutions

22. Jamshidi, P., Pahl, C., Chinenyeze, S., Liu, X.: Cloud migration patterns: a multi-cloud service architecture perspective. In: Toumani, F., et al. (eds.) ICSOC 2014. LNCS, vol. 8954, pp. 6–19. Springer, Cham (2015). https://doi.org/10.1007/978-3-319-22885-3_2

23. Jamshidi, P., et al.: Pattern-based multi-cloud architecture migration. Softw. Pract. Exp. **47**(9), 1159–1184 (2017)

24. Kopp, O., Binz, T., Breitenbücher, U., Leymann, F.: Winery – a modeling tool for tosca-based cloud applications. In: Basu, S., Pautasso, C., Zhang, L., Fu, X. (eds.) ICSOC 2013. LNCS, vol. 8274, pp. 700–704. Springer, Heidelberg (2013). https://doi.org/10.1007/978-3-642-45005-1_64

25. Kounev, S., et al.: Toward a Definition for Serverless Computing. In: Serverless Computing (Dagstuhl Seminar 21201), vol. 11, Chap. 5.1, pp. 56–59. Schloss Dagstuhl - Leibniz-Zentrum für Informatik (2021)

26. Lau, K.K., Wang, Z.: Software component models. IEEE Trans. Softw. Eng. **33**(10), 709–724 (2007)

27. Leymann, F., Barzen, J.: Pattern Atlas. Next-Generation Digital Services. A Retrospective and Roadmap for Service Computing of the Future, pp. 67–76 (2021)

28. Messerschmitt, D.G.: Rethinking components: from hardware and software to systems. Proc. IEEE **95**(7), 1473–1496 (2007)

29. Microsoft: Directory of Azure Services (2022). https://azure.microsoft.com/en-us/services/

30. Morris, K.: Infrastructure as Code. O'Reilly Media, Sebastopol (2020)

31. OASIS: Topology and Orchestration Specification for Cloud Applications (TOSCA) Version 2.0. Organization for the Advancement of Structured Information Standards (OASIS) (2020)

32. Pahl, C., et al.: Architectural principles for cloud software. ACM Trans. Internet Technol. (TOIT) **18**(2) (2018)

33. Richardson, C.: Microservices Patterns. Manning Publications Company, New York (2018)
34. Taibi, D., et al.: Patterns for serverless functions (function-as-a-service): a multivocal literature review. In: CLOSER, pp. 181–192 (2020)
35. Wellhausen, T., Fiesser, A.: How to write a pattern? A rough guide for first-time pattern authors. In: Proceedings of the 16th European Conference on Pattern Languages of Programs, pp. 1–9 (2011)
36. Yussupov, V., et al.: Facing the unplanned migration of serverless applications: a study on portability problems, solutions, and dead ends. In: Proceedings of the 12th IEEE/ACM International Conference on Utility and Cloud Computing (UCC), pp. 273–283. ACM (2019)
37. Yussupov, V., et al.: From serverful to serverless: a spectrum of patterns for hosting application components. In: Proceedings of the 11th International Conference on Cloud Computing and Services Science (CLOSER 2021), pp. 268–279. SciTePress, May 2021
38. Zambrano, B.: Serverless Design Patterns and Best Practices: Build, Secure, and Deploy Enterprise Ready Serverless Applications with AWS to Improve Developer Productivity. Packt Publishing, Birmingham (2018)

Towards Immediate Feedback for Security Relevant Code in Development Environments

Markus Haug[(✉)] [iD], Ana Cristina Franco da Silva[iD], and Stefan Wagner[iD]

Institute of Software Engineering, University of Stuttgart, Universitätsstraße 38, 70569 Stuttgart, Germany
markus.haug@iste.uni-stuttgart.de

Abstract. Nowadays, the correct use of cryptography libraries is essential to ensure the necessary information security in different kinds of applications. A common practice in software development is the use of static application security testing (SAST) tools to analyze code regarding security vulnerabilities. Most of these tools are designed to run separately from development environments. Their results are extensive lists of security notifications, which software developers have to inspect manually in a time-consuming follow-up step. To support developers in their tasks of developing secure code, we present an approach for providing them with continuous immediate feedback of SAST tools in integrated development environments (IDEs). Our approach also considers the understandability of security notifications and aims for a user-centered approach that leverages developers' feedback to build an adaptive system tailored to each individual developer.

Keywords: Software development · IDE · Security · SAST · Notifications

1 Introduction

An essential practice for ensuring IT security in software applications nowadays is the use of cryptography libraries, such as the Bouncy Castle Crypto APIs[1] or the Java security APIs. For example, in the communication among distributed services in cloud environments, the security of information in transit is a highly important requirement [4]. Yet, using cryptography libraries is not easy because of their complexity. They are often used incorrectly, for example, due to misuse of parameters, which can lead to severe security issues [7].

Already during implementation, static application security testing (SAST) tools, such as SonarQube[2] or CogniCrypt [5], can be used to analyze the code in

---

[1] https://bouncycastle.org.
[2] https://www.sonarqube.org.

This work is funded by the BMBF project CRITICALMATE (16KIS0995).

© The Author(s), under exclusive license to Springer Nature Switzerland AG 2022
J. Barzen et al. (Eds.): SummerSOC 2022, CCIS 1603, pp. 68–75, 2022.
https://doi.org/10.1007/978-3-031-18304-1_4

development regarding security vulnerabilities [8]. For this, SAST tools contain comprehensive rule sets, which define, for example, correct or incorrect API usage patterns, and are used to recognize issues and decide when to show security notifications.

Many current SAST tools are designed to be used separately from integrated development environments (IDEs). That is, security analyses are usually performed as additional steps in build processes, for example, in nightly builds. This normally leads to extensive lists of security notifications, which software developers have to inspect manually in a follow-up step. In addition to being time-consuming and cumbersome, the interruption and associated loss of context increase the challenge of understanding and fixing an issue for developers [9].

In this paper, we present an approach that supports software developers in their tasks of developing secure code. Using our approach, developers are continuously provided with immediate feedback from SAST tools in their IDEs. Our approach considers the understandability of security notifications and also leverages developer feedback to build an adaptive system tailored to each individual developer. This approach has been developed as a prototype within the BMBF funded project *Cybersecurity static analysis with immediate feedback* (CRITI-CALMATE[3]).

Within the CRITICALMATE project, we prototyped a novel SAST tool, also named CRITICALMATE. In the following, we will use CRITICALMATE when referring to the tool and CRITICALMATE project when referring to the project.

We conducted the CRITICALMATE project in collaboration with RIGS IT, who have previously developed Xanitizer[4], another SAST tool.

The remainder of this paper is structured as follows: In Sect. 2, we present our approach. We present future improvements to our approach in Sect. 3. Section 4 discusses related work. Finally, Sect. 5 concludes our paper and gives an outlook on future work.

2   Approach

Our approach consists of two major parts regarding notifications of security tools: (i) their efficient integration into developer's IDEs to provide immediate feedback, and (ii) the understandability of security notifications.

2.1   Immediate Feedback

We integrated CRITICALMATE into IntelliJ, Eclipse, and Visual Studio Code through the respective plugin systems. These plugins receive analysis results from our novel static code analysis engine and display them as highlights in the IDE's code editor. The analysis engine as well as the integration plugins aim to perform

---

[3] https://www.forschung-it-sicherheit-kommunikationssysteme.de/projekte/critical mate.

[4] https://web.archive.org/web/20210724231452/https://www.rigs-it.com/xanitizer/.

without any user-noticeable latency. This way, CRITICALMATE can provide software developers with immediate feedback about security vulnerabilities in their code.

One advantage of immediate feedback in IDEs is that the typical workflow interruption while running static code analysis separately is avoided [9]. This shortens the feedback cycle and identifies security issues in the code as early as possible. This allows developers to fix issues while they still have most of the context available.

Furthermore, by identifying and fixing security vulnerabilities early, we avoid creating extensive lists of problems during nightly analysis runs, reducing associated feelings of frustration or overwhelm in software developers.

When a developer feels that an issue reported by CRITICALMATE is a false positive, CRITICALMATE supports suppressing certain types of notifications via in-code annotations. Limiting this suppression to one type of notification strikes a balance between false positive avoidance and security. If developers were able to suppress notifications more broadly, they could inadvertently hide actual security issues alongside false positives.

2.2 Understandable Security Notifications

Several studies in the literature have shown that many usability issues exist in current SAST tools with respect to understandability of security notifications. Tahaei et al. [10] conducted an experiment aiming to understand how helpful static analysis tools notifications (SonarQube[5] and SpotBugs[6]) are to developers. They emphasize as a finding that developers make mistakes even if these were well-known mistakes and had known solutions, which suggests a lack of developer awareness and/or missing support in addressing security issues.

Smith et al. [9] conducted a usability evaluation of four SAST tools. Within the list of found usability issues[7], there are issues related to the content of the notification, such as "Fix suggestions not adequately explained/sometimes missing" or "Verbose XML output distracting".

Figure 1 shows an example code snippet employing the Bouncy Castle Crypto API for asymmetric ElGamal encryption with an elliptic curve (EC). The encryptor needs to be initialized by calling the init() method with suitable parameters, i.e., the public key of the recipient, before encrypting the data. However, the developer forgot to call the init() method in this snippet.

In Fig. 1, we can also see the in-code highlight that the CRITICALMATE analysis engine generates for this example. While the notification correctly identifies the problem, it is difficult to understand, especially for developers who are not well-versed in the field of cryptography. Furthermore, there is no example of how to fix the issue, which has been identified as a problem for understandability above. Consequently, the solution for the issue might not be clear enough because of missing information.

---

[5] https://www.sonarqube.org.

[6] https://spotbugs.github.io.

[7] https://figshare.com/s/71d97832ae3b04e0ff1a.

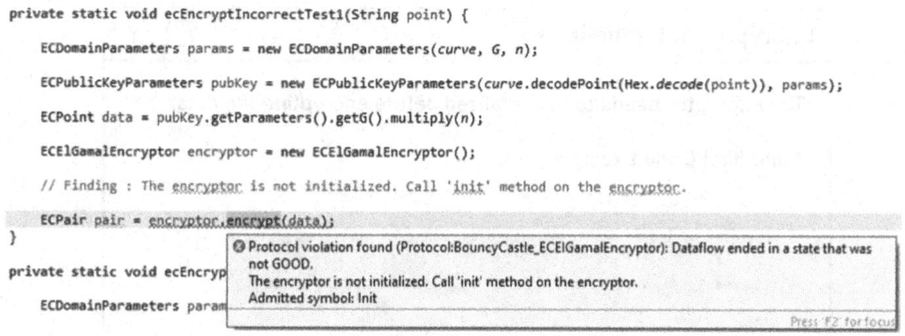

```
private static void ecEncryptIncorrectTest1(String point) {

    ECDomainParameters params = new ECDomainParameters(curve, G, n);

    ECPublicKeyParameters pubKey = new ECPublicKeyParameters(curve.decodePoint(Hex.decode(point)), params);

    ECPoint data = pubKey.getParameters().getG().multiply(n);

    ECElGamalEncryptor encryptor = new ECElGamalEncryptor();

    // Finding : The encryptor is not initialized. Call 'init' method on the encryptor.

    ECPair pair = encryptor.encrypt(data);
}
private static void ecEncryp
    ECDomainParameters para
```

> 🛈 Protocol violation found (Protocol:BouncyCastle_ECElGamalEncryptor): Dataflow ended in a state that was not GOOD.
> The encryptor is not initialized. Call 'init' method on the encryptor.
> Admitted symbol: Init
>
> Press 'F2' for focus

Fig. 1. Security notification regarding misuse of Bouncy Castle Crypto API for elliptic-curve (EC) encryption

Therefore, to support software developers in avoiding misinterpretation of security notifications, we propose an approach for presenting security notifications within IDEs that follows usability guidelines to increase the understandability of the security notifications. In addition to the in-code highlights within an IDE's code editor, our CRITICALMATE prototype offers an on-demand pop-up that provides additional details about each issue.

Figure 2 shows our proposed notification format for the issue highlighted in Fig. 1. Our format is based on the format used in the SonarSource rule repository[8]. In this format, information about the error should be provided in a concise language, as well as code examples of how to fix the error should be provided.

3 Future Work

In this section, we discuss possible improvements to our prototype. We again focus on two general areas, both revolving around adaptivity: (i) adaptive analysis strategies to improve the accuracy and usefulness of analysis results and (ii) adaptive notifications to increase developers' understanding of security issues.

3.1 Adaptive Analysis Strategies

Adaptive analysis strategies could help improve the accuracy of the results and their usefulness to developers working with CRITICALMATE. One major opportunity for improvement is the false positive rate. In SAST tools, the increased analysis performance required for immediate feedback frequently comes at the cost of an elevated false positive rate [1,2]. Generally, such tools have two options to handle a high false positive rate: (i) they implement more accurate analysis strategies, usually at a performance cost, or (ii) they tighten their confidence threshold. As a consequence, they issue fewer notifications, which however can increase their false negative rate. Due to the severe consequences of undetected

---

[8] https://rules.sonarsource.com.

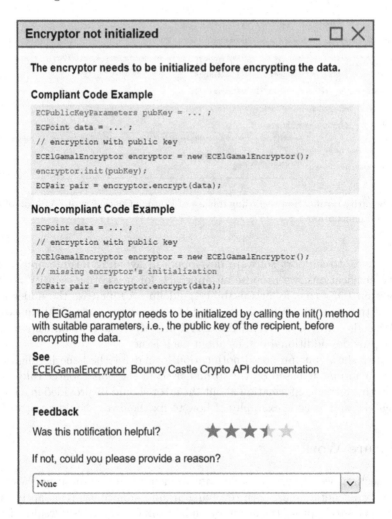

Fig. 2. Notification format using as example an API misuse

vulnerabilities, we want to ensure a low false negative rate. That is, tightening the confidence threshold is not a suitable option.

Furthermore, a high false positive rate reduces user trust in such tools, which might cause adverse effects. For example, developers might disable analyses across their whole projects instead of single notifications because of frustrating high false positive rate. In doing so, they might also inadvertently disable notifications indicating actual security issues in the code.

To handle false positives, we consider an adaptive analysis approach with incremental accuracy. For each class of issues, the analysis could choose a suitable strategy depending on factors, such as time budget, user-defined confidence rating, or recorded false positive rate for a certain combination of issue and strategy. For example, for a class of notifications known to have a low false positive rate, the analysis could choose a less detailed strategy, which would save time for other analyses. In contrast, for a class with a low confidence level, the analysis could choose a more accurate iterative strategy, until it achieves a desired confidence level, as long as the time budget permits this.

To be tailored to software developers, the proposed IDE plugin should be able to learn from software developers' feedback, especially about how they assess notifications as false positives in the context of their development projects. Based on this, the plugin should be able to adapt the classes and amount of shown notifications. For example, the plugin could learn to suppress notifications, which developers frequently classify as false positives.

3.2 Adaptive Notifications

The participants of the study conducted by Tahaei et al. [10] imply that the most helpful part were the provided code examples in the notifications. On the other hand, they indicated that metadata was not relevant for them. Therefore, providing code examples in notifications seems like the best way to help developers understand security issues (cf. Sect. 3.1).

If static analysis tools use fixed code examples in the notifications, however, they risk a mismatch between the example and developers' actual code. This mismatch may create confusion and inhibit understanding rather than promoting it. One solution to tackle this problem would be to create parameterized code example templates that can be dynamically completed to match the specific scanned code snippet and the context of the software project.

This approach could also be taken further by automatically suggesting quick fixes for a given notification. Developers can then choose to apply these fixes directly in their IDE. In some cases, where a concrete fix might not be available, a snippet with placeholders for the developer to fill in could be suggested instead. This would help developers in fixing security issues in their software more quickly and more accurately. Some existing static analysis tools, such as Clippy[9] or rust-analyzer[10] from the Rust programming language ecosystem, already support such features for some problems.

Furthermore, the plugin could also learn the developer's typical workflow, such as if they usually fix the code as soon as notifications are shown or just before committing or sharing their code. Based on this, the plugin could increase the amount of shown notifications when a developer is most likely to react to them. At other times, the shown amount would be reduced, e.g., by disabling highlights in the editor and listing the notifications only in the IDE's error list. This would allow developers to perform their tasks in the way that is most suitable for them. Reducing the amount of information when developers are unlikely to need it, could also mitigate information overload. In combination

---

[9] https://github.com/rust-lang/rust-clippy.
[10] https://rust-analyzer.github.io/.

with an adaptive analysis strategy, this would also allow more detailed analysis which could provide more accurate results.

Finally, the feedback of software developers to a notification, for example, the reason a notification was not helpful, can also be used to learn about the helpfulness of notifications and adapt future notifications' content.

4   Related Work

This section presents related work to SAST tools, which provide an IDE integration and consequently immediate feedback.

Eclipse CogniCrypt[11] is an open-source platform for static code analysis based on CrySL rules [6]. Such rules can describe different error types indicating incorrect usage of cryptography libraries. For example, a *constraint error* indicates that the static analysis detected an incorrect argument in a specific method call.

Find Security Bugs (FSB)[12] is an open-source extension of the SpotBugs static analysis tool for security audits of web application in Java. It can detect security issues, such as those described in the open web application security project (OWASP) Top 10. Furthermore, it provides plugins for its integration in several IDEs, such as for Eclipse and IntelliJ.

The goals of our approach are very similar to both aforementioned works in respect to supporting software developers with immediate feedback within their IDEs. However, in addition, we aim for a user-centered approach that leverages developers feedback to build an adaptive system.

5   Results and Conclusion

In this paper, we introduced an approach for supporting software developers to address possible security issues directly in their IDEs. Through continuous immediate feedback integrated in IDEs, developers can see notifications regarding security issues, such as misuse of cryptography libraries, as soon as code is typed in the code editor and the typed code has been analyzed by a SAST tool. Within the *Cybersecurity static analysis with immediate feedback* (CRITICAL-MATE) project, the University of Stuttgart and RIGS IT have jointly developed a prototype that integrates the analysis results of a novel SAST tool into different IDEs, namely IntelliJ, Eclipse IDE, and Visual Studio Code. Preliminary measurements tell us that security notifications are shown to developers in average under a second. However, there are several factors that influence the response time from triggering the static code analysis until the visualization of the found security notifications. To get more insights about these issues, we plan to conduct further experiments.

---

[11] https://www.eclipse.org/cognicrypt/documentation/codeanalysis.
[12] https://find-sec-bugs.github.io.

Furthermore, we plan to conduct a user study to get insights about the interaction of software developers with the immediate feedback and the adaptivity feature. One possibility is to conduct a study that also conducts emotion recognition based on physiological signals or video input. We can gain valuable feedback by recognizing confusion or frustration [3] of software developers while they are working with selected security notifications for the study.

One big challenge in the aforementioned approach is how to differentiate notifications that are actual false positives and what developers might label as false positives because they do not agree on the issue or perceive them as noise. Furthermore, if there are many notifications regarding the same code snippet, these should be prioritized to be visualized sequentially based on, for example, their severity, to avoid cluttered visualization or missing important notifications.

References

1. Alahmadi, B.A., Axon, L., Martinovic, I.: 99% false positives: a qualitative study of SOC analysts' perspectives on security alarms. In: 31st USENIX Security Symposium (USENIX Security 2022), pp. 10–12. USENIX Association (2022)
2. Aloraini, B., Nagappan, M., German, D.M., Hayashi, S., Higo, Y.: An empirical study of security warnings from static application security testing tools. J. Syst. Softw. **158**, 110427 (2019)
3. Fernandez, R., Picard, R.: Signal processing for recognition of human frustration. In: Proceedings of the 1998 IEEE International Conference on Acoustics, Speech and Signal Processing, ICASSP 1998 (Cat. No. 98CH36181). vol. 6, pp. 3773–3776 (1998)
4. Iankoulova, I., Daneva, M.: Cloud computing security requirements: a systematic review. In: 2012 Sixth International Conference on Research Challenges in Information Science (RCIS), pp. 1–7. IEEE (2012)
5. Krüger, S., et al.: Cognicrypt: supporting developers in using cryptography. In: 2017 32nd IEEE/ACM International Conference on Automated Software Engineering (ASE), pp. 931–936. IEEE (2017)
6. Krüger, S., Späth, J., Ali, K., Bodden, E., Mezini, M.: CRYSL: an extensible approach to validating the correct usage of cryptographic APIS. IEEE Trans. Softw. Eng. **47**(11), 2382–2400 (2019)
7. Nadi, S., Krüger, S., Mezini, M., Bodden, E.: Jumping through hoops: why do java developers struggle with cryptography APIS? In: Proceedings of the 38th International Conference on Software Engineering, pp. 935–946 (2016)
8. Nguyen Quang Do, L., Wright, J., Ali, K.: Why do software developers use static analysis tools? a user-centered study of developer needs and motivations. IEEE Trans. Softw. Eng. 1 (2020)
9. Smith, J., Do, L.N.Q., Murphy-Hill, E.: Why can't Johnny fix vulnerabilities: a usability evaluation of static analysis tools for security. In: Sixteenth Symposium on Usable Privacy and Security (SOUPS 2020), pp. 221–238 (2020)
10. Tahaei, M., Vaniea, K., Beznosov, K., Wolters, M.K.: Security notifications in static analysis tools: Developers' attitudes, comprehension, and ability to act on them. In: Proceedings of the 2021 CHI Conference on Human Factors in Computing Systems, pp. 1–17 (2021)

Data Science and Applications

Unsupervised Labor Intelligence Systems: A Detection Approach and Its Evaluation
A Case Study in the Netherlands

Giuseppe Cascavilla[1,2]([✉]), Gemma Catolino[1,3], Fabio Palomba[5],
Andreas S. Andreou[4], Damian A. Tamburri[1,2],
and Willem-Jan Van Den Heuvel[1,3]

[1] Jheronimus Academy of Data Science, Hertogenbosch, The Netherlands
{g.cascavilla,g.catolino,d.a.tamburri}@tue.nl, W.J.A.M.v.d.Heuvel@jads.nl
[2] Eindhoven University of Technology, Eindhoven, The Netherlands
[3] Tilburg University, Tilburg, The Netherlands
[4] Cyprus University of Technology, Limassol, Cyprus
andreas.andreou@cut.ac.cy
[5] University of Salerno, Fisciano, Italy
f.palomba@unisa.it

Abstract. In recent years, job advertisements through the web or social media represent an easy way to spread this information. However, social media are often a dangerous showcase of possibly labor exploitation advertisements. This paper aims to determine the potential indicators of labor exploitation for unskilled jobs offered in the Netherlands. Specifically, we exploited topic modeling to extract and handle information from textual data about job advertisements for analyzing deceptive and characterizing features. Finally, we use these features to investigate whether automated machine learning methods can predict the risk of labor exploitation by looking at salary discrepancies. The results suggest that features need to be carefully monitored, e.g., hours. Finally, our results showed encouraging results, i.e., F1-Score 61%, thus meaning that Data Science methods and Artificial Intelligence approaches can be used to detect labor exploitation—starting from job advertisements—based on the discrepancy of delta salary, possibly representing a revolutionary step.

Keywords: Case study · Data science · Artificial Intelligence

1 Introduction

In the last decade, the number of labor exploitation victims has risen in the Netherlands[1]. Globally, the report of UNODC (United Nations Office on Drugs and Crime) in 2020 showed how Internet-based trafficking had become increasingly used for illegal activities such as labor exploitation [36]. Traffickers usually target less regulated industries and those featuring seasonal demand for workers.

---

[1] https://tinyurl.com/we359yhe.

© The Author(s), under exclusive license to Springer Nature Switzerland AG 2022
J. Barzen et al. (Eds.): SummerSOC 2022, CCIS 1603, pp. 79–98, 2022.
https://doi.org/10.1007/978-3-031-18304-1_5

Vulnerable sectors include agriculture, food production, cleaning, construction, manufacturing, entertainment, hospitality, retail, transportation, distribution, and consumption supply chains [13]. Recently, there exists a growing trend of recruitment through the web, social media in primis, thus increasing the number of potential victims who can be targeted by labor exploitation [9]. The absence of geographical boundaries and the spread of open-access online domains make illicit behaviors accessible to a broad range of individuals that may facilitate crime [26]. In addition, the multijurisdictional context of the Internet is still an open challenge, thus complicating the prosecution of the perpetrators. However, technology improved getting short-term job arrangements, resulting in a growth in self-employed individuals. So, more effort is needed to prevent and address issues like labor exploitation, legal worker classification, wage, benefits required, and educate workers about their rights. United Nations did the first step to recognize common labor exploitation practices. Indeed, several institutions tried to define a list of forced labor and human trafficking indicators. They converged in a list of 67 indicators for human trafficking[2]. They are divided into six categories based on the type of recruitment, i.e., deceptive, coercive, abuse of vulnerability, exploitative conditions of work, forms of coercion, and abuse of vulnerability at the destination. These indicators can provide a complete understanding of the commonly utilized practice for forced labor.

The primary purpose of this paper is to shed light on coercive labor practices in the dutch economic sectors of unskilled labor. The goal of this work is double. On the one hand, we want to frame deceptive behaviors in a social media context and what are the risk factors involved in looking at online job advertisements on Dutch market labor. On the other hand, we want to define an approach that automatically detects deceptive practices based on the delta salary. In particular, we extracted information about job advertisements from Facebook groups and pages, focusing our attention on Dutch market labor. Then, we preprocess these data and apply topic modeling—applying Latent Dirichlet Allocation (LDA) and Latent Semantic Indexing (LSI)—to extract the most relevant feature that characterizes job advertisement, possibly compared to the risky indicators cited above. Finally, based on the features extracted above, we constructed a logistic regression model for assessing whether those can predict potential discrepancy in terms of salary—according to the Ducth National Salary Tables[3]—thus possibly indicating the risk of labor exploitation. Results showed how features like job class, external link represents info that characterizes job advertisements and should be carefully monitored. Finally, our logistic regression model showed encouraging results, i.e., 61% F-Measure, thus meaning that AI approaches can be used to detect labor exploitation announcements based on the discrepancy of delta salary. Indeed, detecting and preventing labor exploitation starting from job advertisements, thus represents a revolutionary step that can help decrease this issue. We are already collaborating with Dutch Police

---

[2] https://www.ilo.org/wcmsp5/groups/public/---ed_norm/---declaration/document s/publication/wcms_105035.pdf.

[3] https://www.cbs.nl/en-gb/labour-and-income.

to provide an intelligence dashboard that consists of an AI model for real-time crawling data from social media and highlights possible labor exploitation in the dutch labor market. i.e., SENTINEL Project.

Structure of the Paper. In Sect. 2, we briefly introduce the existing literature in the context of our study. Section 3 concerns the methodology of our research and Sect. 4 shows the results our experimentation. We discuss and conclude our paper in Sect. 5.

2 Related Work

This section provides a brief grounding on what has been done so far by the existing literature in labor exploitation identification.

2.1 Labour Exploitation Identification

The online recruitment of an exploitable workforce takes part on employment websites, online agencies, and social networks [19]. The existing academic literature experimented with strategies to infer deceptive recruitment for labor exploitation [38]. The state of the art experimented with strategies to infer deceptive recruitment for labor exploitation. Volodko et al. [38] addressed the problem showing the indicators for labor exploitation by the existing literature may be commonplace characteristics of online job advertisements for people looking for jobs abroad. They manually labeled all the job advertisements from the most famous Lithuanian website. They experimented with Poisson regression to test if the characteristics of one advertisement can give enough information to predict the number of labor trafficking indicators present.

Kejriwal et al. [23] developed a search engine to address the problem of collecting evidence about labor exploitation but, at the same time, minimizing investigative effort. The system exploits ontologies, knowledge graphs, and word embedding to extract information from Open and Dark Web for human trafficking identification. In addition, they used several strategies such as keyword strategy to extract information to create an investigation schema that helps the graph algorithm analyze the crawled web corpus.

Tong et al. [35] introduced a multi-modal deep learning algorithm to detect suspected human trafficking advertisements automatically. The approach uses both text and images and shows a high accuracy compared to models that use one of the sources. Nevertheless, the approach is hardly interpretable, especially when evaluating the impact of the features in a different context. Zhu et al. [41] proposed a language model-based approach for creating a phrase dictionary for identifying human trafficking indicators in adult service ads. The model showed a good performance and a reasonable interpretation of the keywords retrieved as potential trafficking indicators, thanks to the pipeline developed for automatically detecting and extracting data from potential fraudulent websites. This pipeline also detects and clusters human trafficking activities into unknown criminal organizations.

Siddiqui et al. [33] highlighted the importance of pre-processing tasks when dealing with unstructured or semi-structured text in order to separate relevant snippets of information from the unorganized text and find a way to improve the decision-making process in regard criminal fight.

The state of art on labor exploitation identification mainly concerns sexual trafficking [7]. Sweileh et al. [34] showed how labor trafficking is under-represented compared to sex trafficking. One reason is that indicators of sexual exploitation are more discernible and less ambiguous in the online textual context of working offers Di Nicola et al. [12]. Burbano et al. [4] make a corpus in Spanish language from social media text and build a predictive model in order to identify automatically.

2.2 Social Media Topic Detection

A recent challenge in research is to detect topics from online social networks. These topics are mainly connected to disaster events, urban planning, public health, political or marketing studies [24]. The open challenge is to interpret a massive volume of unstructured data [20], but without knowing what should be the final pattern as in the information retrieval method [22]. Since the quantity of data available in social media is exponentially growing [6] there is a need to recognize the necessity to employ tools for automatic topic discovery. Thus, the goal is to detect topics that are high-level patterns of textual data. For this reason, topic models represented a powerful techniques for discovering hidden text patterns [18]. The idea behind topic modeling is to create a thematic structure that defines a determined amount of underlying concepts through an efficient process that takes less representation space and noise and, consequently, can manipulate large amounts of data without human supervision.

Latent Dirichlet Allocation (LDA) is the dominant topic modeling technique in this particular field of research [37]. Shahbazi et al. [32] collected contents from different social media to conduct a semi-automatic process. Rohani et al. [30] addressed the problem to detect topics from a large variety of semantic text by proposing a topic modeling technique based on LDA. Statistical topic modeling based on LDA is also effective in crime prediction. Gerber et al. [14] showed that the combination of the standard approach—based on kernel density estimation—with additional Twitter features improved spatial-temporal crime prediction in one city in the United States. Once assessed the probability of each word belonging to a certain topic is, the topic modeling process evaluates each topic's cohesion in each neighborhood.

Social network such as Twitter has been used for extracting any information: Wang et al. [39] showed the possibility to predict hit-and-run crime incidents; Godin et al. [15] provided a method for recommending hashtags for tweets in a fully unsupervised approach based on LDA; Cordeiro et al. [8] improved tweet event description by extracting latent topics using LDA from the tweets text for each hashtag signal obtained after wavelet analysis; Prier [28] detected tobacco-related topics in order to provide a better understanding about public health problems in the United States. Cvijikj et al. [10] proposed a trend detection algorithm that can collect data from Facebook and detect disruptive events and popular topics in a near-real-time interval since Facebook does not provide real-time streaming access as the other social media. One problem with discovering topics from social media is the granularity that every topic can have once determined the number of topics in a corpus. Deng et al. [11] proposed a three-level LDA topic model combined with keyword matching and coherence analysis to identify topics and sub-topics and provide a good level of interpretability and a better understanding of the evolution that any topic can have over time. Keyword matching can also be done through the use of co-occurrences between pairs of the discussion topics in a key graph-based model approach [25], or through the use of algorithms such as Rapid automatic extraction algorithm (RAKE) [21].

3   Methodology

In this section, we present the methodology of our research.

3.1   Research Questions

The aim of this work is *to understand what indicators can be employed to detect labor exploitation in online job offers and define an approach to detect possibly labor exploitation alerts through salary discrepancy.* To this end, we defined the following research questions:

RQ1 - *Which are the most common features that characterize deceptive online job advertisements?*
RQ2 - *Can we use a logistic regression analysis to detect deceptive online job post practise?*

To answer **RQ1**, we collected data from Facebook public groups and pages on Dutch market labor. We filtered out all the posts that did not match the online job posting that had not been recalled by the existing literature demonstrated in Sect. 2. After scraping and gathering the data, we probed and extracted meaningful features for our further analysis. Indeed, we used NLP techniques to extrapolate meaningful information from the unstructured text. Next, we performed topic modeling analysis using LDS and LSI to explore the most common and insightful features that characterize job advertisements for spotting potential labor exploitation from social media job postings.

Based on the feature extracted above, we answer **R2** constructing a logistic regression model for identifying potential discrepancies between the salary proposed by the online announcements and the national Dutch working wage calculated by the Dutch "Centraal Bureau voor de Statistiek" (CBS)[4].

---

[4] https://www.cbs.nl/en-gb/labour-and-income.

3.2 Data Collection

In order to extract the information about job advertisements, we chose Facebook. The reason behind our choice is related to its popularity. Indeed, it is the world's most widely used social media platform, especially in the context of non-sexual labor work. For the data collection, we used a scraper written in *Python* as programming language[5]. For identifying Facebook groups and pages that post unskilled job offers in the Netherlands, we defined a query with simple keywords that would capture the context of our research e.g., job, offer. Then we double-checked the results to check whether a group or a page contained some job offers, e.g., post every week. Out of more than 200 groups, we kept 20 of them. To scrape the job offer posts of every group, we increased the number of `pages` in a range from 200 to 500 depending on the limit of the posts that one group had, and set the `posts_per_page` as 500 in order to avoid to lose data from groups that mainly contain short text. The number of entries scraped was initially 10301. To decrease the number of entries, we applied the criteria listed below. For ensuring data quality extraction, we defined the following criteria:

- The post is from groups and/or pages that have a clear mention of job announcements for the Netherlands or the Benelux region
- The post contains at least 100 characters
- The post is from a group or page that shows some activity in 2021 and has two posts per month or an average of one post per week
- The post is unique and not a duplicate

To guarantee the last criterion, we removed duplicates once we merged all the posts from different sources of groups and pages. We used the *cosine similarity* to filter out further posts that show strong similarities with each other. Nonetheless, we cannot exclude missing relevant posts. The scraper provided a JSON file as output in which the text, the post id, and the timestamp are stored. We then proceed to pre-process the qualified posts. The dataset is available online using the online appendix [1].

3.3 Data Preparation

Data preprocessing is essential since we deal with unstructured data, i.e., posts, that need to be remodeled to be input for the topic modeling analysis. In addition, raw data extracted from the collection phase need to be transformed into an understandable format. Therefore, we deployed Regular Expression (RegEx) to extract relevant features:

- We assigned a label as a new key for the contact information for each job offered by matching ad hoc regular expressions in strings of text;
- We considered as a piece of contact information two details: external website and phone contact;

---

[5] https://github.com/kevinzg/facebook-scraper.

- For each contact information, we yielded a positive value if the expression found the pattern in the string and a negative instead;

Afterward, we employed a language detector to recognize which language was used in the job announcements, i.e., *Java* library ported from Google's language detection and recreated to *Python*[6]. Since this language detection algorithm is non-deterministic, it is not always reliable. Therefore, the first and the second authors of this paper manually double-checked half of the posts to check whether the language detected was the correct one. Moreover, the detection can result in ambiguous and not comprehensive as some posts can contain not only one language. Therefore, we gave priority to labels with a different language other than English and/or Dutch. Finally, we translated data into English to use them as input for the topic modeling task. We employed Google translate API for doing this task[7]. Posts written on social media might contain typos/errors. Hence, we extended the translation with a spelling corrector[8]. Furthermore, we identified any possible duplicates, filtered out them. **2873** represent the final number of posts we got.

Subsequently, we extrapolated the salary offered in each post. Once again, regular expressions came in handy when dealing with numeric characters with a specific meaning according to their position in the text. We developed a heuristic approach to get only the digits that represent the salary and nothing else, such as the phone number or the date:

- We first retrieved all the words in a consecutive or closed position to every number for every post;
- We selected only the words that related to a money offer such as *euro*, *gross*, *hourly*;
- We retrieved the digit in a new feature, and we kept all the keywords necessary to calculate the salary and convert it hourly and into the gross form

Since we want to have an accurate conversion from a net wage to a gross one, we collected the data from a gross/net converter website for each amount of hourly wage and each year[9]. Then, we matched the net wage with the salary obtained from the preprocessing and the year with the one from the timestamp retrieved with the scraper; finally, we obtained the gross salary. As for the posts that did not explicitly specify whether the salary was grossly or net, we reasonably assume it as gross wage. We kept the timestamp as the next feature. In particular, we consider the year as the most informative part of the timestamp. Moreover, we found five main languages, with varying degrees, consistently present in the dataset, five different type of job post and the amount of post on each year. These features are not related to the salary, hence we defined them as "other" as shown in Table 1.

---

[6] https://github.com/shuyo/language-detection.
[7] https://py-googletrans.readthedocs.io/en/latest/.
[8] https://textblob.readthedocs.io/en/dev/.
[9] https://thetax.nl.

Table 1. Top 5 frequency of the other features

Language	Count	Job type	Count	Year	Count
Polish	1459	Manufacturing	976	2020	803
English	815	Transportation and storage	603	2021	795
Dutch	447	Wholesale and retail trade	448	2019	575
Romanian	80	Construction	354	2018	259
Lithuanian	61	Agriculture, forestry and fishing	205	2016	198

The type of job represents the last feature. We performed a heuristic approach to extract this information together with manual labeling:

- We took into consideration the type of job that, according to the existing literature, is most likely to be at risk for labor exploitation;
- We considered the United Nations' classification of the job sector[10], and we extracted all the keywords related to the type of job previously considered;
- We then matched these keywords with each post in our dataset, filtering out all the rest of the words.

Once we had only these relevant keywords, we could manually label each post within the appropriate job sector.

3.4 [RQ1]. Topic Modeling for Deceptive Online Job Advertisements

After extracting the data, we tried to find the essential information that characterizes online job advertisements using topic modeling, possibly spotting potential signals of labor exploitation. The usage of topic modeling showed promising results in uncovering hidden communities of tweets in social media [30]. We exploited two topic modeling techniques, Latent Dirichlet Allocation (LDA) and Latent Semantic Indexing (LSI).

LDA is an unsupervised learning that views documents as bags of words. It is a generative probabilistic model of a corpus based on a three-level hierarchical Bayesian model. The probabilistic topic model estimated by LDA consists of two tables (matrices). The first table describes the probability or chance of selecting a particular part when sampling a particular topic (category). The second table describes the chance of selecting a particular topic when sampling a particular document or composite. Indeed, it determines the proportion of a collection of topics for each document of corpus-based on the distribution of the keywords [2]. Once the number of topics is given, the document's topic distribution is reorganized. Finally, the keywords are distributed inside the topics to have the ideal output of topic-keywords structure.

LSI is the second method that we implemented. It attempts to solve the issues of lexical matching by retrieving information using statistically determined conceptual indexes rather than individual words. It represents a method that maps

---

[10] https://unstats.un.org/unsd/publication/seriesm/seriesm_4rev4e.pdf.

documents into a latent semantic space [31]. Since this new space has fewer semantic dimensions than the original one, this technique works as a dimensionality reduction. A truncated singular value decomposition (SVD) evaluates the structure of the words in each document given. The vectors created from the truncated SVD are then used for retrieval. The result is that these vectors produce a more reliable performance in understanding the meaning compared to the individual phrases since they can handle the synonymy problems.

Data Preprocessing. Before deploying the topic modeling, we preprocessed our data. First, we considered the unstructured text filtered by the keywords from the previously extrapolated features. Then, we prepared the text data for the preprocessing tasks.

The first operation is to correct wrongly translated words: they are translated without a proper or reasonable meaning concerning the context in the text. For this reason, we created an initial list of the unique words from the raw corpus of text, and then we detected the language of each word. The words that were not detected in English were discarded or corrected based on a manual check. Then, we ordered the words by frequency, checking if some uncommon words appeared in an unexpected frequency, and replaced them with the correct word.

Another step performed consisted of removing the stopwords, i.e., the most common words such as articles, pronouns, and prepositions. We included as stopwords words such as *'work'*, *'job'* and *'Netherlands'* since they often appeared, not adding any additional information to the text. Removing this low-level information from the text also helped reduce the number of tokens used and streamline the following steps. We removed punctuations, and we tokenized each post in a list of words with the use of the Gensim library[11]. We computed the bigrams and trigrams, i.e., the sets of two and three adjacent words. We tried different value of the n-gram parameters' function `min_counts` and `threshold` to achieve an optimal combination of n-grams words. We performed a lemmatization of the word since we wanted to produce words that could be easily readable and recognizable. Finally, we created the dictionary and the corpus using `id2word`, which maps the unique id of each word to a token.

Applying Topic Modeling. Once we completed the preprocessing steps, we trained the LDA model. The initial task is to set the number of topics. In order to define the optimal number of the topic, we ran a grid search setting the minimum and the maximum number of topics and the `step` as 1. We gradually reduced the number of topics to 15 once we measured the coherence score, i.e., the degree of semantic similarity between high scoring words in the topic, for each amount of topics that the LDA model was generating.

As for LSI, We replicated the same preprocessing implementation for LDA. We used Gensim library to implement the model[12]. In this case, we explored different values for the hyperparameters step, i.e.,   `chunksize` and `decay`.

---

[11] https://pypi.org/project/gensim/.

[12] https://radimrehurek.com/gensim/models/lsimodel.html.

Chunksize indicates the number of posts used in each training chunk, and it can affect the speed of the training, while decay value gives a weight of existing observations relatively to new ones.

Once we had the topics, we evaluated the goodness of the model. We used two evaluation metrics: the perplexity score, which captures the level of generalization of the model, and the coherence score.

The perplexity score is a statistical measure that estimates the distribution of words in the documents and tells how the model can represent the statistics of the held-out data [2]. Since it has been proved that this metric may not yield human interpretable topics and it can be not positively correlated with the human judgments [5], we include other metrics along with the perplexity score. The metric that evaluates the coherence score is 'c_v'. It measures the score using a normalized pointwise mutual information (NPMI), and the cosine similarity once obtained the co-occurrence between words [29]. Due to the space limitation, we do not report the formula.

3.5   [RQ2]. Building a Logistic Regression Model

This RQ aims to predict deceptive behavior, considering as dependent variables the most tangible value that we can get from an online job announcement: the salary. To obtain our dependent binary variable, we relied on data regarding the employment, working hours, and wages in the Netherlands[13]. In particular we procured the hourly wage per class of job and per year. We calculated the difference between these values and the salary extracted from our dataset.

The predictive variable was named *delta salary*: when the salary offered in a job post is larger than the one displayed by the national statistic agency, we attributed a positive value, we gave a negative value otherwise.

In order to classify this variable, we deployed a logistic regression model. This technique can estimate the probability of occurrence, including making a connection between features and the likelihood of specific outcomes. The features that we considered are the ones obtained from the data preparation phase and the topics obtained from the LDA topic model, and they are:

- Topic
- Year
- Language
- Job Class
- Presence of phone contact
- Presence of external url

In this way, we wanted to discover whether it is possible to find a hidden pattern between potential labor exploitation indicators and if there is a chance to improve the accuracy of the investigation in this area of research. At the same time, having a tangible asset as the salary identification can help to assess the economic impact better and better understand the business model employed.

---

[13] https://opendata.cbs.nl/statline/#/CBS/en/dataset/81431ENG/table?ts=1637795 200937.

Before running the model, we initially explored the data and checked possible class unbalancing. Unfortunately, the negative value overcame the positive ones. However, the ratio was not excessively unbalanced (70%–30%). Moreover, oversampling with artificial data could deteriorate the quality of the dataset. On the other side, undersampling could discard potentially meaningful data and undermine the model's accuracy. We then proceeded to encode the variables. We first converted the categorical variable such as the *job class*, the *language* and the *topic* into one hot encoded variables, *time* into ordinal encoded variable and *phone contact* and *external url* into simple dummy variables. As a consequence, the number of variables exponentially increased. Thus, we measured a possible correlation among the variables and performed a recursion feature elimination to select the meaningful variables and avoid high dimensionality problems. We used the Sklearn library to implement it[14].

The recursion feature elimination selects features by recursively evaluating smaller groups of features. First, the estimator is trained on the original set of features to determine the importance of each feature. Then, the least significant feature is removed from the current group of features. The process is repeated until the given set of features is attained. We decided to keep half of the features out of those previously made. We divided the dataset into training and testing data, finally implementing the model. We removed the features that exhibit p-values higher than 0.05 and re-run the model. Then we removed topic features to compare with the previous model and evaluated whether the model showed any difference in terms of explainability. We then evaluated our final model to predict the accuracy. We also wanted to see what is the accuracy of both of the binary predictive classes. Thus we calculated the precision, recall, and F1-score. We finally evaluated the sensitivity/precision trade-off using the ROC curve.

4   Results

This section presents the results obtained according to the methodology described in Sect. 3.

4.1   Topic Modeling

In this section, we show the results from the experimentation presented in the methodology in the Sect. 3. We started to experiment with LDA[15]. In particular, we initially defined the optimal `threshold` of both bi-grams and tri-grams. We experimented with several sets of values. The values outside the range between 10 to 100 displayed worse scores and poorer interpretation, so we focused on those inside the range. We reported the results in Table 2. In this case, we chose 80 as the optimal choice since it showed a better coherence score, even though it was very close to the other values. Once selected the *threshold* of the n-grams,

---

[14] https://scikit-learn.org/stable/modules/generated/sklearn.feature_selection.RFE.html.

[15] https://github.com/giuseppecascavilla/topic_modelling.

we further kept experimenting using α and η hyperparameters. We tried several values of α and η. Since we reasonably assumed that the distribution for words in topics and documents is sparse, we expected to have a better score with a value of α and η less than 1. Table 3 shows the results of the tuning. While the optimal number of topics changes from a range of values from 2 to 6, the coherence scores are very close. The coherence score showed the same trend for the experimentation with different values of the hyperparameters. It kept increasing for the first few topics, before having a fall after the seventh topic, as we can see from the Fig. 1.

Table 2. LDA: experimentation with n-grams threshold

LDA			
Threshold	Coherence	Perplexity	N. of Topics
10	0.421	−7.924	5
50	0.552	−7.750	5
80	0.577	−7.537	4
100	0.557	−7.428	2

Once selected the *threshold* of the n-grams, we further kept experimenting using α and η hyperparameters. We tried several values of α and η. Since we reasonably assumed that the distribution for words in topics and documents is sparse, we expected to have a better score with a value of α and η less than 1. The coherence score showed the same trend for the experimentation with different values of the hyperparameters. It kept increasing for the first few topics, before having a fall after the seventh topic, as we can see from the Fig. 1.

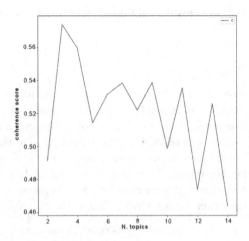

Fig. 1. Coherence scores of topics for LDA model (with $\alpha = 0.5$, $\eta = 0.01$)

The coherence scores between the optimal number of topics and the number of topics close to the optimal one do not flat out. Thus, despite the fact that the optimal number of topics often differs from one experimentation to another, the optimal range of topics remains the same. The coherence scores provides an overview of the number of topics available in the dataset.

The perplexity score changed only when the value of η was set as the lowest (0.01), and it confirms the assumption about the sparsity of the distribution of the words in each topic. Consequently, this leads to believe that the size of vocabulary for each topic is variable and topics contain uncertain word combinations. Regarding the model, the optimal number of topics have the same range of a number of the ones with the LDA experimentation, as we can see from the Table 4. The coherence scores showed a slightly better performance, especially when the *chunksize* is small and the *decay* is not more than 0.5.

Table 3. LDA: experimentation with α and η and *threshold* of bi-grams and tri-grams as 80

LDA				
α	η	Coherence	Perplexity	N. of Topics
Symmetric	*Symmetric*	0.547	−7.605	2
Auto	*Auto*	0.577	−7.536	4
0.01	*Symmetric*	0.539	−7.474	6
0.01	*Auto*	0.546	−7.498	3
0.5	*Auto*	0.546	−7.498	3
2	*Auto*	0.576	−7.905	6
0.01	0.01	0.564	−10.201	5
0.5	0.01	0.573	−10.223	3
2	0.01	0.533	−10.407	2
2	0.5	0.571	−7.554	4
2	2	0.576	−7.791	3

Table 4. LSI: experimentation with *decay* and *chunksize*

LSI			
Decay	Chunksize	Coherence	N. of Topics
0.1	10	0.627	6
0.1	50	0.591	4
0.1	100	0.559	3
0.5	10	0.624	4
0.5	50	0.605	5
0.5	100	0.622	4
1	10	0.552	3
1	50	0.530	3
1	100	0.522	10

As mentioned in Sect. 3.4, the purely quantitative metrics can limit the overall evaluation. Consequently, we looked for topics in detail through the observation-based. We considered the top 15 words of each topic, and we evaluated whether any word was shared among the topics. We made use of the Word Cloud to visualize better the top words (Fig. 2).

Fig. 2. Word Cloud of the 3 topics of the best LDA model

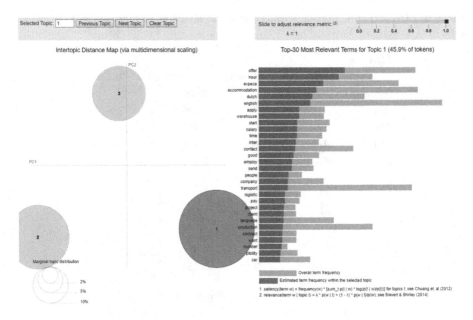

Fig. 3. Visualization of the LDA model

The majority of the topics could not identify as a determined class of job or a specific working condition. Few words were not shared among the topics, and only a few of them can be representative of a kind of job, working condition, or an evident writing pattern. The LDA best model had **3** topics, a perplexity score of −**10.223** and a coherence score of **0.573**. By observing the top 15 words, at most one word per topic, *'warehouse'* and *'shift'* for example, was relevant to differentiate the topics. We further visualized the LDA model in an intertopic distance map (Fig. 3). It provided more insight regarding the top 15 words previously analyzed. Despite most of the top words being shared in every topic, different words had different saliency levels. For example, the word *'accommo-dation'* has a high value of relevance but a saliency close to 0. On the contrary, term such as *'production'* has a high relevance as well as a high saliency towards a specific topic, which makes it more informative. To access the interactive file of our LDA topic modelling please refer to [1] file name `everything.html`.

4.2 Logistic Regression Results

Regarding the regression analysis, we implemented the procedure previously described in 3.5. We used a *Python* library[16] to evaluate whether the features built can be significant to reveal if the salary offered in a job announcement is appropriate to the national values. We considered 26 features created after the econding phase. We also included topics from the LDA model.

Before the implementation, we considered reducing the dimensions to avoid using irrelevant features that would have only increased the time complexity. We used the recursive feature elimination, which is a wrapper-type algorithm that searches for a subset of features by starting with all features and subsequently removing them until a fixed number is provided [16], which in our case is 14, more than a half.

We implemented the model. Out of the 14 features that we initially had, we removed the ones with a *p-value* higher than 0.05, which indicates the statistical significance for a confidence interval of 95%. As a result, 6 variables are removed. Detailed results are available in the online appendix [1]. After this step, we wanted to check whether the model changed the significance for the remaining variables, so we took into consideration the *Pseudo-R^2* to evaluate the change of the interpretability of the model [27]. The *Pseudo-R^2* of the model with 14 features is 0.385, while the one of the models without significant features is 0.263. The value showed a decrease. However, it is still in a good fit range for the machine learning estimation, as it is demonstrated to be between 0.2 and 0.4 [17]. The significant variables kept by the model were 7, 3 regarding the language of the text, 3 about the type of the job and the last one is the first topic of the LDA model. We consider the Durbin Watson statistic is for the auto-correlation in the model's output. The value is −1.942, which was a sign of zero or low level of auto-correlation in the residuals.

As for 'topic' variable, its regression coefficient was negative, which indicates a negative proportional relationship between the text similar imputable to this topic and the *delta salary*. Since we wanted to evaluate the importance of the variable in the logistic model, we ran the regression without the topic. There is a slight reduction of the value of the *Pseudo-R^2* (0.249) and a slight increase of the log-odd, from 0.440 to 0.446, which means that the topic had some importance in the prediction. Detailed results are available in the online appendix [1]

We analyzed several metrics used in a binary classification task namely accuracy, recall, precision and F1 score.

---

[16] https://www.statsmodels.org/dev/example_formulas.html.

As we can see from Table 5, while the negative *delta salary* had high values of precision, recall, and F1 score, the positive class had a low value of F1 score, which is caused by a low recall. Moreover, since the amount of data leans towards the negative class, the score of the macro average is lower than the one of the weighted average.

Table 5. Classification results

# of class	Class	Precision	Recall	F1-score
2	Negative *Delta salary*	0.81	0.98	0.88
	Positive *Delta salary*	0.76	0.25	0.38
Macro average		0.79	0.61	0.63
Weighted average		0.80	0.80	0.76

Detailed results are available in the online appendix [1]

5   Discussion

Our initial investigation showed a match between the labor indicators stated by the literature that we reviewed and the one from social media and how they can affect the job research in the unskilled job market. From our research study we found that human judgment still plays a big role in the evaluation and interpretation. For example, the presence of the wage can indicate that we are more likely to deal with unskilled job offers than skilled ones [3,40] By combining other indicators such as the type of job, the description, and the national salary for that job, we can assess if the offer is adequate to the national standard.

Offering a low-paid job but still above the minimum wage does not implicitly entail illegal work. We have then to discern what kind of job is more susceptible to salary discrepancy. In this regard, we need to shed light on a better evaluation of the recruitment process's weakness and what the main actors are involved for a further investigation.

Besides the salary, the richness of the information in a job description can also play an important role during the evaluation. Job announcements with short text descriptions were difficult to frame into a job category since they contained very few keywords regarding the job and, in most cases, they belonged to more than one job type. This announcement shortness problem leads the categorization ambiguous, compromising the next steps. The topic modeling phase suffered from the presence of entries with a short text. Some of them were discarded due to the lack of real information. However, others were kept since they were job offers, and ignoring them could have reduced the variety and the true representation in the social media context.

Stopwords are also important factors in topic modeling. There are words such as 'english', 'contact', 'company' or 'worker'. These words can be considered general words in a job description and are not insightful. However, considering them on a par with *stopwords* and removing them can lead to a complete outcome, with different topics from a less rigorous *stopwords* selection. The n-gram threshold is also a parameter that affects the output. Increasing the threshold we had a fewer number of topics and a higher coherence score, but the topics are difficult to interpret as the variety of most relevant and salient words is really low.

It was not the only time that we encountered the conflict between better performance with quantitative metrics and questionable performance with human judgment. When experimenting with LDA hyperparameters, we noticed that a better model was given with a low value of η, since it reduced the perplexity, which is connected to the model's generalization. However, the results showed topics with defined characteristics but very ambiguous from each other. Overall we can state that we Topic 1 is more related to the type of **job offer** and the amount of **hours**, hence we have also terms like **salary** offered in a job post. Topic 2 appears to be more related to the type of job, indeed in this topic we have terms like **production** and **transport** that give the idea of the main type of job offered. In the last topic, Topic 3, we find prevalence of languages like **English** and **Dutch**. Topic 3 is representative if related to the type of languages requested to work in Netherlands. The complete analysis is available in the Appendix online [1].

We aimed to capture in a so-called topic the type of job and the job description's linguistic features simultaneously. Both LDA and LSI models displayed good results with quantitative metrics, i.e., coherence and perplexity but hard interpretation and human evaluation of the data, mostly because of the lack of interpretable embedding. One problem is that we do not have clear evidence that components from one topic have a positive or negative sense. We tried to determine an explanation in this sense by including the topics as features in the regression model. In fact, we had a clear relationship between statistically significant topics and wages offered in the job announcement.

Nevertheless, metrics used along with the intertopic distance map, such as saliency and relevancy, provided more information about a single word in each topic. In this way, we discovered more insightful patterns in each topic. This last evidence showed the potential that topic modeling could achieve for this particular field of research.

As we can see from the results of our prediction model, other information can be relevant to assessing the job announcement's fairness. Different types of language might affect the salary offered. Although our dataset cannot be considered a complete representation of the job market, it is interesting that language is a significant aspect of the data. Considering that every kind of analysis needs language conformity to provide a comparison in a final evaluation, translating the text into language might risk losing essential information for the analysis.

Finally, we believe that our approach—which needs further studies—can represent the starting point for future investigation on how AI can help police to detect and prevent labor exploitation starting from job advertisements, thus representing a revolutionary step that can help decrease this issue. We are already collaborating with Dutch Police to provide an intelligence dashboard that consists of an AI model for real-time crawling data from social media and highlights possible labor exploitation in the dutch labor market. i.e., SENTINEL Project (see the acknowledgment). These studies will also converge in providing a more general framework and tool that different countries' police can use.

6   Conclusion

In this work, we provide a promising approach for detecting and analyzing potential labor exploitation indicators in social media. First, we examined indicators of potential labor exploitation from the current literature, and we investigated their presence in real data. Then we extracted and pre-processed data from Facebook groups and pages that offer job advertisements in the dutch labor market. To extract important feature that characterizes labor, we apply topic modeling techniques, i.e., Latent Dirichlet Allocation and Latent Semantic Indexing. Then, based on the topic extracted, we constructed a logistic regression model for predicting salary discrepancy from the wage expected to the national standard. The results of our model are encouraging (F1 Score 61%), thus meaning that the Artificial Intelligence approaches should be considered for any criminal investigation. In future works, we want to consider other types of social networks and try different parameters configurations when running a machine learning model.

Acknowledgements. We thank Davide Carnevale for the work done during his master thesis. The work is supported by EU Twining DESTINI project, and, the Dutch Ministry of Justice and Safety through the Regional Table Human Trafficking Region East Brabant sponsored the project SENTINEL.

References

1. Appendix: unsupervised labor intelligence systems: a detection approach and its evaluation (2022). https://doi.org/10.6084/m9.figshare.19481339.v1
2. Blei, D.M., Ng, A.Y., Jordan, M.I.: Latent dirichlet allocation. J. Mach. Learn. Res. **3**, 993–1022 (2003)
3. Brenčič, V.: Wage posting: evidence from job ads. Can. J. Econ./Revue canadienne d'économique **45**(4), 1529–1559 (2012)
4. Burbano, D., Hernandez-Alvarez, M.: Identifying human trafficking patterns online. In: 2017 IEEE Second Ecuador Technical Chapters Meeting (ETCM), pp. 1–6. IEEE (2017)
5. Chang, J., Gerrish, S., Wang, C., Boyd-Graber, J.L., Blei, D.M.: Reading tea leaves: how humans interpret topic models. In: Advances in Neural Information Processing Systems, pp. 288–296 (2009)
6. Chinnov, A., Kerschke, P., Meske, C., Stieglitz, S., Trautmann, H.: An overview of topic discovery in twitter communication through social media analytics. In: Americas Conference on Information System (2015)
7. Cockbain, E., Bowers, K., Dimitrova, G.: Human trafficking for labour exploitation: the results of a two-phase systematic review mapping the European evidence base and synthesising key scientific research evidence. J. Exp. Criminol. **14**(3), 319–360 (2018)

8. Cordeiro, M.: Twitter event detection: combining wavelet analysis and topic infer-
   ence summarization. In: Doctoral Symposium on Informatics Engineering, vol. 1,
   pp. 11–16 (2012)
9. Council of Europe: Third Report on the Progress Made in the Fight Against Trafficking in Human Beings. European Commission (2020)
10. Cvijikj, I.P., Michahelles, F.: Monitoring trends on facebook. In: 2011 IEEE Ninth
    International Conference on Dependable, Autonomic and Secure Computing, pp.
    895–902. IEEE (2011)
11. Deng, Q., Gao, Y., Wang, C., Zhang, H.: Detecting information requirements for
    crisis communication from social media data: an interactive topic modeling app-
    roach. Int. J. Disast. Risk Reduct. **50**, 101692 (2020)
12. Di Nicola, A., et al.: Surf and sound. The role of the internet in people smuggling
    and human trafficking. eCrime (2017)
13. Forte, E., Schotte, T., Strupp, S.: Serious and organised crime in the EU: The
    EU serious and organised crime threat assessment (SOCTA) 2017. Eur. Police Sci.
    Res. Bull. **16**, 13 (2017)
14. Gerber, M.S.: Predicting crime using twitter and kernel density estimation. Decis.
    Support Syst. **61**, 115–125 (2014)
15. Godin, F., Slavkovikj, V., De Neve, W., Schrauwen, B., Van de Walle, R.: Using
    topic models for twitter hashtag recommendation. In: Proceedings of the 22nd
    International Conference on World Wide Web, pp. 593–596 (2013)
16. Guyon, I., Weston, J., Barnhill, S., Vapnik, V.: Gene selection for cancer classifi-
    cation using support vector machines. Mach. Learn. **46**(1), 389–422 (2002)
17. Hensher, D.A., Stopher, P.R.: Behavioural Travel Modelling. Routledge, London
    (2021)
18. Hong, L., Davison, B.D.: Empirical study of topic modeling in twitter. In: Pro-
    ceedings of the First Workshop on Social Media Analytics, pp. 80–88 (2010)
19. Hughes, D.M.: Trafficking in human beings in the European Union: gender,
    sexual exploitation, and digital communication technologies. SAGE Open **4**(4),
    2158244014553585 (2014)
20. Immonen, A., Pääkkönen, P., Ovaska, E.: Evaluating the quality of social media
    data in big data architecture. IEEE Access **3**, 2028–2043 (2015)
21. Jeong, B., Yoon, J., Lee, J.M.: Social media mining for product planning: a product
    opportunity mining approach based on topic modeling and sentiment analysis. Int.
    J. Inf. Manage. **48**, 280–290 (2019)
22. Kasiviswanathan, S.P., Melville, P., Banerjee, A., Sindhwani, V.: Emerging topic
    detection using dictionary learning. In: Proceedings of the 20th ACM International
    Conference on Information and Knowledge Management, pp. 745–754 (2011)
23. Kejriwal, M., Szekely, P.: An investigative search engine for the human trafficking
    domain. In: d'Amato, C., et al. (eds.) ISWC 2017. LNCS, vol. 10588, pp. 247–262.
    Springer, Cham (2017). https://doi.org/10.1007/978-3-319-68204-4_25
24. Khanjarinezhadjooneghani, Z., Tabrizi, N.: Social media analytics: an overview of
    applications and approaches. In: Proceedings of the 13th International Joint Con-
    ference on Knowledge Discovery, Knowledge Engineering and Knowledge Manage-
    ment (IC3K 2021) - Volume 1: KDIR, pp. 233–240I (2021)
25. Ko, N., Jeong, B., Choi, S., Yoon, J.: Identifying product opportunities using social
    media mining: application of topic modeling and chance discovery theory. IEEE
    Access **6**, 1680–1693 (2017)
26. Latonero, M.: Human Trafficking Online: The Role of Social Networking Sites and
    Online Classifieds. SSRN 2045851 (2011)

27. McFadden, D., et al.: Conditional Logit Analysis of Qualitative Choice Behavior. Academic Press, New York (1973)
28. Prier, K.W., Smith, M.S., Giraud-Carrier, C., Hanson, C.L.: Identifying health-related topics on twitter. In: Salerno, J., Yang, S.J., Nau, D., Chai, S.-K. (eds.) SBP 2011. LNCS, vol. 6589, pp. 18–25. Springer, Heidelberg (2011). https://doi.org/10.1007/978-3-642-19656-0_4
29. Röder, M., Both, A., Hinneburg, A.: Exploring the space of topic coherence measures. In: Proceedings of the Eighth ACM International Conference on Web Search and Data Mining, pp. 399–408 (2015)
30. Rohani, V.A., Shayaa, S., Babanejaddehaki, G.: Topic modeling for social media content: A practical approach. In: 2016 3rd International Conference on Computer and Information Sciences (ICCOINS), pp. 397–402. IEEE (2016)
31. Rosario, B.: Latent semantic indexing: an overview. Techn. rep. INFOSYS **240**, 1–16 (2000)
32. Shahbazi, Z., Byun, Y.C.: Analysis of domain-independent unsupervised text segmentation using LDA topic modeling over social media contents. Int. J. Adv. Sci. Technol **29**(6), 5993–6014 (2020)
33. Siddiqui, T., Amer, A.Y.A., Khan, N.A.: Criminal activity detection in social network by text mining: comprehensive analysis. In: 2019 4th International Conference on Information Systems and Computer Networks (ISCON), pp. 224–229. IEEE (2019)
34. Sweileh, W.M.: Research trends on human trafficking: a bibliometric analysis using scopus database. Glob. Health **14**(1), 1–12 (2018)
35. Tong, E., Zadeh, A., Jones, C., Morency, L.P.: Combating human trafficking with deep multimodal models. arXiv preprint arXiv:1705.02735 (2017)
36. United Nations: Global Report on Trafficking in Persons 2020. UN (2021). https://books.google.nl/books?id=gGxczgEACAAJ
37. Vayansky, I., Kumar, S.A.: A review of topic modeling methods. Inf. Syst. **94**, 101582 (2020)
38. Volodko, A., Cockbain, E., Kleinberg, B.: "spotting the signs" of trafficking recruitment online: exploring the characteristics of advertisements targeted at migrant job-seekers. Trends Organ. Crime **23**(1), 7–35 (2020)
39. Wang, X., Gerber, M.S., Brown, D.E.: Automatic crime prediction using events extracted from twitter posts. In: Yang, S.J., Greenberg, A.M., Endsley, M. (eds.) SBP 2012. LNCS, vol. 7227, pp. 231–238. Springer, Heidelberg (2012). https://doi.org/10.1007/978-3-642-29047-3_28
40. Zhang, S.X., Cai, L.: Counting labour trafficking activities: an empirical attempt at standardized measurement. In: Forum on Crime and Society, vol. 8, pp. 37–61. United Nations (2015)
41. Zhu, J., Li, L., Jones, C.: Identification and detection of human trafficking using language models. In: 2019 European Intelligence and Security Informatics Conference (EISIC), pp. 24–31. IEEE (2019)

MicroStream vs. JPA: An Empirical Investigation

Benedikt Full, Johannes Manner$^{(\boxtimes)}$ ⓘ, Sebastian Böhm, and Guido Wirtz ⓘ

Distributed Systems Group, University of Bamberg, Bamberg, Germany
ben.fu@t-online.de,
{johannes.manner,sebastian.boehm,guido.wirtz}@uni-bamberg.de

Abstract. MicroStream is a new in-memory data engine for Java applications. It directly stores the Java object graph in an optimized way, removing the burden of having to map data from the Java object model to the relational data model and vice versa, a problem well known as the impedance mismatch. Its vendor claims that their product outperforms JPA-based systems realized with Hibernate. They furthermore argue that it is well-suited for implementing microservices in a cloud-native way where each service complies with the decentralized data management principle of microservices.

Our work empirically assessed the performance of MicroStream by implementing two applications. The first one is a modified version of MicroStream's BookStore performance demo application. We used it to reproduce the data the MicroStream developers used as backing for their performance claims. The second application is an OLTP system based on the TPC-C benchmark specification.

MicroStream does not provide any sophisticated features for concurrent data access management. Therefore, we created two distinct MicroStream-based approaches for our OLTP application. For the first solution, we used a third-party transaction management system called JACIS. The second solution relies on structured modelling and Java 1.0 concurrency concepts.

Our results show that MicroStream is indeed up to 427 times faster when comparing the service execution time on the server with the fastest JPA transaction. From a user's perspective, where network overhead, scheduling etc. impact the overall server response time, MicroStream is still up to 47% faster than a comparable JPA-based solution. Furthermore, we implemented concurrent data access by using an approach based on structured modelling to handle lock granularity and deadlocks.

Keywords: Cloud-native applications · Java persistence · In-memory data engine · JPA · Concurrency control

1 Introduction

In 2019, the Java-native persistence solution *MicroStream (MS)* was released. It was integrated with Helidon, a set of open-source libraries for writing cloud-native

© The Author(s), under exclusive license to Springer Nature Switzerland AG 2022
J. Barzen et al. (Eds.): SummerSOC 2022, CCIS 1603, pp. 99–118, 2022.
https://doi.org/10.1007/978-3-031-18304-1_6

microservices, in late 2021[1]. At its core, MS is a storage engine for managing and persisting Java object graphs. As it was developed specifically for handling Java objects, persisting data does not involve object-relational mapping (ORM). This fact is invoked by the framework developers as a major factor for MS's superior performance when compared to conventional relational persistence based on the Java Persistence API (JPA) standard. The developers of MS even claim that their persistence solution is "[...] up to 1000× faster than Hibernate + EHCache."[2] They support this by providing results acquired using their own, non-standardized performance evaluation solution, the *BookStore Performance Demo (BSPD)* application[3]. Our overall motivation for this work is to assess the marketing claim of MS as well as to compare the two persistence solutions with each other. We are aware that MS (in-memory) and JPA (ORM-based) solutions are two types of data management frameworks. Nevertheless both approaches allow a developer to work with their business objects in an object-oriented way. This is different from other in-memory data management solutions like Redis, where only key-value pairs can be stored, leading to a fragmentation of the domain model into disjunct objects. Furthermore the design principles of microservices, especially the decentralized data management principle, encourage developers to use the best data management solution for the use case at hand. This aspect fosters our motivation to look at MS as a candidate for a Java-native persistence solution.

To the best of our knowledge, no other publications have investigated this persistence solution and its vendor's claims regarding their product's performance. Therefore, the research questions of this work are:

- **RQ1** - Is a MicroStream-based solution up to a thousand times faster than a comparable JPA-based implementation utilizing Hibernate?
- **RQ2** - How can we achieve concurrency control for a mutable data model with the MicroStream in-memory data engine?
- **RQ3** - What are potential usage scenarios where MicroStream-based persistence should be used instead of JPA-based persistence?

Evaluating the performance of any component or system is rather challenging. There seems to be no general consensus on how performance data must be measured and interpreted [20]. Vendors sometimes provide custom applications which are supposed to highlight the strengths of their products, while at the same time ignoring or downplaying the products' weaknesses. For performance comparisons between their product and competing systems, vendors may use their own, non-standardized evaluation design implementations which raise questions regarding the bias and reliability of the data acquired. Furthermore, the performance of any system depends on the workload and application scenario [17].

---

[1] https://medium.com/helidon/helidon-2-4-0-released-18370c0ebc5e.

[2] https://microstream.one/.

[3] https://github.com/microstream-one/bookstore-demo-performance.

Benchmarks are tools used for evaluating and comparing the performance of similar systems. A benchmark should allow its users to measure performance in a standardized, reproducible, and simplified way [17]. The scope of a benchmark, and thus the applicability of its results, are usually limited to some specific usage scenario. Our research focuses on the context of Online Transaction Processing (OLTP) applications - software systems in which multiple clients can access resources concurrently.

For our work, we used a modified version of the BSPD application[4] to acquire some baseline performance data. We then implemented the *Wholesale Supplier (WSS)* benchmark[5], an OLTP benchmark based on the well-established, standardized TPC-C benchmark[6] [15]. This benchmark was then used to evaluate the performance of two different MS-based implementations in relation to a JPA-based implementation. Besides gathering and analyzing performance data, we share our expertise for identifying potential usage patterns and best practices for working with MS.

The paper is organized as follows. Section 2 describes previous work in the area of persistence solution evaluation and approaches to deal with concurrency control. Section 3 provides a more detailed introduction to the BSPD and WSS applications and how they were used to acquire performance data. This data is introduced in Sect. 4 and its implications are the foundation to answer our research questions in the subsequent part, Sect. 5. Besides answering the research questions, we also discuss potential threats to the validity of our work. Section 6 concludes the paper and provides an overview of possible future work.

2   Related Work

2.1   Performance Evaluation

Evaluating performance in the context of computer systems—and more specifically, persistence solutions—has been of concern to developers, vendors, and researchers for decades [17].

Benchmarks were developed to provide convenient means for evaluation and to enable fair comparisons of the performance of different solutions. Standardization efforts began during the 1970s [20], driven by groups and councils from industry and academia [17]. The Transaction Processing Performance Council (TPC) was formed in 1988 as a body for defining standards for evaluating the performance of systems in the context of OLTP applications. One of their most successful publications is the TPC-C benchmark, a specification-based benchmark for evaluating persistence solutions in the context of OLTP applications, released in 1992 [15].

---

[4] https://github.com/fullben/bookstore-demo-performance.

[5] https://github.com/fullben/java-persistence-benchmark.

[6] The specification for the TPC-C benchmark can be found at http://www.tpc.org/tpc_documents_current_versions/current_specifications5.asp.

Besides standardized benchmarks published by councils such as the TPC, various research projects have released or used benchmarks. One of the earliest benchmarks looking into the performance of relational databases are the so-called *Wisconsin benchmarks* published in 1983 [2]. The *HyperModel benchmark* from 1990 was used to evaluate object-oriented database management system (DBMS) in the context of engineering applications [1]. Another important benchmark in this context is the *OO1* benchmark from 1992, which—like the previously mentioned HyperModel benchmark—can be used for evaluating persistence solutions in the context of engineering applications (e.g., CAD and CASE applications). Its authors—Cattell and Skeen—deemed all existing applications insufficient for evaluating database systems for this usage scenario and, therefore, developed their own benchmark [7]. Based on the OO1 benchmark, Carey, DeWitt, and Naughton developed *OO7*, another benchmark for evaluating the performance of object-oriented databases in the context of engineering applications, released in 1993 [5]. While OO7 was quickly adopted by various vendors of object-oriented databases, its authors hoped that they would be able to eventually pass on their benchmark to some standards body [6]. Although this has not happened to this day, besides vendors, various researchers have used the benchmark for their own research projects [9,10,16].

Besides performance-focused work, researchers have also published evaluations that primarily rely on the qualitative comparison of the features of the systems being evaluated [8,14]. Other works use both a benchmark-based performance evaluation and a feature comparison [4,16].

While most of the previously described works deal with the evaluation of persistence solutions, only a few have been performed in the context of the Java environment: Jordan used a set of criteria and a custom implementation of the OO7 benchmark to evaluate Java-based persistence technologies such as EJBs, JDBC, JOS, and JDOs [16]. Based on this work, Zyl et al. compared the performance of object-oriented databases and relational databases by using yet another, custom Java-based implementation of OO7 [24].

2.2 Concurrency Control

In database research, topics like the granularity of locks, transaction management, or principles such as ACID have been discussed in the context of concurrent data access management for decades [12]. In JPA-based solutions the concurrency handling of updating data is delegated to the DBMS. Modern in-memory databases have similar problems to solve [18]. Handling concurrency control in an optimistic way is often discussed based on a multiversion strategy [19].

Since MS does not expose any meaningful concurrency control features, users of the persistence solution are forced to rely on external transaction management systems with an adapter for MS, like the Java ACI Store (JACIS) library[7]. Alternatively, developers may take it upon themselves to implement thread-safe

---

[7] https://github.com/JanWiemer/jacis.

data access in their applications. For this, they can rely on Java language features such as locks and concurrent collections [11]. This leads to a system design where business logic and concurrency control concepts are mixed in the source code. Best practices and strict design rules are necessary to avoid concurrency errors which are hard to test and resolve at runtime.

3 Methodology

3.1 BookStore Performance Demo Application

The vendor of MS has published the so-called *BookStore Performance Demo* application on GitHub. This application is used to back their claims regarding the superior performance of MS when compared to JPA-based persistence on their website, see **RQ1**.

The application is implemented in Java 8 using SpringBoot and both MS and JPA for persistence. The JPA-based, relational persistence uses Hibernate as JPA implementation and a PostgreSQL DBMS for managing the relational database. The business model of the BSPD application is that of a company selling books in stores located in multiple countries. It is worth mentioning that the model structures for the MS-based implementation are largely immutable to increase thread-safety and ease the burden of manual synchronization.

At BSPD application startup, an initial set of model data is generated for the MS-based persistence implementation. Once written to storage, this data is then also written to the JPA-based implementation, thus ensuring that both persistence implementation variants have the same initial set of data. After this setup has been completed, users can use the Vaadin-based web interface of the application to trigger one of seven predefined read-only queries. The selected query is executed for both, the MS-based and the JPA-based persistence implementations, and usually repeated multiple times. The execution durations for these queries are then reported back and visualized in the web interface. The actual result data of the queries is ignored. And although the queries are designed to be parameterized, the application selects the actual parameter values to be used automatically.

We developed an extension of this application[8]. It makes no significant modifications to the behavior of the existing application components. For executing the seven defined queries parameterized, we added a dedicated service layer. This service layer allows for query execution against both, the MicroStream-based and the JPA-based data. We made these services available as part of a new API. The endpoints of the API can be used to trigger the queries with appropriate parameters, provided via HTTP request properties. Additionally, we wrote a JMeter script that can be used to simulate multiple clients interacting with this API concurrently. The clients use the API in a two-step process:

1. Setup phase: A set of data is acquired from the API in order to define the value ranges for the parameters of the queries.

---

[8] https://github.com/fullben/bookstore-demo-performance.

2. Measurement phase: Each client randomly selects one of the seven queries and randomly chooses valid parameters before calling the appropriate API endpoint.

With this performance measurement approach, more data can be generated than with the original implementation. This should potentially reduce the impact of errors introduced by sources of uncertainty such as the host platform or the JVM JIT-compiler activity during the initial moments of the application run-time [3].

3.2   Why Another Custom Benchmark?

As indicated in Sect. 2.1, there is a variety of benchmarks for evaluating persistence solutions. So why did we see the need for implementing our own, custom benchmark?

Solely relying on the BSPD application would not have been appropriate, as it is a non-standardized, vendor-provided solution.

Most of the benchmarks described in Sect. 2.1 focus on the area of engineering applications. As our goal was to use a benchmark relevant for OLTP applications, using benchmarks developed for evaluating the performance of persistence solutions in the context of CAD or related software was not an option. Besides this obvious mismatch in focus, OO7 and its predecessors were initially published during the early 1990s. As the field of computing is vast and evolves quickly, benchmarks must either evolve to remain relevant or risk becoming outdated [15].

We, therefore, decided to implement a custom benchmark modelled after the specification-based TPC-C benchmark. The business model and workloads of TPC-C defined by the specification are relevant for a typical OLTP use case. Additionally, the business scenario of the TPC-C benchmark requires a mutable data model, as opposed to the immutable data model of the BSPD application. Furthermore, as the benchmark is specification-based, users must create a complete implementation themselves, allowing for a high degree of freedom in regard to technologies used by the benchmark implementation.

It has to be mentioned that the WSS benchmark is not fully compliant with the TPC-C benchmark specification. The reasons for this can primarily be found in our disagreement with certain requirements and structures defined in the specification. The specification heavily relies on the terminology of the relational data model. For example, it defines many primary composite keys for the data model entities. While this approach may have appeared intuitive in 1992, we were able to convert it to an object-oriented model. This allowed us to drop the foreign keys since these keys represent other objects which are class members in our approach. We also modified the overall data model by removing a model object we deemed unnecessary (*NewOrder*, used to explicitly indicate that an order is new and for artificially providing an opportunity for deleting data) and adding two new objects (*Employee* and *Carrier*). These two map entities which are implicitly part of the TPC-C business model, but not modelled as entities in the benchmark specification.

3.3   Wholesale Supplier Benchmark

Just like the TPC-C specification, the WSS benchmark models the order-entry system of a wholesale supplier.

In the business model of our WSS application, the employees of a company use computer terminals to perform their work tasks, such as adding a new order of a customer or updating an order's payment data. These tasks are referred to as *transactions*.

Table 1. The business transactions of the WSS benchmark.

	Transaction type	Read-only	Minimum % of mix
WSS1	Order-Status	Yes	4
WSS2	Stock-Level	Yes	4
WSS3	New-Order	No	45
WSS4	Payment	No	43
WSS5	Delivery	No	4

The terminals are clients of the main application that implements the business logic and manages data maintained by some persistence solution. For communication with the terminals, the application exposes a web API, secured with basic authentication. The API has two distinct sections: The first provides a set of read-only endpoints for accessing most of the data maintained by the application. The second section has endpoints that enable the parameterized execution of five predefined business transactions which are listed in Table 1, together with their execution probability. For referring to these transactions in later sections of the paper, we numbered them with our application prefix (WSS1 to WSS5). Of these five transactions, two are read-only and three are read-write actions. The server is implemented in Java 11 using SpringBoot. We implemented the application by providing two generic core modules, on which actual WSS server implementations must be based. The first of these two is a component for data generation which can be used to create the initial population of the database in a persistence solution independent model representation structure. This component relies on the JavaFaker library[9] for some of the random data generation. This data can then be converted to any solution-specific model. In the second component, we defined the overall architecture of the server. This includes the API structure, security, data transfer structures, and services.

For the WSS benchmark, we created three actual implementations of the WSS server:

1. *JPA*: Uses JPA-based persistence, with Hibernate as JPA implementation. Spring Data JPA is used for data access. The relational database is managed by a PostgreSQL DBMS. Concurrent data access is facilitated by employing the transaction mechanism defined by JPA.

---

[9] https://github.com/DiUS/java-faker.

2. *MS-JACIS*: Relies on MS for data storage and uses the JACIS library for data access synchronization by means of transactions on transient data. As JACIS uses Java object cloning for transaction isolation, we were forced to completely decouple the data model classes of this implementation. In any regular implementation (e.g. JPA-based implementation) an *Order* class would have a field referencing the appropriate *Customer* object. But in the case of this implementation, the *Order* only has a field containing an artificial identifier for the related *Customer* object. This approach makes simple object graph navigation impossible, which has significant performance implications.
3. *MS-Sync*: Also uses MS for data storage. Concurrent data access is achieved by using synchronization features provided by the Java environment. Primarily, locks and the *synchronized* keyword are used with the aid of Fig. 1.

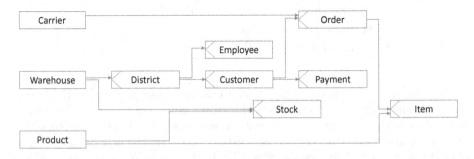

Fig. 1. Simplified Structured Entity Relationship Model of our WSS application.

For the MS-Sync variant, we analyzed the data model by using the Structured Entity Relationship Model (SERM) notation format [23], as depicted in Fig. 1. In this diagram, we have independent entity types like the carrier or the warehouse, which can also be identified by the shape of their boxes. Furthermore, there are entity-relationship types such as the district, which is dependent on the warehouse and would therefore hold the foreign key of the warehouse in a relational model. This notation gave us a direction of dependence which was helpful when determining the ordering of our locks in the concurrent Java implementation of our application. It is important to note that we used a simplified version of SERM. The arrows in Fig. 1 do not indicate the cardinality since we only want to visualize the interdependence of the individual classes of the data model.

Besides the server, we developed a JMeter script that can be used to simulate the employee terminals. Just as in the case of the BSPD application framework, each simulated terminal has two main phases of execution: the setup phase and the measurement phase.

For each of the actual server implementations, we have also provided a Docker Compose file which can be used to configure and launch the server and any necessary auxiliary systems as Docker containers.

3.4   Experimental Setup

For our experiments we used two bare-metal Linux machines with an Ubuntu 20.04 server image. The primary machine (*H90*) was a Fujitsu Esprimo P757 with an Intel Core i7-7700 CPU with 4 cores and 210 GFLOPS peak performance. We used a LINPACK benchmark to assess the peak performance and to verify the linear scaling behavior of our machines [22]. H90 had 32 GB of RAM and used a SSD with 256 GB as primary drive. The other machine, referred to as *H50*, was a Fujitsu Esprimo P700 with an Intel Core i7-2600 CPU with 4 cores and approximately 92 GFLOPS peak performance. It had 16 GB of RAM and a 240 GB SSD as primary drive.

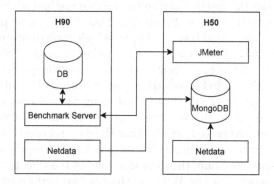

Fig. 2. Overview of the experimental setup, consisting of two physical machines. Note that the *DB* on H90 was, depending on the actual setup, either a SQL-based DBMS or the files (database) used by MicroStream to store data.

For monitoring, Netdata[10] was installed on both machines. Both Netdata agents sent their recorded data to the MongoDB instance on H50 once per second[11].

We used version 1.1.1 of the BSPD[12] and version 2.1.1 for the WSS application[13]. Both the BSPD and WSS benchmark are similar in their overall structure. They both have a Java application managing data operations and a JMeter script simulating clients interacting with this application. Due to this, the setup for measuring the performance with the two systems was very similar. We used the

---

[10] https://www.netdata.cloud/.

[11] Netdata claims that it only consumes 1% CPU utilization of a single core (https://github.com/netdata/netdata).

[12] https://github.com/fullben/bookstore-demo-performance/releases/tag/1.1.1.

[13] https://github.com/fullben/java-persistence-benchmark/releases/tag/2.1.1.

medium data generation option for BSPD. For the WSS, we scaled our model by changing the warehouse count, as defined by the TPC-C specification. Overall, we generated over 2.5 million objects: 5 warehouses, 50 districts (10 per warehouse), 50 employees (one per district), 100,000 products, 150,000 customers, and 150,000 orders. The remaining objects were order items, stock information, and payments. The impact of these settings on the used memory for the different applications will be discussed later.

Since we wanted an isolated workbench for the benchmark servers, we only deployed the benchmark server (BSPD or WSS) and their respective database on H90. The JMeter instance for executing the appropriate client-simulating script was installed on H50 and invoked the queries via the previously mentioned server APIs. This setup is depicted in Fig. 2.

Our measurement methodology focused on two metrics. Firstly, we recorded the user-perceived server response time via JMeter. Since this User-perceived Response Time (URT) contains a lot of uncontrollable effects like the physical transmission time, the middleware layers of our application etc., we also decided to additionally wrap the method call to the service method within the business logic layer to measure the Server Processing Time (SPT). This processing time value only included the actual time the business logic took to process the request. We used JMeter to save these two metrics and other data to a CSV file. For both applications, we simulated concurrent users executing the queries.

In the case of the BSPD application, we performed two distinct types of executions: one targeting the data persisted using MS, and another one aimed at the data maintained by the JPA-based persistence implementation. Each of these runs were executed twice to ensure that the data remained consistent. Both data sets proofed to be very similar, thereby indicating reproducibility of our results. We therefore used only the data from one of the runs for the evaluation included in this paper. For the WSS benchmark, we performed three distinct types of runs, one for each of the three implementations: *JPA*, *MS-JACIS*, and *MS-Sync*. As with the BSPD runs, we also performed each of these runs twice to ensure data consistency. After each run, we shut down the containers on the H90 machine and deleted the volumes containing the data written by the persistence solution of the current application implementation.

4   Results

All collected data and some diagrams visualizing CPU utilization, memory, disk IO, bubble plots for the different runs and applications as well as the scripts we used for generating the tables and plots can be found on our raw data page[14], where you can also download all data. For the discussion in this paper, we only used a subset of this data. CPU utilization, memory, and disk IO were measured for the machines in total since there are no other applications running on the machines apart from JMeter on H50 and the benchmark server on H90 as depicted in Fig. 2.

---

[14] https://spboehm.github.io/jpa-microstream-doc/.

In the BSPD application, the CPU utilization when using the JPA-based solution (~20%) was quite different from that of the MS-based implementation (~8%). This additional CPU usage in the case of the JPA-based solution is most likely caused by the DBMS and ORM overhead. In both cases, approximately 3,600 MB of RAM were occupied. Our WSS applications had a low CPU utilization (in all cases <5%), but varying memory demands. The JPA-based solution consumed the least amount of memory with ~5,725 MB, whereas the MS-JACIS implementation consumed ~11,600 MB of RAM. The MS-Sync solution used ~9,500 MB. Comparing this last value to those of the other solutions, we see that the in-memory data engine requires much more RAM than the relational database. Furthermore, the memory overhead of decoupled data model in the JACIS variant becomes evident.

Table 2. BSPD performance data for JPA and Microstream. We used our server processing time (SPT) metric to measure the execution time.

JPA/MS	Median (values in millisecond)	Speed-up
[BSPD1] (6931/8380)	68.12/2.84	24.03
[BSPD2] (6935/8383)	3.64/0.91	3.99
[BSPD3] (6934/8382)	7.87/0.93	8.42
[BSPD4] (6936/8385)	2.8/0.12	23.3
[BSPD5] (6931/8376)	38.24/14.59	2.62
[BSPD6] (6929/8376)	305.06/0.72	426.61
[BSPD7] (6933/8381)	3.26/1.11	2.93

Table 2 summarizes the measured query processing times from our BSPD application. Each line of the table includes abbreviations representing the seven queries, *get book sales* (BSPD1), *get books by title* (BSPD2), *get books in price range* (BSPD3), *get customer page* (BSPD4), *get employee of the year* (BSPD5), *get purchases of foreigners* (BSPD6), and *get revenue of a shop* (BSPD7). In parentheses after the transaction identifier, the number of requests made per solution is depicted (JPA value first, followed by the corresponding MS value). The execution time of JPA requests is higher than that of MS requests, which explains the different number of requests as we used a fixed experiment duration. The last column shows the speed-up of our MS-based solution compared to the JPA-based solution for the BSPD application. We submitted the requests for every user in sequence. So one user of our application does only make a single request at a time. To stress the concurrency aspect, we configured JMeter with ten concurrent users.

We used R for data evaluation and to generate boxplots to visualize our measurements. Computing only the arithmetic mean for our transactions was too coarse-grained and over-represented outliers. Therefore, we decided to include the median for the BSPD application as shown in Table 2.

Table 3. Raw data of the boxplots from Fig. 3. The transactions are as follows: WSS1-GET order-status, WSS2-GET stock-level, WSS3-POST new-order, WSS4-POST payment and WSS5-PUT delivery. After the transaction identifier, the second line in the table header are the number of transactions executed for JPA, MS-JACIS and MS-Synch during our eight hours experiment. The first line of each cell contains the server-side processing time (SPT) in milliseconds for the individual solutions. Line two represents the slowdown (red) and speedup (green) of MS-JACIS and MS-Sync compared to JPA. Lines three and four follow the same structure as one and two but are based on the response times measured client-side (URI).

JPA/MS-JACIS/MS-Sync	[WSS1] (479/479/479)	[WSS2] (478/478/479)	[WSS3] (5388/5386/5390)	[WSS4] (5147/5145/5148)	[WSS5] (479/478/479)
Lower whisker	7.22/76.3/0.01 10.56/580.19 81/145/66 1.79/1.23	31.61/134.63/1.77 4.26/17.86 107/205/70 1.92/1.53	13.76/29.19/3.62 2.12/3.8 88/97/72 1.1/1.22	8.13/5.41/3.32 1.5/2.44 83/74/73 1.12/1.14	52.02/138.93/20.12 2.67/2.59 126/208/89 1.65/1.42
Lower quartile	8.15/85.06/0.03 10.44/307.81 85/157/73 1.85/1.16	35.55/144.84/1.96 4.07/18.17 113/218/76 1.93/1.49	18.96/33.72/4.58 1.78/4.14 97/106/78 1.09/1.24	9.74/8.17/4.76 1.19/2.05 87/81/79 1.07/1.1	58.26/148.97/21.09 2.56/2.76 135/221/95 1.64/1.42
Median	8.65/87.8/0.03 10.15/264.3 87/162/76 1.86/1.14	36.77/148.25/2.03 4.03/18.14 115/223/78 1.94/1.47	21.72/35.16/4.94 1.62/4.39 100/109/80 1.09/1.25	10.41/9.96/5.22 1.05/1.99 89/84/81 1.06/1.1	60.44/152.12/21.52 2.52/2.81 138/226/97 1.64/1.42
Upper quartile	9.27/91.09/2.63 9.82/3.53 88/165/78 1.88/1.13	38.19/152.05/2.09 3.98/18.25 117/227/80 1.94/1.46	24.25/36.75/5.24 1.52/4.63 103/112/82 1.09/1.26	11.03/11.69/7.42 1.06/1.49 90/86/83 1.05/1.08	62.58/155.68/22.08 2.49/2.83 141/230/99 1.63/1.42
Upper whisker	10.69/99.45/6.11 9.3/1.75 92/176/85 1.91/1.08	42.15/162.32/2.27 3.85/18.58 123/239/86 1.94/1.43	32.14/41.29/6.21 1.28/5.18 112/121/88 1.08/1.27	12.87/16.92/11.3 1.31/1.14 94/93/89 1.01/1.06	68.72/165.09/23.55 2.4/2.92 150/243/104 1.62/1.44

For WSS, we included all boxplot details for the quartiles (25%, median, 75%) and the whiskers (max. 1.5 times the size of the box).

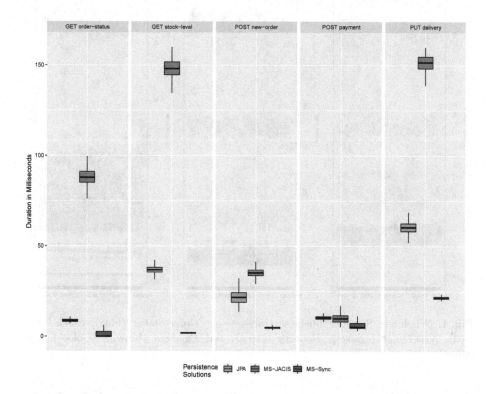

Fig. 3. Wholesale Supplier performance data of the five transactions depicted as box-plots for JPA, MS-JACIS and MS-Sync. We used our server processing time (SPT) metric to measure the execution time.

Figure 3 depicts the results of our WSS application benchmark, while Table 3 shows the raw boxplot data. We see for all transactions that our synchronous implementation with basic Java concurrency features is the fastest compared to the JPA and MS-JACIS implementations. Furthermore, MS-JACIS performed worse for most of the transactions, despite WSS4, leading to a consistent winner's podium for most transactions. Another view on the same data is presented in Fig. 4, where we see the server execution time over time when benchmarking our WSS application. For a better resolution of the Figure, we decided to exclude 0.2% of the outliers. The execution times for the JPA-based solution decreases slightly at the beginning when the JIT compiler still optimizes code and stabilizes after two hours. For the in-memory solution, only a minor increase is visible.

The structure of Table 3 is the same as for Table 2. WSS1 to WSS5 are in the same order as the headlines of the boxplots in Fig. 3. Each cell consists of four lines of data. The first line contains the processing time on the server (SPT) for

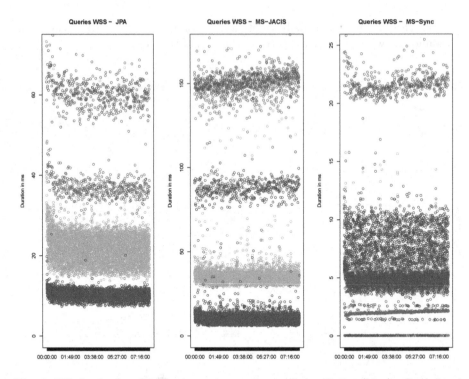

Fig. 4. Wholesale Supplier business transactions: *Order-Status* (blue), *Stock-Level* (red), *New-Order* (orange), *Delivery* (green), and *Payment* (brown). (Color figure online)

JPA, MS-JACIS, and MS-Sync requests. The second line compares MS-JACIS and MS-Sync to JPA. Green values indicate that the corresponding solution is faster by a factor of x compared to JPA, whereas red values stipulate that the solution is slower by a factor of x. The next two lines of each cell show the client-side measured response times (URT). This user-perceived performance includes network transfer, scheduling within the application, etc.

5   Discussion

5.1   MicroStream vs. JPA

First, we want to address MS's claim to be a thousand times faster than a Hibernate-based solution. Table 2 shows the adapted BSPD results. We can see that transaction **BSPD6** experienced the most significant speedup. Using the median values, MS is over 400 times faster than the JPA solution. This query navigates many nested objects which need to be read from the relational database via complex joins, whereas the MS solution can work on the Java object graph by using the Java Streams API. For all other queries executed by the BSPD, MS is faster than the JPA-based solution, but only by factors of tens, not thousands. This insight can be used to partially address **RQ1**. In order to provide a complete answer to the research question, it is important to consider another aspect. In the preceding parts of the discussion we referred to the processing time on the server. For a realistic scenario, we argue that the user-perceived performance must be compared. We did not use the user-perceived response time for a BSPD comparison since the response time measured by JMeter is only recorded on a millisecond basis with integer precision. This distorts the comparison with the server processing time which is sometimes only a small fraction of a millisecond like in **BSPD4**. We also looked at the user-perceived performance (UPT), which on average is a few milliseconds higher than the values measured server-side. The response handling and scheduling on the server adds about 5 ms per query (median of all queries).

Therefore, to fully address the first research question, in addition to the data acquired with the BSPD application, we must also consider the results gathered with the WSS application which contains a mutable data model. Additionally, as mentioned in the concurrency control Sect. 2.2, MS does not offer any sophisticated concurrency control or transaction management facilities. For this reason, we decided to use a suitable transaction framework with a MS adapter (implemented in the MS-JACIS variant) as well as a solution based on low-level synchronization utilizing the Java 1.0 capabilities (implemented in the MS-Sync variant). Especially for transaction WSS1, we see a situation where MS performs best, see boxplots in Fig. 3 and detailed data in Table 3, when looking at the first line of data in each cell which represents the service time on the server (SRT). This is similar to the BSPD application, where MS is a few hundred times faster than the JPA-based implementation. On the other side, MS-JACIS performs worse by a factor of 8–11 compared to JPA, and even worse when comparing it to MS-Sync. JACIS appears to be currently the only available solution for using transactions on transient objects in the context of MS-managed data. The performance data we acquired indicates that JACIS as a third-party transaction middleware cannot compete with JPA-based solutions. Therefore, we exclude the JACIS-based solution (MS-JACIS) and corresponding data from all further analysis.

When looking at user-perceived performance in the third and fourth line in each cell, the quotient is not greater than 1.47 (median of **WSS2**) for MS-Sync compared to JPA. Also, when looking at the millisecond values, it is evident that the response overhead ranges between 65 and 85 ms and has a dominant impact on calculating the quotients and the speedup for the user. Nevertheless, based on our results, we have to conclude that MS is not 1000× faster than a JPA solution. This gives an answer to **RQ1**. We found only a few transactions (**BSPD6** and **WSS1**) where MS is a few hundred times faster when assessing the service execution time and none where it is faster by a factor of a thousand. Furthermore, it must be considered that these speedups are not the actual, user-perceived times. In the case of user-perceived response times, we see an improvement between 10% (median of WSS4) and 47% (median of WSS2) when comparing JPA and MS-Sync. Therefore, MS appears to be capable of outperforming JPA-based persistence, albeit not by as much of a margin as claimed by the vendor of MS.

In a first version of this paper we experienced a linear increase in execution time for WSS5 - the delivery transaction. The first executions took ∼75 ms and after 6 h benchmark, the execution time increase linearly to ∼130 ms. At the beginning the assumption was that the increase is caused by WSS3, the new-order transaction, where over time the number of orders increased and therefore the filtering and sorting is more time consuming. Considering the number of initial orders (150,000) with the newly created orders (3,376), the increase was not justifiable. A detailed description and figures for this step-by-step investigation can be found on our GitHub IO Page[15]. When searching for the cause after looking at database fragmentation, index fragmentation and the LAZY and EAGER loading capabilities of JPA, we changed the service implementation as well as the native JPA query. Our assumption was that the many database queries and the ordering within one query (ORDER BY SQL feature) caused the performance problem. Connecting to a remote machines causes IO waits, therefore we reduced the number of database queries to a minimum and executed the benchmark again. The collected performance data showed that we fixed this performance problem. Our process here is noteworthy in a sense that a reproducible benchmark design like in our case depicted in Fig. 2 supports developers to find performance issues before deploying an application to production.

5.2   Concurrency Best Practices

When using MS, one of the greatest challenges is the issue of concurrency control. Therefore, in **RQ2** we ask the question *how can we achieve concurrency control for a mutable data model[...]*? In this Section, we want to address this question and share best practices we identified when implementing the WSS application.

For an immutable data model like BSPD, the concurrency issue is reduced to a minimum since immutable data is inherently thread-safe. We assume that immutable data models are rarely used in OLTP applications. Therefore, developers must explicitly handle concurrency control in their business code and deal with thread management in Java. From lecturing a bachelor's course on concurrency programming [21][16], we know how challenging it is to implement a thread-safe solution with low-level constructs like the *synchronized* keyword. For the sake of simplicity and extensibility, we suggest centralizing all concurrency logic in a single class. This gives a developer the chance to read all code which changes data concurrently in a single or limited number of files. From a portability investigation [13], we know that the lower the number of locations where source code has to be read or changed, the less error prone is the implementation. In the case of WSS this class is called *DataConsistencyManager*. Another important aspect is to prevent the application from becoming deadlocked. We

---

[15] https://spboehm.github.io/jpa-microstream-doc/.
[16] https://github.com/johannes-manner/ConcurrencyTopics.

used the SERM notation to derive the sequence and hierarchy of lock objects used in our implementation.

Listing 1.1. Lock granularity best practice for MicroStream's concurrent data access.

```
// method for updating order status and customers
public void deliverOldestOrders (... oldestOrders, ...) {
  synchronized (this.storageManger) {
    for (OrderData order : oldestOrders) {
      ...
      synchronized (customer.getId()) {
        synchronized (order.getId()) {
          ...
    this.storageManger.storeRoot();
  }
}
```

When implementing read or write operations, we used the locks from the independent objects towards the dependent objects (Fig. 1) to build nested concurrency blocks within the code as shown in Listing 1.1. For the granularity of locks, we used the identifier of our business objects, a UUID string which is declared as *final* and does not change its identity. This results in an encapsulated concurrency design since the distinct lock object for each Java object is identical for the whole lifecycle of the object. For operations on collections where we want to update several objects of a collection atomically, we used an additional *collection lock object* like the *stockLock* we implemented in our WSS application. This enabled us to handle our collections in a thread-safe manner. A major limitation is how MS writes data to persistent storage. While a write operation is ongoing, the managed Java object graph cannot be modified from other threads. Therefore, we use another lock object (the *storageManager*) since we can only have a single write operation at a time.

When implementing a custom synchronization solution, testing is of utmost importance. Since a verification of the correctness of a parallel program is difficult, brute force testing is one option to assume thread-safety of an implementation with a certain level of confidence. For this, developers can use frameworks such as jcstress[17]. We implemented a stress test for the most critical concurrent operation, the updating of the product stock quantity in our WSS application.

5.3 Usage Scenarios

RQ3 is concerned with possible usage scenarios for MS. The vendor of MS states on their website, that MS is especially suited for "Micro persistence for microservices & serverless Java functions"[18]. When having microservice principles in mind and considering the decentralized data management aspect, their assessment is comprehensible, but the nature of the data model is important for designing an MS solution. As already indicated by the MS vendor's own demo

---

[17] https://github.com/openjdk/jcstress.
[18] https://microstream.one/.

application (BSPD), good use cases for MS-based persistence may be scenarios with mostly immutable data models. This eases the concurrency control issues as well as the single writing thread bottleneck. When using JACIS, we experienced certain limitations, namely data model decoupling and performance issues. We therefore think that in its current state, JACIS is not a viable option for resolving the concurrency control issue in the context of MS-based persistence. Developers may alternatively use our best practices for implementing a thread-safe solution. But low-level concurrency programming is difficult to get right [11], which in our opinion will therefore limit the adoption of MS as a solution for data storage. For integrating the solution with other databases or systems, the current version of MS provides support for various storage targets, but these adapters often do not support the actual data model of those databases. For example, this means that while MS supports certain relational DBMSs as storage targets, the data stored in these targets by MS is not written as relational data. Additionally, a generic CSV export is offered for data migration. We assume to see more adapters and features with future MS releases, which may also support migration to data models of other persistence solution. This may in turn prove beneficial for the adoption of MS as a persistence solution.

5.4   Threats to Validity

During our comparison of MS and JPA, we had to make choices regarding aspects such as the amount of data used by our benchmark applications, or the execution duration of our benchmark runs. It must be assumed that these choices had an impact on the performance of the systems and therefore, our conclusions. The following listing contains the most important threats to validity from our point of view:

No Lazy References - MS offers lazy references with a semantic similar to JPA's LAZY fetch type for loading data at a later point in time (on demand) which introduces delays since the data is read from disk. For our WSS demo application, we decided not to use this feature since we were able to maintain the entire model data in RAM.

Custom Benchmark Application - We implemented a custom benchmark application and used the BSPD application for reproducing the speedup factor. Although the WSS application is self-audited due to tests, unidentified issues and bugs may still remain. Other applications might face different speedups or even slowdowns. Therefore, the applicability of the results of this work are most likely limited to the current capabilities of the data engine within the context of our modernized implementation of a well-known specification-based benchmark (TPC-C).

Used Experimental Setup - The machines used for our experiments obviously had an impact on the performance of our applications. This might have led to situations where the current experimenter hardware may have favoured one storage approach over the other (disk-based vs. in-memory). In the case of MS, as mentioned in Sect. 5.2, only a single thread can write to disk, as MS will otherwise recognize that parts of the object graph are being modified concurrently and will throw an exception. During the development phase of our test environment, when executing concurrency tests, we faced the situation that disk IO was at maximum capacity when writing the changes, whereas CPU utilization peaked at around 25%. Therefore, the bottleneck in this scenario might have been the disk IO capabilities. Furthermore, while assessing **RQ1**, we were unable to find the hardware configuration used by MS to run their MS version.

6   Conclusion and Future Work

In this paper, we performed a comparison of MS and JPA. First, we evaluated the claims of the MS vendor about the performance superiority of their product over JPA-based solutions. Secondly, we implemented a custom benchmark with a mutable data model, a typical OLTP use case. For this implementation, we found that the MS-based solution does indeed exhibit performance superior to that of a JPA-based approach. When looking at the SPT of the evaluated business function only, in the best case MS was able to outperform JPA by the factor of 400. However, looking at URT, we only observed a speedup of no more than 47%. While this is far from the promise made by the MS vendor, the speedup may still be relevant for latency-critical systems.

For future work, we have three aspects in mind. First, we want to investigate major factors influencing the response time. An abstract model of these factors should include aspects such as payload size, its serialization, and overall HTTP message size. Secondly, we want to compare MS with other in-memory database engines. Lastly, the machines where the benchmarks are executed directly influence the results. Therefore, we want to implement a tool to detect bottlenecks for different hardware configurations based on the benchmarked application. The insights gained in this process can lead to an abstraction from the hardware used. This can help to decompose a machine in relevant components like the CPU, memory, disk, network IO, etc. to build a machine configuration meta model for benchmarks.

References

1. Anderson, T.L., Berre, A.J., Mallison, M., Porter, H.H., Schneider, B.: The Hyper-Model benchmark. In: Bancilhon, F., Thanos, C., Tsichritzis, D. (eds.) EDBT 1990. LNCS, vol. 416, pp. 317–331. Springer, Heidelberg (1990). https://doi.org/10.1007/BFb0022180
2. Bitton, D., et al.: Benchmarking database systems - a systematic approach. Technical report, University of Wisconsin-Madison, Department of Computer Sciences (1983)
3. Blackburn, S.M., et al.: Wake up and smell the coffee: evaluation methodology for the 21st century. Commun. ACM **51**(8), 83–89 (2008)
4. Boicea, A., et al.: MongoDB vs Oracle - database comparison. In: Proceedings of EIDWT. IEEE (2012)

5. Carey, M.J., et al.: The OO7 benchmark. ACM SIGMOD Rec. **22**(2), 12–21 (1993)
6. Carey, M.J., et al.: A status report on the OO7 OODBMS benchmarking effort. In: Proceedings of OOPSLA (1994)
7. Cattell, R.G.G., Skeen, J.: Objects operations benchmark. ACM Trans. Database Syst. **17**(1), 1–31 (1992)
8. Cooper, B.F., et al.: Benchmarking cloud serving systems with YCSB. In: Proceedings of SoCC (2010)
9. Daynes, L., Czajkowski, G.: High-performance, space-efficient, automated object locking. In: Proceedings of ICDE (2001)
10. DeWitt, D.J., et al.: Parallelizing OODBMS traversals: a performance evaluation. VLDB J. Int. J. Very Large Data Bases **5**(1), 3–18 (1996)
11. Goetz, B., et al.: Java Concurrency in Practice. Pearson Education (2006)
12. Gray, J.N., et al.: Granularity of locks in a shared data base. In: Proceedings of VLDB (1975)
13. Hartauer, R., et al.: Cloud function lifecycle considerations for portability in function as a service. In: Proceedings of CLOSER (2022)
14. Hecht, R., Jablonski, S.: NoSQL evaluation: a use case oriented survey. In: 2011 International Conference on Cloud and Service Computing (2011)
15. Huppler, K.: The art of building a good benchmark. In: Nambiar, R., Poess, M. (eds.) TPCTC 2009. LNCS, vol. 5895, pp. 18–30. Springer, Heidelberg (2009). https://doi.org/10.1007/978-3-642-10424-4_3
16. Jordan, M.: A comparative study of persistence mechanisms for the Java^{TM} platform. Technical report, Sun Microsystems Laboratories (2004)
17. Kounev, S., Lange, K.-D., von Kistowski, J.: Systems Benchmarking: For Scientists and Engineers. Springer, Cham (2020). https://doi.org/10.1007/978-3-030-41705-5
18. Larson, P., Levandoski, J.: Modern main-memory database systems. Proc. VLDB Endow. **9**(13), 1609–1610 (2016)
19. Larson, P., et al.: High-performance concurrency control mechanisms for main-memory databases. Proc. VLDB Endow. **5**(4), 298–309 (2011)
20. Lilja, D.J.: Measuring Computer Performance: A Practitioner's Guide. Cambridge University Press, Cambridge (2000)
21. Manner, J., Böhm, S.: Lecture notes: concurrency topics in Java. In: Bamberger Beiträge zur Wirtschaftsinformatik und Angewandten Informatik, no. 106. Otto-Friedrich-University (2022)
22. Manner, J., Wirtz, G.: Why many benchmarks might be compromised. In: Proceedings of SOSE (2021)
23. Sinz, E.J.: Datenmodellierung im Strukturierten-Entity-Relationship-Modell (SERM). Otto-Friedrich-Universität, Bamberg (1992)
24. van Zyl, P., et al.: Comparing the performance of object databases and ORM tools. In: Proceedings of SAICSIT (2006)

From Data Asset to Data Product – The Role of the Data Provider in the Enterprise Data Marketplace

Rebecca Eichler[1]([✉]), Christoph Gröger[2], Eva Hoos[2], Holger Schwarz[1], and Bernhard Mitschang[1]

[1] University of Stuttgart, Universitätsstraße 38, 70569 Stuttgart, Germany
{rebecca.eichler,holger.schwarz,
bernhard.mitschang}@ipvs.uni-stuttgart.de
[2] Robert Bosch GmbH, Borsigstraße 4, 70469 Stuttgart, Germany
{christoph.groeger,eva.hoos}@de.bosch.com

Abstract. In the big data era companies have an increasing volume of data at their disposal. To enable the democratization of this data so it can be found, understood and accessed by the majority of employees, so-called data providers must first publish the data and provide provisioning options. However, a lack of incentives and increased effort for the data providers to share their data hinders the democratization of data. In this work, we present the current state and challenges of a data provider's journey, derived from a literature study as well as expert interviews we conducted with a globally active manufacturer. To address these challenges, we propose the use of an enterprise data marketplace, a platform for sharing data within the company. By presenting a functionality framework for such a marketplace and by highlighting how it can integrate with a company's data catalog, we outline how a marketplace can support the data provider. We implemented a prototype of an enterprise data marketplace and determined the feasibility of three scenarios to relieve the data provider. Finally, an assessment based on the prototype yields that the data marketplace supports the provider throughout the provider's journey, addresses major challenges, and thus, contributes to the overall goal of data democratization within enterprises.

Keywords: Data marketplace · Data catalog · Data sharing · Metadata management

1 Introduction

Data contains the potential to provide companies with important knowledge, for example, to optimize processes or develop new business models [1]. Therefore, data democratization initiatives that have the goal of empowering and motivating employees to find, understand, access, use and share data across the company [2] are gaining importance. To drive democratization aspects such as data sharing across the company, the use of enterprise data marketplaces has been proposed [3].

© The Author(s), under exclusive license to Springer Nature Switzerland AG 2022

J. Barzen et al. (Eds.): SummerSOC 2022, CCIS 1603, pp. 119–138, 2022.
https://doi.org/10.1007/978-3-031-18304-1_7

In general, data marketplaces are metadata-driven self-service platforms for trading data and data related services [3, 4]. Enterprise data marketplaces are specifically designed to facilitate the exchange of data and data related services within a company [5]. Within enterprise data marketplaces company employees take on the roles of data marketplace administrators, data consumers and data providers. In the context of providing data, we distinguish three roles: Firstly, data is created by a data producer [6] which can be both a person or system, e.g., a manufacturing machine. The person responsible for this data is called the data owner [6]. Responsibility includes various aspects such as legal or technical topics, yet the owner may delegate the realization thereof to, e.g., data stewards who maintain data on behalf of the data owner [6]. The data owner may be the data producer. Lastly, the employee that makes the data available is the data provider [7]. The data provider may also be the data owner or data producer, for example, they could be the owner but not the producer.

In an external data marketplace, in which data is exchanged across institutions, the main incentive for data providers to supply data is the monetization of data and the resulting profit [8, 9]. Within a company, however, monetization inhibits data democratization, as money presents a barrier to the data consumer. Therefore, data monetization is only envisaged to a limited degree within the enterprise data marketplace.

However, without monetization one main motivation for data providers to share data within the company disappears. Fernandez et al. [9] also discuss that providers lack information on how consumers require data and are disincentivized to share data which may leak confidential information. In addition, providers may be reluctant to share data as releasing data implies revealing own processes and quality standards [8]. Ultimately, the provider has the additional effort but no advantage by offering the data. This lack of incentives and increased effort on the part of the data providers therefore hinders the democratization of data. For this reason, in this paper we examine the role of data providers in the enterprise data marketplace, the challenges and efforts they face and how they can be supported in sharing data.

To this end, we offer the following contributions: Based on a literature study and expert interviews conducted with a globally active manufacturer, we developed (1) *a data provider's journey* which reflects the steps and roles involved in publishing and provisioning data, presented in Sect. 2. From this journey, we derive (2) *current challenges* the provider is faced with in Sect. 2 and propose the use of an enterprise data marketplace to address these. To investigate how a data marketplace assists the provider, (3) *we have developed a functionality framework* which also differentiates the marketplace functionality from other corporate data related tasks in Sect. 3. In the same section, we also (4) *introduce a distinction between data assets and data products* in order to leverage the existent enterprise tool landscape, particularly existing data catalogs, to support the provider. Lastly, we have developed a prototype to (5) *assess the extent to which an enterprise data marketplace supports the data provider* and to address the challenges in Sect. 4. Section 5 addresses related work and Sect. 6 concludes this paper.

2 Providing Data in the Enterprise

In order to identify the data provider's assignments and associated processes for publishing and provisioning data within an enterprise, we conducted a literature study, as described in Sect. 5, including [3, 9–12]. Yet, we found that many articles focus on the consumer perspective not the provider perspective or only give abstract insight into the provider's processes. Therefore, we also conducted expert interviews with employees of a global manufacturer to gain a more detailed and practical perspective.

The manufacturer is active in a variety of sectors like the mobility or industrial sector and operates a global manufacturing network. A lot of data are collected and stored across the industrial value chain, e.g. by internet of things (IoT) devices or operational systems like enterprise resource planning (ERP) systems. The manufacturer's business strategy is to become a data-driven Industry 4.0 company and they aim to create an environment where data can be shared freely and efficiently within the company. As part of these efforts, the IT system landscape for handling data is already enhanced with tools such as data catalogs and enterprise data marketplaces are being actively investigated (see our previous work [13] for more details on the manufacturer's case and [14, 15] for details on data-driven manufacturing and Industry 4.0). The exchange with experts from various key data-related roles in an industrial enterprise, including enterprise and solution architects, as well as data scientists and business analysts, gives us a representative view of current processes for publishing data in industrial enterprises from different perspectives.

Based on the conducted interviews, we derived the data provider's processes within industrial enterprises, which we have merged into an overarching data provider journey as presented in Sect. 2.1. It entails the essential steps and the parties involved in the journey. Thereupon, the data provider's challenges in this journey are examined in Sect. 2.2. Building on this, the following sections in this paper examine the extent to which an enterprise data marketplace can address these challenges.

2.1 The Data Provider Journey

The data provider's journey of making data available in the company, as illustrated in Fig. 1, consists of two processes: *publishing* the data, i.e. making it public within the company so it can be found, and *provisioning* the data, i.e. making it available to consumers so these can work with it. These parts contain a set of steps which are carried out by various roles in the company such as the data provider, the data owner, IT or operations, legal experts or management. To illustrate the journey by way of an example, we demonstrate it with the scenario of a data steward. The data steward wants to provide machine sensor data from running productions lines proactively to support machine maintenance use cases, e.g., predictive maintenance. For warranty cases concerning the machines, the sensor data are stored in a database for up to 15 years.

Part one, the publishing process, comprises two segments: *documenting* the data, and *making it known* to other employees so the data can be found, understood and requested. To begin with, the data provider must *assemble documentation*. This is essentially meta-data on various aspects of the data such as descriptions of the content, the data's quality or lineage, the underlying data model, technical descriptions, and lifecycle specifications. Basically, this constitutes all the information which a data consumer will require to understand and work with the data. For example, these metadata could be descriptions of the machines which provide the sensor data, their semantics, e.g., machine temperatures or torque, and lifecycle information that these are stored up to 15 years. If the data is documented sufficiently, the data provider will next specify the *legal framework* in which the data may be used. This entails topics such as specifying access rights, the allowed usage or the data's security class, defining the data's sensitivity, e.g. whether it is ranked as public, internal or confidential. Specifications such as these are relevant for ensuring personal related data privacy and compliance to legal regulations such as the General Data Protection Regulation (GDPR) [16]. In this step, the provider may seek the assistance and guidance of legal experts. In our example, the sensor data is not personal data and ranked as internal, so all employees can access it, and there are no limitations to the usage.

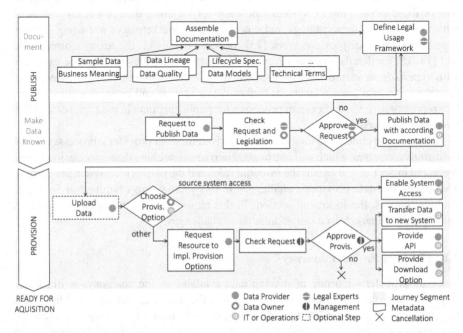

Fig. 1. The image depicts the steps and parties involved in the journey for publishing and provisioning data within an enterprise.

Having clarified the legal issues, the data must next be published, so the data can be found, understood and requested by company employees. To begin with, the data provider must issue a *request to publish data*. On the one hand, the provider must attain the consent of the data owner to publish the data. On the other hand, legal experts have to verify the authorization of the requester to release the data and whether the publication of this data is compliant with legal regulations. If the request is rejected, the legal framework must be adjusted. If it is approved, the provider may *publish the data*. This entails entering the data into an enterprise data inventory through which the data becomes discoverable. For this, a minimum amount of metadata must be provided, such as the name and location of the data source, the type, e.g., oracle database, a short description what it contains and who owns the data. To enable better understanding, the metadata assembled in step one can be added as well. Assistance from IT may be required for integration into the inventory as this may require technical expertise. In continuation of our example, the steward contacts the data owner and legal experts, e.g., by email asking for the permission to publish the data. Given approval, the steward registers the data in an inventory adding information where the data source, in this case an oracle database with the machine sensor data, is located, a description of the data on the production lines, the name of the owner and so on.

At this point, employees can find and understand data through the inventory and provided metadata. The data provider now enters the second part of the journey and must provide a *provisioning* option for the data in the event that there is an access-request. As the data might currently be hosted on a local machine, it may first have to be *uploaded* to some system through which it can be made accessible, e.g., a data lake. If data is uploaded to a different system the inventory must be updated. Next, the *provisioning option must be chosen*. As the responsible person for the data, the owner has to decide with potential help from IT if *direct access to the source system* can be granted through a user account. This might, for instance, not be desirable due to a potential system overload or the risk of data manipulation in operational systems. For instance, in the case of the sensor data, direct access is not possible for risk that it may be manipulated and jeopardize the machine warranty. Based on the decision, the provider either enables system access for the data consumers or implements an alternative access method. Providing another access method may be resource intensive, e.g., by requiring a team of developers, and therefore *resources must be requested*. Given admission by management, access methods like the *transfer* of the data into another system like a data lake, or the implementation of an *API* for access without a specific user account or *download options* can be carried out by IT. By way of example, the steward requests resources to provide an API through which the machine sensor data can be accessed. As machine maintenance is of high relevance, the resources are granted and the API development approved. If management rejects the request and no provisioning option can be guaranteed, it would be useful to indicate this circumstance in the inventory or to remove the data from it accordingly. Subsequent to performing these steps, employees can find, understand and receive access to the data.

2.2 Challenges in the Data Provider Journey

Within this section, the challenging aspects for the provider in terms of cost and circumstance are derived from the provider journey, presented in the previous section.

The (1) *assembly of metadata* is the first challenge for the data provider. Although documentation is a best practice in many processes, it is often neglected. To ensure the usability of the data, however, a certain degree of documentation is indispensable. Since the provider is not necessarily an expert for the data, he has to rely on other employees such as the data producer or a data steward to provide this documentation.

Besides assembling documentation, (2) *supplying provisioning options* apart from direct system access, is also costly. This task requires an IT project, e.g., for the implementation and realization of pipelines for moving data or developing an API. This may be a useless expense as it is unknown whether the data is of interest to other employees and hence, the provisioning options may not be required.

In practice, there are tools for publishing data which are based on a data inventory. One of these tools is a data catalog such as Alation[1] or the Collibra Data Catalog[2]. These are tools for maintaining inventories of data with discovery, administration, governance functionality and more [12, 17]. Catalogs support finding and understanding data, however, are not built to access data. For this reason, there are further publishing tools such as enterprise data marketplaces through which the data can be requested and accessed. Examples are Snowflake[3] or the Dawex Data Exchange Platform[4]. Companies are in the process of building a tool landscape for finding, understanding and accessing data using tools such as these [13]. For the provider, this means that the data must be registered in several tools such as the data catalog and the enterprise data marketplace. Therefore, challenge three refers to the effort of *(3) registering data in several publishing tools* which partly require the same metadata.

Finally, *(4) the process involves several parties* which need to be found, contacted and coordinated. With each new party the process becomes more complex and time-consuming as each introduces latencies when processing their tasks.

3 Providing Data Through the Enterprise Data Marketplace

As data marketplaces are platforms for exchanging data, they have functionality for making data available as required in the data provider journey [18]. Therefore, we examine how a data marketplace built to exchange data within a company, i.e., an enterprise data marketplace [5], can support the data provider in their journey and to what extent it addresses the providers' challenges. To examine data marketplaces' ability to support the data provider, it is necessary to understand what functionality a data marketplace offers. Therefore, we present a marketplace functionality framework in Sect. 3.1. Based on this framework, Sect. 3.2 discusses how an enterprise data marketplace can be built on existent tools in the company, such as a data catalog. In Sect. 3.3, we outline three provisioning scenarios in this platform tool constellation, which advantages it confers and how it works in the favor of the data provider.

3.1 Data Marketplace Functionality

The content of this subsection refers to data marketplaces in general, i.e., not explicitly to enterprise data marketplaces. We conducted a literature study, described in Sect. 5, to examine existing functionality lists for data marketplaces such as those presented in [5, 18–22]. According to literature and reports, marketplaces provide a range of functionality such as the up- and download of data [18], functionality for selling and buying data, governance topics like license management, monetization aspects like pricing, revenue allocation and sharing functions [9, 22], functionality for data cleansing and preparation [5, 18–20, 22] or integration [18] and analytics [21].

---

[1] https://www.alation.com/.

[2] https://www.collibra.com/us/en/platform/data-catalog.

[3] https://www.snowflake.com/workloads/data-sharing/?lang=de.

[4] https://www.dawex.com/en/data-exchange-platform/.

When comparing these lists, it is noteworthy that the extent of functionality differs. Common features include the trading and exchange aspects of data, such as buying and selling of data. Differences arise around features like data preparation which is listed on occasion or data analytics functionality which is listed in individual cases. It is also noticeable that functionality is described at different levels of detail. For example, Meisel and Spiekermann [18] provide a very detailed list of functionality, e.g., with specifics that data cleansing functionality includes duplicate and pattern recognition or plausibility check features, whereas that of Wells [5] is at a higher level of abstraction in which, e.g., data curation and preparation are the granular listed functionality. The structure also differs, with some articles listing functionality by role, i.e., data provider and consumer [19, 20] and others breaking it down by functional group [18], such as marketplace infrastructure, interfaces and security and so on.

To assess how the marketplace supports the data provider, we need an attribution of functionality by role. Furthermore, we considered the range of the above mentioned functionality in the light of the company's experience. In this context, we notice that some lists go beyond the scope of the marketplace as we understand it. From our point of view, a data marketplace is purely a broker for data and data related services. It is a platform on which data providers can publish data and services and data consumers can find, understand and gain access to these. How the data is, for instance, prepared or integrated with other data is, in our opinion, beyond the scope of the marketplace as a broker. Finally, we noticed that literature devotes little detail to the topic of metadata in the context of data marketplaces. Since finding and understanding data is a crucial feature of the marketplace, and this is dependent on metadata supplied by the data provider, we consider metadata management to be a relevant underlying and role independent functionality in the marketplace. Therefore, we have created a functionality framework that takes these three aspects into account: the division by role, the delineation of functionality that lies within and outside the marketplace, and the metadata management which is the basis for the role-specific features.

To create the functionality framework, we incorporated the common parts from the different functionality lists derived from the literature study and allocated them to the roles of the data consumer, data provider and administrator. The functionality that was only partially represented, such as rating or data cleaning, were examined whether they belonged in the functional scope of a broker and were accordingly included or excluded. In this context, we also had to find a common level of abstraction that subsumes the more detailed tasks. Additionally, we extended functionality such as the necessary metadata features based on input from the expert interviews and the role-based functionality. The resulting functionality framework, illustrated in Fig. 2, provides insight what functionality is needed and is therefore a guideline for implementing a data marketplace, but also provides a basis for comparing commercial tools, as well as a basis to evaluate what functionality is already offered by other tools within a company and which functionality is specifically missing.

The Functionality Framework. The functionality framework, shown in Fig. 2, displays the marketplace's functionality in the blue box and other functionality outside of it. Data governance and data management including data quality or data lifecycle management take place outside its functional scope as these concern the management as opposed to the exchange of data. Equally, activities that follow the acquisition of data such as data preparation or exploration are out of scope as these involve data processing which goes beyond data sharing. To enable an integrated data processing toolchain, the marketplace nevertheless provides interfaces to tools that perform tasks outside the marketplace context, such as preparation tools.

Within the marketplace, we distinguish between *consumer-side functionality*, *provider-side functionality* and *administration functionality*. This functionality is accessible through a *portal*, i.e., a graphical user interface, and an API. The *metadata management functionality* and *privacy, security and compliance* extend across these areas.

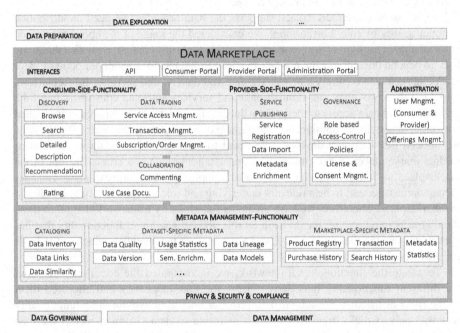

Fig. 2. The image depicts the data marketplace functionality framework.

Consumer-Side-Functionality. The consumer-side functionality includes *discovery*, *data trading* and *collaboration* features. The consumer can *browse* or *search* for data and services in the marketplace, like the machine sensor data provided by the data steward in the provider journey example. For each search result, there is a *detailed description* with an integrated view of all available metadata. For example, the de-tailed description could contain a description of the machine and the according production line with technical details how and where the data is stored or operational information such as the data's lineage. The marketplace can also offer service *recommendations* based on the conducted search, previous acquisitions and those of similar users. In order to support data democratization in the sense of collaboration and knowledge sharing [2], the marketplace also offers functionality such as *commenting* to both the consumer and producer. Furthermore, consumers can *rate* data and *document their use case*, thereby enabling other users to see if the data has been used for similar use cases. In our example, a user could specify how they used the data in a machine maintenance use case. These functionalities are only available to the consumer and thus, placed in the consumer-side box in Fig. 2. The data trading functionality like the collaboration functionality are overarching in Fig. 2, as they are available to both the consumer and producer. On the consumer-side *service-access-management* signifies the ability to request and receive access details and a license to use data, e.g., by ordering it through a shopping cart. Additionally, the consumer can *manage transactions* related to reimbursements for services, as well as active, expired and pending orders through the *subscription and order management*. In continuation of the example, the user can order the machine sensor data through the shopping cart and request access, then pay for this data through the transaction management and after receiving access, view the active subscription on this data with according details.

Provider-Side-Functionality. The provider functionality involves *publishing, governance* and *data trading* functionality. For publishing services such as data-as-a-service or professional services like courses for data preparation, the provider uses the *service registration*. In this step, the marketplace adds the service, mostly a data source or a specific dataset, to the marketplace service inventory so it can be found via the search. In our example the data steward registers the machine sensor data in the marketplace which is thereby added to the marketplace inventory. Although the marketplace will reference most data as opposed to storing it, it does have a *data import* feature for cases like the upload of a locally stored singular csv file. In our example, the database in which the machine sensor data is stored is registered instead of uploading the data directly. The *metadata enrichment* allows the provider to add additional metadata to ensure a better understanding of the data. This may include a variety of metadata such as a content description, technical details as well as information about the data provenance. These could for instance be descriptions of the machine and production line, the database and the lineage showing how the data originates in the machine and is moved to the database by a specific script. Besides service registration, the marketplace offers governance functionality which supports the specification as well as compliance to aspects defined within the data's legal usage framework explained in the provisioning journey. A provider can define *role-based access control*, usage rights within *policies* and package these in *licenses* for specific services. This functionality does not replace the underlying data governance, it merely enables the implementation of the marketplace-specific governance aspects. For instance, the decision who is allowed to do what with the machine sensor data is part of the governance outside the marketplace. Within the marketplace the steward in our example merely specifies that only people from department x are allowed to use it for maintenance use cases. Like the consumer, the provider has functionality to support them in the trading of data. For instance, the provider can manage access requests, i.e., receive notifications, consult an overview and accept or decline these requests. If monetisation or other forms of reimbursement are included in the marketplace the provider can monitor transactions for the offerings. For example, the steward can view closed and outstanding invoices for the sensor data. Having provided access to the data, a provider can then handle the subscriptions and orders on the offered services. This includes an overview of who is subscribing to which data, options to contact all subscribers or functionality to terminate subscriptions and revoke access rights. In terms of collaboration, the provider can also enter into a comment dialog with the data consumers.

Metadata Management Functionality. A data marketplace requires a variety of metadata to support the above-mentioned functionality. This comprises general metadata for *cataloging* as known from a data catalog tool like an inventory, *dataset-specific metadata* such as a business description and *marketplace-specific metadata* like the purchase history. Metadata for cataloguing can refer to a range of datasets and helps to provide an overview of existing offerings. It includes a *data inventory*, e.g., a list of contained data sets, *data links* that indicate whether data sets are related as well as *data similarity* information, which reveals replicated and similar data sets. Dataset-specific metadata refers to a specific dataset and helps users to understand and trust this data. Amongst others, this covers *data quality, lineage* and *versions*. It is important to understand that the maintenance of the dataset-specific metadata is not part of the marketplace, merely, that it is relevant for the consumer in the sense of finding and understanding data. Therefore, this metadata has to be supplied by the provider and the marketplace must support some form of indexing and integrated processing and presentation of these. For instance, data quality metrics like completeness or accuracy can be extracted from tools that maintain data quality. The marketplace-specific metadata comprises a *product registry, purchase history, transaction history, search history and metadata statistics*. The statistics indicate to what extent the metadata is complete or contain user statistics such as how often a service has been viewed. The regulation of privacy, security and compliance, and the administration features are not discussed in detail due to lack of space. With this framework we have gained insight which explicit functionality a marketplace should offer to the user and which implicit functionality like the metadata management is required.

3.2 Data Catalogs as a Foundation for Enterprise Data Marketplaces

When examining the listed metadata management functionality within the functionality framework, it becomes apparent that there is a considerable overlap with functionality offered through a data catalog. Besides data asset inventories these have discovery, administration, governance, collaboration functionality and more [12, 17]. They contain a large part of the metadata also required in the data marketplace. Since a marketplace also requires an inventory, a data catalog is thus a component of the data marketplace [5]. Inversely this means, the data marketplace builds on a data catalog and extends it with further functionality like data trading features.

Nowadays, companies have one, or are in the process of building data catalogs [13]. Accordingly, when an enterprise data marketplace is developed, this platform can be built on top of the existing data catalogs and use them as their data inventory. Thereby, functionality is reused and extended as opposed to duplicated. Furthermore, the catalog metadata can be reused in the marketplace. This means, the marketplace can read the catalog entries so these are found in the marketplace search.

In order to enable access to the data, the marketplace requires metadata which is not part of a data catalog. This includes, for instance, details on the *provisioning options* such as an API, download or source system access and the according *access procedures* that go with these options. Also, *contractual information* such as the *price*, if data is monetized, the *license*, or *subscription options* as well as the *terms of use* such as the *permitted usage* or *conditions of use*. We call these metadata product metadata. They include all information which is required to sell or make data available for access and use. In this sense, we distinguish between *data assets* and *data products*. The distinction is displayed in Fig. 3. As the term suggests, data as an asset has a potential financial value for a company [23]. They are registered and maintained through a data catalog and are therefore, enriched with a minimum of metadata for finding and understanding them, such as the *content description, lineage* or *data owner* [12]. Data products are data assets which have been prepared for access and provisioning and have been enriched through the data marketplace with according product-specific metadata. Metadata to both of these types belong to the dataset-specific metadata in the functionality framework, in Fig. 2. To conclude, this means that data assets can be found through the data catalog and data products through the marketplace. If the marketplace builds on the data catalog and uses it as its inventory, then data assets can also be found in the marketplace, even if they are lacking product metadata. In order for consumers to gain access to these assets, the provider must however, first turn them into a data product by adding provisioning options and enriching these with product metadata.

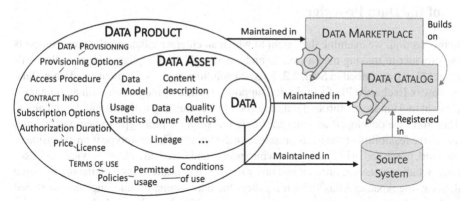

Fig. 3. The figure illustrates the distinction of data assets and data products with exemplary metadata, as well as the systems in which these are maintained. Metadata which are connected through dashes belong to a specific topic that is portrayed though capital letters.

3.3 From Data Asset to Data Product

Data assets can be transformed into a data product in different ways, therefore, we illustrate three main transformation scenarios. Within the first scenario, the provider *explicitly registers the data in the marketplace* and directly specifies all the product metadata, such as the permitted usage, license etc. By implication, the data is then also registered in the catalog. In the second scenario, the data provider *registers the data within the catalog* and does not concern himself with the data marketplace. The data is therefore a data asset. Now, some employee, e.g., a data scientist, can search for data in the marketplace and finds the data asset. The employee can then send a request to access this data to the provider who is then prompted to specify the product metadata. Having turned the data asset into a data product, access can be granted to this data. The third scenario assumes that *another employee can fill in the required product metadata* and send a request for asset-product transition to the provider. For instance, a data steward may know the product metadata and can fill this in for the data owner. The owner is notified and can accept or reject the proposed metadata. If accepted the data is turned into a product, if not it remains a data asset which cannot yet be accessed. As underlined by these three scenarios, the distinction of data assets and data products yields several advantages:

- The marketplace references data even if it has not been explicitly registered in it, but only in the data catalog.
- Consequently, the providers initially only have to register the data in the catalog so it can be found and understood within the enterprise.
- The provider only has additional effort for adding product metadata and providing provisioning options when the data are actually relevant and are requested.

4   Assessing How an Enterprise Data Marketplace Assists the Role of the Data Provider

In this section, we examine the extent to which an enterprise data marketplace supports the provider in making data available and whether the marketplace addresses the challenges (1–4), described in Sect. 2.2. Existent solutions such as the mentioned Snowflake or Dawex Exchange Platform do not support a seamless integration with a company's existent tool landscape through out of the box loose coupling with existent data catalogs. Therefore, we developed an enterprise data marketplace prototype to demonstrate and assess the feasibility of the ideas presented in the Sect. 3. The prototype is an extension to our work presented in [24]. It is built with Spring[5] and based on a micro services architecture including a search, product and order service. It is implemented on the open-source data catalog Apache Atlas[6] which registers the data assets. Product metadata is stored in the marketplace's metadata repository, set up with a Neo4J[7] graph database and the metadata is modeled according to our metadata model HANDLE [25]. The enterprise data landscape is simulated by a variety of databases and a data lake which are registered in the catalog.

4.1   Prototypical Demonstration – From Data Asset to Data Product

As argued in Sect. 3.2, it is beneficial to build the enterprise data marketplace on a company's established data catalog. In this case, we built the enterprise data marketplace on Apache Atlas and use it as the data catalog for the marketplace. If a search query

---

[5] https://spring.io/.

[6] https://atlas.apache.org/.

[7] https://neo4j.com/.

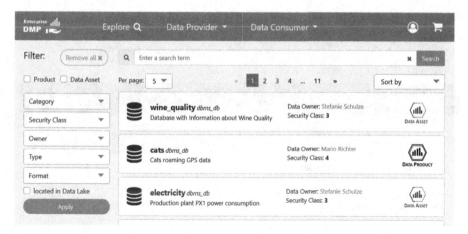

Fig. 4. Illustration of the data asset and data product distinction in the dataset search.

is issued in the marketplace it is forwarded to Atlas. The corresponding search results are displayed in the marketplace search results view. The marketplace can identify the data assets for which it contains the corresponding product metadata and labels these as data products, as can be seen in Fig. 4 on the right hand side of each search result. As explained in the following, the prototype supports several scenarios as to how data is provided and an asset becomes a product.

Scenario One. As specified in Sect. 3.3, the data provider can register the data product in the marketplace. To do this, the provider can select "Add new Product" in the menu under "data provider" and is directed to a data registration wizard. The wiz-ard guides the provider through 3 steps, as displayed in Fig. 5. The first step prompts the provider to specify whether the data is already registered as an asset and if so, to enter the asset-id. In the second step the provider is led to a form for either registering or editing the asset if it already exists. In this case, the form fields are prepopulated with the metadata loaded from the catalog. If the data is not registered as an asset, the provider fills out the form with according metadata such as a data description, data owner, security class and so on. The metadata is sent to the catalog in which it is registered as an asset. The provider is then guided to the third wizard page for adding product metadata, as illustrated in Fig. 5. This step is optional as the data can already be found through the marketplace search. To register the product, the *terms of use* are specified in which the provider indicates if it is *personal data*, the *permitted usage*, *conditions of use* and a *license*. For example, the GDPR allows people to influence how their personal data is processed [26]. By way of example, the data is personal and the processing has been restricted to the evaluation of user statistics which is specified in the field *permitted usage*. Also, only persons from a specific team may access this data, therefore this is also specified in the field *conditions of use*. If none of the licenses fit the requirements, the provider can also create a customized license. Besides the terms of use, the *data delivery options* are specified. This includes information on the data's *update cycle*, the *provisioning options* and *description of the access procedure*. Having specified this information, the provider clicks on the button

"Add As Product" so the metadata is stored in the metadata repository, creating a data product.

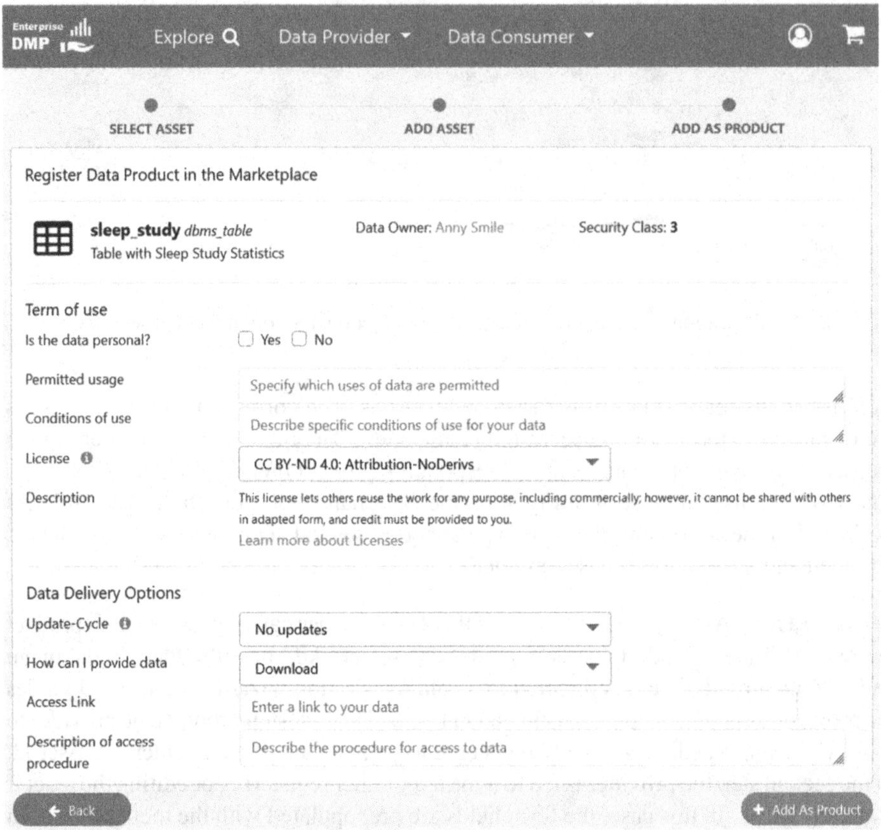

Fig. 5. Wizard for enriching data assets with product metadata to create data products.

Scenario Two. In the second scenario, data is only registered through the data catalog. For this purpose, the provider dials into the Atlas GUI and fills in the corresponding 15 form fields for registering data assets. As explained above, this data can then be found in the marketplace and is flagged as an asset. If this dataset is then requested in the marketplace by a data consumer, the provider receives an access request and is prompted to add the product metadata and is automatically forwarded to the corresponding form fields in the wizard as depicted in Fig. 5.

Scenario Three. The third scenario entails that another employee can fill in the required product metadata for the provider. If a user selects a search result as shown in Fig. 4, they are taken to a detailed page with overview metadata providing detail on the dataset. This

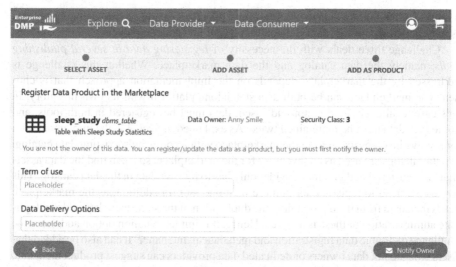

Fig. 6. This image depicts the form for creating data products which is shown if the user is not the data owner. For space reasons the form fields are replaced by placeholders. The form is identical to the form displayed in Fig. 5.

detail page also specifies whether the result is an asset or a product. In the case that it is an asset, a button is displayed "add product metadata". Clicking on this button will take the user to the registration wizard where the user can navigate to the "add product" form. If the user is not the data owner, this is displayed with a message as shown in Fig. 6. The form is submitted using the "Notify Owner" button. The owner then receives the request and can accept, reject or edit the metadata before creating the product. As shown in this chapter, a data marketplace can be built on top of an external data catalog and the three scenarios as described in Sect. 3.3 are supported in this catalog-marketplace constellation.

4.2 Addressing of the Challenges in the Data Provider Journey

In this section, we discuss to which extent the enterprise data marketplace addresses the challenges in the data provider journey, as given in Sect. 2.2. The first challenge signifies the *assembly of documentation*, i.e., metadata. In effect, this task is supported to a certain extent through tools which can automatically capture metadata. For instance, the data catalog Alation uses AI to suggest business glossary terms and suggests links to relevant data [27]. Since this concerns the first step of the provider journey and the marketplace is only utilized throughout later steps, the assembly of metadata is not supported through the marketplace.

Challenge two refers to the *effort of supplying provisioning options*, even if these may not be required. This issue is addressed by the enterprise marketplace through the differentiation of data assets and data products. It is dealt with by allowing the provider to supply product metadata and thereby make provisioning options available only when a request is made for a data asset. Therefore, the effort relating to provisioning options is only undertaken if this data is actually relevant for other employees.

Challenge three deals with the necessity of *registering data in several publishing tools*, namely the data catalog and the data marketplace. Whether this challenge is addressed by the marketplace depends on the implementation approach that is chosen. The marketplace can be built as a standalone platform with its own inventory. In this case, challenge three is not addressed, data must be registered in both tools, and some metadata must be maintained twice. As explained in Sect. 3.2, the implementation alternative involves integrating the marketplace with a company's existing data catalog. If data catalogs are used as an inventory for the marketplace, so it can find the data assets that are registered in them, the provider only has to register data in the data catalog. This avoids the need to register data in more than one tool. In addition, as the marketplace reads metadata from the data catalog, the duplication of the same metadata and the duplicate administration of these is avoided. Hence, this implementation option addresses the challenge of double data registration and metadata maintenance. It can also be added that users who are not data owners or dedicated data providers can suggest product metadata, which eliminates the need for the data provider to do this. In this case, the data provider only has to accept or reject the request.

That the data provider's journey *involves several parties* which have to be found, contacted and coordinated constitutes challenge four. There are two steps, which involve a request to third parties that can be partially automated through the marketplace. This includes the *request to publish data*. For this, however, the owner and the legal experts must be known and specified. If this is the case, the marketplace represents a platform via which a workflow for the request and approval of such processes can be implemented. The same is true for the *request for resources*. If the people from management are known and can be identified in the marketplace, then the marketplace can also ensure a regulated workflow for the resolution of this subject matter.

Consequently, all of the challenges are addressed through various tools and the marketplace specifically addresses the challenges two through four.

5   Related Work

We conducted a literature study based on the snowball method and considered both scientific articles and white papers. The goal of democratizing data is related to the FAIR principle, i.e., making data findable, accessible, interoperable and reusable, which was introduced in the context of scientific data [12]. Labadie et al. [12] discuss the FAIR principles in the enterprise context and how these are addressed through data catalogs, yet they do not consider data marketplaces. Data marketplaces have been investigated in various contexts. Some research focuses on the overall picture and identifies the main characteristics [23, 28–31], trends and emerging markets [23, 29, 31], challenges [23, 31] and research fields [32] around data marketplaces. Other research examines the marketplace in a specialized context such as marketplaces for open data [33] or for data of the internet of things [34–38]. The application of different technologies in the data marketplace, such as the use of distributed ledger technology is also studied [35, 39]. These research articles cover a wide range of topics, but do not discuss the distinguishing features of enterprise data marketplaces.

A report published by Wells [5] distinguishes internal marketplaces, synonymous to enterprise data marketplaces, and external markets. While highlighting topics such as components and involved technologies of these marketplaces like data catalogs or data lakes it does not discuss how these can be used to an advantage in the enterprise data marketplace. The same is true for the article by Gröger [3] in which he presents the enterprise data marketplace as a central element in the data ecosystem of industrial enterprises. Like Wells, Fernandez et al. [9] differentiate internal marketplaces in their work based on the data exchange boundaries and the incentive to share data and discuss challenges and the research agenda for constructing data marketplaces. However, they do not take into account the specifics of embedding a marketplace into a company's tool landscape. How the data marketplace can be integrated into a company's system landscape and how it can be used to its advantage has not been explored.

Data marketplaces are metadata-driven platforms [3] and the necessity for metadata management in data marketplaces is expressed in several research articles. For instance, metadata is discussed in the context of data trading challenges and provenance [19], data integration [18] or decentralized marketplaces and storing it in the blockchain [35]. The functional frameworks presented in [18] and [5] also list metadata management as a required feature. Most of the research around data marketplaces, however, only provides a high-level view on metadata management. In contrast, [40] introduces a detailed metadata model for describing data goods, to facilitate the selection and trading of data and Fernandez et al. [9] describe a metadata engine for maintaining the lifecycle of datasets. To the best of our knowledge, none of the work provides a detailed overview of necessary metadata management features in marketplaces or take peculiarities of enterprise data marketplaces into account.

As discussed in Sect. 3.1 several research articles provide a list of data marketplace functionality [5, 9, 18–22]. However, as already explained, the aspect of metadata management functionality is not addressed sufficiently, and the delimitation of the tasks of the data marketplace as a data broker is not clearly defined.

The role of the data provider is differentiated in a number of research articles such as [18, 23, 32, 41]. For instance, Lange et al. [32] differentiate the role of the data provider and derive a provider challenge, such as the difficulty of pricing data when lacking knowledge on the data value for the consumer. Furthermore, they introduce several marketplace types based on different data providers such as commercial, public or private data providers. Yet, these research articles do not examine the provider in the enterprise context. In contrast, Wells [7] discerns three types of providers for the enterprise data marketplace, the internal providers, people and systems in the company, open data providers which supply free external data and commercial data providers that offer fee or subscription-based external data. But he does not look at the processes and specific challenges that data providers face in the enterprise. Fernandez et al. [9] consider the provider in internal and external marketplaces and tackle the provider challenge that sharing data is hard as the providers lack information and incentives to make data available so it increases the consumer's utility. They propose bonus points or time as an incentive of internal providers to share data. However, further specifics of the enterprise data marketplace and the provider's processes therein are not examined. Hence, this article has covered this gap in existing literature by examining the current processes for providing data within an enterprise and the corresponding challenges and how these are addressed by an enterprise data marketplace.

6   Conclusion

Data democratization initiatives with the goal to facilitate a broader availability and accessibility of data within a company are becoming increasingly important. The data provider journey we presented illustrates the current processes for providing data within an industrial enterprise and the challenges a provider faces which impede data democratization. In this work, we propose the use of an enterprise data marketplace to support the data provider throughout this journey. Our marketplace functionality framework illustrates the overall as well as provider specific functionality and shows that an enterprise data marketplace is based on metadata management functionality. Through a prototypical implementation we demonstrate the integration of a marketplace with an existent data catalog, the differentiation of data assets and data products, and how this enables several application scenarios which support the data provider in publishing and provisioning data. Consequently, we have demonstrated how the enterprise data marketplace can leverage the existent tool landscape to ease the publication and provisioning of data and is, therefore, a platform which enables data democratization within enterprises. In future, we intend to investigate incentivation mechanisms for data providers to share data within the enterprise and how the marketplace can leverage further tools and systems in the enterprise system landscape such as a data lake, a business glossary or knowledge graph.

References

1. Cao, L.: Data science: a comprehensive overview. ACM Comput. Surv. **50**, 1–42 (2017)
2. Lefebvre, H., Legner, C., Fadler, M.: Data democratization : toward a deeper understanding. In: Proceedings of the International Conference on Information Systems (ICIS) (2021)
3. Gröger, C.: There is no AI without data. Commun. ACM **64**, 98–108 (2021)
4. Stahl, F., Schomm, F., Vossen, G., Vomfell, L.: A classification framework for data marketplaces. Vietnam J. Comput. Sci. **3**(3), 137–143 (2016). https://doi.org/10.1007/s40595-016-0064-2
5. Wells, D.: The Rise of the Data Marketplace: Data as a Service. Eckerson Gr. (2017)
6. Abraham, R., Schneider, J., vom Brocke, J.: Data governance: a conceptual framework, structured review, and research agenda. Int. J. Inf. Manage. **49**, 424–438 (2019)
7. Wells, D.: Dynamic Data Marketplace Fast Data for Fast Business. Eckerson Gr. (2018)
8. Trauth, D., van Ouwerkerk, N., Mönckemeyer, F., Herrmann, K.: Putting a price tag on data. In: Trauth, D., Bergs, T., Prinz, W. (eds.) Monetarisierung von technischen Daten. Springer, Heidelberg (2021). https://doi.org/10.1007/978-3-662-62915-4_14
9. Fernandez, R.C., Subramaniam, P., Franklin, M.J.: Data market platforms: trading data assets to solve data problems. Proc. VLDB Endow. **13**, 1933–1947 (2020)
10. Gröger, C., Hoos, E.: Ganzheitliches Metadatenmanagement im Data Lake: Anforderungen, IT-Werkzeuge und Herausforderungen in der Praxis. In: Proceedings of the 18. Fachtagung für Datenbanksysteme für Business, Technologie und Web (BTW) (2019)
11. Zeng, J., Glaister, K.W.: Value creation from big data: looking inside the black box. Strateg. Organ. **16**, 105–140 (2018)

12. Labadie, C., et al.: FAIR enough? Enhancing the usage of enterprise data with data catalogs. In: Proceedings of the IEEE 22nd Conference on Business Informatics (CBI). pp. 201–210 (2020)

13. Eichler, R., et al.: Enterprise-wide metadata management: an industry case on the current state and challenges. In: Proceedings of the 24th International Conference on Business Information Systems (BIS), pp. 269–279 (2021)

14. Hoos, E., Gröger, C., Kramer, S., Mitschang, B.: ValueApping: an analysis method to identify value-adding mobile enterprise apps in business processes. In: Cordeiro, J., Hammoudi, S., Maciaszek, L., Camp, O., Filipe, J. (eds.) ICEIS 2014. LNBIP, vol. 227, pp. 222–243. Springer, Cham (2015). https://doi.org/10.1007/978-3-319-22348-3_13

15. Gröger, C., Schwarz, H., Mitschang, B.: The manufacturing knowledge repository consolidating knowledge to enable holistic process knowledge management in manufacturing. In: Proceedings of the 16th International Conference on Enterprise Information Systems, vol. 1, pp. 39–51 (2014)

16. General Data Protection Regulation (GDPR). https://gdpr.eu/tag/gdpr/. Accessed 28 Mar 2022

17. Zaidi, E., et al.: Data Catalogs Are the New Black in Data Management and Analytics. Gartner. (2017)

18. Meisel, L., Spiekermann, M.: Datenmarktplätze - Plattformen für Datenaustausch und Datenmonetarisierung in der Data Economy. Fraunhofer ISST (2019)

19. Koutroumpis, P., Leiponen, A., Thomas, L.: The (Unfulfilled) Potential of Data Marketplaces. ETLA Work. Pap. (2017)

20. Roman, D., et al.: ProDataMarket: a data marketplace for monetizing linked data. In: Proceedings of the ISWC 2017 Posters Demonstration and Industry Tracks Co-located with 16th International Semantic Web Conference 1963 (2017)

21. Saxena, S.: Enterprise Data Marketplace: Democratizing Data within Organizations. Tata Consultancy Service (2018)

22. Spiekermann, M., Lehmann-Brauns, S., Tontsch, R., Otto, B., Hoffmann, M.: Datenmarktplätze in Produktionsnetzwerken. Plattf. Ind. 4.0. (2020)

23. Spiekermann, M.: Data marketplaces: trends and monetisation of data goods. Intereconomics **54**(4), 208–216 (2019). https://doi.org/10.1007/s10272-019-0826-z

24. Eichler, R., et al.: Data shopping — how an enterprise data marketplace supports data democratization in companies. In: Proceedings of the 34th International Conference on Advanced Information Systems Engineering (CAiSE). pp. 19–26 (2022)

25. Eichler, R. et al.: Modeling metadata in data lakes—a generic model. Data Knowl. Eng. **136** (2021)

26. Art. 6 GDPR - Lawfulness of processing - GDPR.eu. https://gdpr.eu/article-6-how-to-process-personal-data-legally. Accessed 7 Sep 2021

27. Alation: Data Stewards. https://www.alation.com/solutions/data-stewards/. Accessed 12 Mar 2020

28. Schomm, F., Stahl, F., Vossen, G.: Marketplaces for data: an initial survey. ACM SIGMOD Rec. **42**, 15–26 (2013)

29. Stahl, F., et al.: Marketplaces for digital data: quo vadis? Comput. Inf. Sci. **10** (2017)

30. Fruhwirth, M., Rachinger, M., Prlja, E.: Discovering business models of data marketplaces. In: Proceedings of the 53rd Hawaii International Conference on System Sciences (HICSS) (2020)

31. Driessen, S.W., Monsieur, G., Van Den Heuvel, W.-J.: Data market design: a systematic literature review. IEEE Access. **10**, 33123–33153 (2022)

32. Lange, J., Stahl, F., Vossen, G.: Datenmarktplätze in verschiedenen Forschungsdisziplinen: Eine Übersicht. Informatik-Spektrum **41**(3), 170–180 (2018). https://doi.org/10.1007/s00287-017-1044-3

33. Zuiderwijk, A., et al.: Elements for the development of an open data marketplace. In: Proceedings of the Conference for E-Democracy and Open Governement. pp. 309–322 (2014)

34. Zheng, Z., et al.: Challenges and opportunities in IoT data markets. In: Proceedings of the 4th International Workshop on Social Sensing (SocialSense). pp. 1–2 (2019)

35. Ramachandran, G.S., Radhakrishnan, R., Krishnamachari, B.: Towards a decentralized data marketplace for smart Cities. In: Proceedings of the IEEE International Smart Cities Conference (ISC2). pp. 1–8 (2018)

36. Alrawahi, A.S., Lee, K., Lotfi, A.: AMACoT: a marketplace architecture for trading cloud of things resources. IEEE Internet Things J. **7**, 2483–2495 (2019)

37. Krishnamachari, B., et al.: I3: an IoT marketplace for smart communities. In: Proceedings of the 16th ACM International Conference on Mobile Systems, Applications, and Services (MobiSys). pp. 498–499 (2018)

38. Schmid, S., et al.: An architecture for interoperable IoT ecosystems. In: Proceedings of the 2nd International Workshop on Interoperability and Open-Source Solutions for the Internet of Things (InterOSS-IoT), pp. 39–55 (2016)

39. Roman, D., Stefano, G.: Towards a reference architecture for trusted data marketplaces: the credit scoring perspective. In: Proceedings of the 2nd International Conference on Open and Big Data (OBD). pp. 95–101. IEEE (2016)

40. Spiekermann, M. et al.: A metadata model for data goods. In: Multikonferenz Wirtschaftsinformatik (MKWI). pp. 326–337 (2018)

41. Muschalle, A., Stahl, F., Löser, A., Vossen, G.: Pricing approaches for data markets. In: Castellanos, M., Dayal, U., Rundensteiner, E.A. (eds.) BIRTE 2012. LNBIP, vol. 154, pp. 129–144. Springer, Heidelberg (2013). https://doi.org/10.1007/978-3-642-39872-8_10

Data-Aware Service Placement in the Cloud-IoT Continuum

Jacopo Massa(✉), Stefano Forti, and Antonio Brogi

Department of Computer Science, University of Pisa, Pisa, Italy
`jacopo.massa@phd.unipi.it`

Abstract. We present a declarative solution to determine, in a data-aware manner, application service placements and SDN data routings over Cloud-IoT infrastructures while meeting functional (software, hardware, IoT) and non-functional (security, latency, bandwidth) application requirements. The solution employs continuous reasoning to speed up the reconfiguration of application placements and routing decisions at runtime, when needed. An open-source Prolog prototype is presented and assessed over a scenario based on lifelike data.

Keywords: Data-aware application placement · Cloud-IoT continuum · Continuous reasoning

1 Introduction

The explosion of the Internet of Things (IoT) has given rise to the so-called *data deluge* [36], with more than 500 billion connected devices producing tons of data, which cannot always be suitably transmitted, stored, and processed by employing traditional Cloud architectures [43]. To tame this problem, Cloud-IoT computing paradigms – e.g. Fog [3], Edge [29], Osmotic computing [39] – have been proposed. They exploit heterogeneous computing capabilities along the Cloud-IoT continuum (e.g. data centers, ISP routers, gateways, access points, smartphones) to process data as close as possible to their sources, avoiding unnecessary data transfers.

In such context, much research has focussed on supporting decision-making on where to place application services along Cloud-IoT infrastructures so to meet a set of application requirements, e.g. availability of the required *hardware/software capabilities*, suitable *latency* and *bandwidth* among interacting services, or security policies [5,31]. Guaranteeing such requirements can benefit from considering *where* to (temporarily or permanently) store data to be

This work has been partly supported by the EU Horizon 2020 Research and Innovation program, under project ACCORDION (G.A. 871793), and by project *Energy-aware management of software applications in Cloud-IoT ecosystems* (RIC2021PON_A18), funded with ESF REACT-EU resources by the *Italian Ministry of University and Research* through the *PON Ricerca e Innovazione 2014–20*.

© The Author(s), under exclusive license to Springer Nature Switzerland AG 2022
J. Barzen et al. (Eds.): SummerSOC 2022, CCIS 1603, pp. 139–158, 2022.
https://doi.org/10.1007/978-3-031-18304-1_8

processed along the Cloud-IoT continuum. However, despite taming the data deluge and achieving *data-awareness* are among the main motivations of Cloud-IoT computing [42], to the best of our knowledge, the characteristics of the data (e.g. security needs, volume, velocity) processed by the application have only marginally been used to drive placement decisions [31].

Placing application services by taking into account volume, velocity and variety of data [16] can reduce access latencies and *data gravity* issues (i.e. the need to move or replicate data among various services that use them), thus improving application performance [32]. Besides, *software-defined networking* (SDN) can help by instructing *ad-hoc* routing paths for different applications to guarantee suitable bandwidth and latency for data transfer at runtime [30,33]. Finding a *data-aware* service placement and an associated SDN routing that meet application requirements is hence a challenging (NP-hard) problem to attack.

Focussing on data and their characteristics, this article presents:

1. a novel *declarative model* of *Cloud-IoT infrastructures* and *multi-service applications* and a declarative strategy to determine placement and SDN routing decisions in a data-aware manner, meeting all application (hardware, software, IoT, security, latency and bandwidth) requirements,
2. an incremental *continuous reasoning* approach, as in [7], to speed-up decision-making at runtime when a migration is needed only for a portion of application services that cannot currently meet their requirements, taming the exp-time complexity of the placement and routing problem, and
3. an open-source *prototype* (DAPlacer) of the above, assessed over a scenario based on lifelike data.

Overall, the novelty of this work is in that it follows a *data-aware* approach accounting for the characteristics of different types of data (e.g. size, frequency, security requirements) to derive QoS (e.g. latency, bandwidth, security) requirements of the application services to be placed, and for priorities to determine which services to migrate first, when needed.

The rest of this article is organised as follows. We first illustrate a lifelike scenario for our problem (Sect. 2), and describe the methodology of DAPlacer over such a scenario (Sect. 3). Then, we assess our prototype at increasing infrastructure sizes and show the benefits of continuous reasoning in speeding-up decision-making (Sect. 4). Last, we briefly discuss some related work (Sect. 5) and conclude with some directions for future work (Sect. 6).

2   Motivating Scenario and Problem Considered

Consider the museuMonitor application sketched in Fig. 1, managing a smart museum by orchestrating three services:

- a dataStorage service that collects and manages environment data from IoT devices, i.e. exhibition information, temperature, humidity and lighting of exhibited artifacts, and physical presence of people in different rooms so to track their interest for different sections,

- an interface service that collects and streams video footage from museum cameras, and offers a GUI to access the system, and
- a controller service that streams data to *AR glasses* wore by visitors to provide them with exhibition information, and to drive them interactively across the museum.

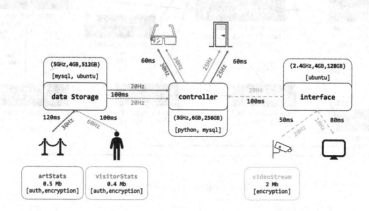

Fig. 1. Example application.

Each service has its *hardware, software, IoT* requirements. For instance, the dataStorage service needs a 5 GHz CPU, 5 GB of RAM and 512 GB of storage space, and to reach out sensors linked to museum artifacts and visitors.

Interacting services collect, manage and exchange data among them and with the IoT devices they are bound to at runtime. Different data types flow from/to IoT devices across application services as indicated by the arrows in Fig. 1, with different colours and dashes, each characterised by a *unit data size* and by associated *security requirements*. Data flow hops are characterised by maximum tolerated *latencies* and by specific *data rates*.

For instance, consider the green dotted line that binds the visitorStats data type with the dataStorage service, passing through the controller service to reach out both *AR glasses* and smart door devices. The visitorStats data type has a size of 0.4 Mb and requires encryption and authentication to be available for the services that process it. The associated data rate varies hop by hop, i.e. it corresponds 60 Hz for the hop from the sensors to the dataStorage, 20 Hz from the dataStorage to the controller service, and 25 Hz from the controller to actuators. Similarly, latency constraints vary from 100 ms for the first two hops, to 60 ms for the last one.

Now consider the Cloud-IoT infrastructure of Fig. 2 to deploy the above application. It is a portion of a real Cloud-IoT infrastructure at UC Davis [12,26]. Such an infrastructure consists of heterogeneous computing *nodes*, interconnected via wired and wireless *links*. Nodes are characterised by their software, hardware, IoT and security capabilities. Physical links between those nodes are described by the latency and bandwidth they feature. For instance, the studentCenter node

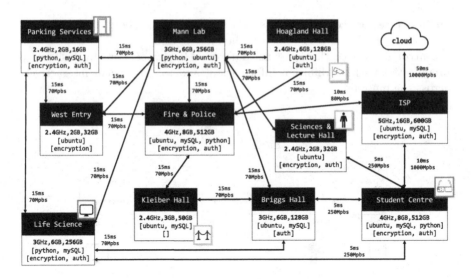

Fig. 2. Example infrastructure.

offers a 4 GHz CPU, 8 GB of RAM and 512 GB of storage space, and reaches out an *AR glasses* device. Its connection with the briggsHall node features an average latency of 5 ms and a bandwidth of 250 Mbps.

Application management must continuously decide onto which node(s) to place museuMonitor services, and how to route traffic between them onto the substrate infrastructure. This is needed to always fulfill application service requirements by continuously matching them against infrastructure capabilities. In the following, we present a declarative solution to the problem of *continuously* determining application placements and associated traffic routings:

> A *placement* of a multi-service application onto a Cloud-IoT infrastructure is a complete mapping from application services to Cloud-IoT nodes that meet all application hardware, software, IoT and data security requirements.

> A *data routing* for a given eligible placement is a mapping from application data flows between services to routes across the physical links between their deployment nodes. It must ensure that all data flows meet the required end-to-end network QoS (based on data volume and velocity) from IoT sensors, through application services, reaching out target actuators (if needed).

Our approach is *data-aware* as it considers QoS requirements dictated by the data types handled by an application, viz. security, volume and velocity, instead of set requirements. Besides, by employing *continuous reasoning*, our solution can locally and continuously handle changes in the application requirements (e.g. increased data frequency or volume, new security need) and infrastructure resources (e.g. node or link overloading, deactivation of a security countermeasure) that might affect the runtime application performance. Last, but not least, we allow specifying migration priorities that can be determined by considering different factors (e.g. business criticality, service migration and data transfer times) to reduce downtime and unavailability.

3   Modelling and Prototype

In this section, we describe our data-aware modelling of Cloud-IoT applications and infrastructures (Sect. 3.1) and detail[1] how DAPlacer determines *data-aware* placements of application services and routings (Sect. 3.2), also illustrating how it employs *continuous reasoning* to speed-up runtime decision-making (Sect. 3.3).

3.1   Model

Application. An application is denoted by Prolog[2] facts

```
application(AppId, [ServiceIds]).
```

where AppId is a unique application identifier, and ServiceIds is the list of identifiers of the services that compose the application.

Services and their requirements are denoted as in

```
service(ServiceId, [SWReqs], HWReqs, [DataTypes], MigrationCost).
```

where ServiceId is a unique service identifier, SWReqs and HWReqs are its software and hardware requirements, DataTypes the list of data types processed by the service, and MigrationCost is a measure of the migration cost of ServiceID e.g. based on the data/code transfer times, or on the impact on the application availability. The higher its migration cost, the better to avoid migrating a service.

---

[1] Due to space limitations, only the main predicates of DAPlacer are presented. The prototype is open-sourced at https://github.com/di-unipi-socc/daplacer.

[2] Prolog is a declarative programming language based on first-order logic. Prolog programs consist of *clauses* of the form a :- b1, ..., bn. stating that a holds if b1 ∧...∧ bn holds. Clauses with empty premise (n = 0) are called *facts*. Predicate definitions can also contain *disjunctions* (denoted by ;) and negations (denoted by \+). Variables start with upper-case letters. Prolog programs can be queried, and the Prolog interpreter tries to answer each query by applying SLD resolution [20] and by returning a computed answer substitution instantiating the variables in the query. For instance, the query ?- nice(W). on the program

    nice(X) :- honest(X), gentle(X).
  honest(alice).   honest(barbara).   gentle(barbara).

returns the computed answer substitution {barbara/ W }, obtained by first rewriting the query by applying the first clause for honest/1 and failing, and then applying the second clause for honest/1 and then the clause defining gentle/1.

Data types are denoted by facts like

```
dataType(DataId, Size, [SecReqs]).
```

where `DataId` is a unique identifier, `Size` is the unit data size in `Mb`, and `SecReqs` are the security requirements associated by such data type, which are inherited by the service that processes it.

Applications can require runtime bindings with (one or more) IoT devices, which can be declared as in

```
requirement(ReqId, IoTDeviceType, [DataIds]).
```

where `ReqId` is the unique identifier of the requirement, `IoTDeviceType` specifies the type of IoT sensor/actuator needed by the application, and `DataIds` is the list of data types that should be provided by such an IoT device.

Finally, interactions between application services, and between services and IoT requirements are denoted by facts like:

```
e2e(A, B, MaxLatency, [DataInfo]).
```

where `A` and `B` are unique identifiers of interacting services or IoT requirements, `MaxLatency` is the maximum tolerated latency for such interactions, and `DataInfo` is a list of pairs (`DataId`,`DataRate`) that identify the data type exchanged during the interaction along with their rate expressed in Hz. Note that this is important as, for instance, a same service or IoT sensor can be queried for data at different rates from different services, or at different moment in times.

Example. The `museuMonitor` application of Fig. 1 (Sect. 2), with its three services (viz. `interface`,`controller`,`dataStorage`), is defined[3] by

```
application(museuMonitor, [interface,controller,dataStorage]).
```

Similarly, the software, hardware and IoT requirements, and the migration cost of the `dataStorage` service are declared by

```
service(dataStorage, [mySQL,ubuntu],(5,4,512),[artStats,visitorStats], 100).
```

Note that `dataStorage` processes two different data types from exhibition artifacts and visitors' monitoring – i.e. `artStats`, `visitorStats` – both requiring encryption and authentication mechanisms to manage users' authentication. Those are declared, with their data size and security requirements, as in:

```
dataType(artStats, 0.5, [encryption]).
dataType(visitorStats, 0.4, [auth, encryption]).
```

---

[3] The full application declaration is available at https://github.com/di-unipi-socc/daplacer/blob/main/app.pl.

Those data types require runtime bindings – rVst and rArt – to actual IoT devices. Such requirement is specified as in:

```
requirement(rVst, smartphone, [visitorStats]).
requirement(rArt, heat, [artStats]).
```

where visitorStats requires binding to visitors' smartphones and visitorStats require binding to a system of thermometers installed at each exhibited artifact.

Finally, end-to-end interactions between the runtime binding requirements above and the dataStorage service are declared as in

```
e2e(rVst, dataStorage, 100, [(visitorStats,60)]).
e2e(rArt, dataStorage, 120, [(artStats,30)]).
```

where the maximum tolerated latency is 100 ms and 120 ms respectively for rVst and rArt, and visitorStats are transmitted 60 Hz and artStats 30 Hz. Similarly, the end-to-end interaction between the dataStorage and the controller service is set to have a maximum tolerated latency of 100 ms and to transmit data 20 Hz by a fact of the form: ⋄

```
e2e(dataStorage, controller, 100, [(artStats,20), (visitorStats,20)]).
```

Infrastructure. Cloud-IoT infrastructures are modelled as graphs. First of all, infrastructure node can be declared by facts like:

```
node(NodeId,[SWCaps],HWCaps,[SecCaps],[IoTCaps]).
```

where NodeId is the unique node identifier and SWCaps, HWCaps SecCaps and IoTCaps are respectively its software, hardware security and IoT capabilities. Communication links between nodes are denoted by facts like:

```
link(NodeId1, NodeId2, FeatLat, FeatBW).
```

where FeatLat FeatBW define the end-to-end latency and bandwidth featured by the communication link between nodes NodeId1 and NodeId2. Devices connected to a node could be *sensors* or *actuators*:

```
sensor(SensorId, Type, [DataIds]).
actuator(ActuatorId, Type).
```

identified by a SensorId (or ActuatorId) and the device type Type. Sensors are also associated with the list of data they can generate (i.e. DataIds).

Example. Such an infrastructure, like the one shown in Fig. 2, can be represented starting from sensors and actuators, by facts like

```
sensor(art42, heat, [artStats]).
actuator(video3, display).
```

where `art42` is a monitoring temperature system that manages `artStats` data type, and `video3` shows information as it is a visual display. IoT devices need to be hosted on some infrastructure nodes, which are defined with their software, hardware, security and IoT capabilities, as follows:

```
node(kleiberHall, [ubuntu, mySQL], (2.4, 3, 50), [], [art42]).
node(briggsHall, [ubuntu, mySQL], (3, 6, 128), [auth], []).
```

Note that `kleiberHall` node hosts `art42` sensor and has empty security capabilities. Conversely, `briggsHall` node provides higher hardware capabilities and `auth` as security capability, but does not host any IoT device.

Finally, links between nodes are represented as in

```
link(kleiberHall, briggsHall, 15, 70).
```

which means that `kleiberHall` and `briggsHall` nodes are connected with a link offering 15 ms of latency and 70 Mbps of bandwidth.   ◇

Deployment Information. As mentioned before, applications can require runtime bindings (via `requirement/3` facts) to actual IoT sensors and actuators from/to which collect/transmit data. Such a piece of information should be provided at *deployment time*, when looking for eligible placements and routings, by facts like

```
dataBinding(ServiceId, ReqId, IoTId).
```

where `ServiceId` is the identifier of the service bound to a physical IoT device `IoTId` of a certain type and managing the same data types as stated in the application requirement `ReqId`.

Example. For instance, the runtime binding of the `rArt` requirement of `museuMonitor` is specified as in

```
dataBinding(dataStorage, rArt, art42).
```

where `art42` is an actual temperature monitoring system available in the Cloud-IoT infrastructure of Fig. 2 at node `kleiberHall`.   ◇

3.2   Placement and Routing

Based on the modelling above, predicate `placement/8` (line 1) of DAPlacer implements the backtracking *generate and test* strategy illustrated in Fig. 3 to determine eligible placements and data routings for a given application onto a target Cloud-IoT infrastructure. Such a strategy consists of three steps:

```
1  placement(Ss, (HW,BW), PrevBW, Rs, P, (NewHW,NewBW), NewRs, NewP) :-
2    compatible(Ss,SNs),
3    servicePlacement(SNs, HW, NewHW, P, NewP),
4    findRoutes(Ss, NewP, BW, PrevBW, Rs, NewBW, NewRs).
```

Fig. 3. Bird's-eye view of DAPlacer placement strategy.

1. predicate `compatibles/2` (line 2) determines for each application service S the subset of *compatible* infrastructure nodes that can support its requirements. The list of services and their compatible nodes Compatibles (line 8) is sorted into SNs from the service with less compatible nodes to the one with more (line 9), so that they are considered from the most difficult to the less difficult to be placed in the next step,
2. predicate `servicePlacement/5` (line 3) determines an eligible placement NewP, starting from an empty placement P, for each application service in the sorted list SNs along with the associated hardware allocation NewHW,
3. based on the found placement, predicate `findRoutes/7` (line 4) determines an associated eligible SDN data routing NewRs, starting from both empty routing R and bandwidth allocation PrevBW, checking that each route respects network QoS requirements, retrieving also the associated bandwidth allocation NewBW.

Next, we detail the functioning of the predicates mentioned in 1–3.

Placement. Predicate `placement/8` exploits `compatibles/2` (so `findCompatibles/2`, lines 6–10) to perform a pre-processing step that determines, for each application service in Ss, a subset of nodes where to suitably place it (lines 7–8). The subset is built by using `lightNodeOK/3` predicate that starts by checking the existence of service S (line 16) and then performs all the controls for software (line 18), hardware and security requirements. Hardware requirements are *softly* checked by `checkHW/2` (line 20) as it does not consider the rest of the application, but it only ensures that node N has enough hardware resources to host service S.

Security requirements SecReqs are dictated by the data types processed by a service (i.e. DataIds). DAPlacer collects those via predicate `getSecReqs/2` and checks them against the security capabilities SecCaps available at node N (line 19).

Then, `servicePlacement/5` (lines 11–14) actually determines the eligible placement, looking for compatible nodes found in the previous pre-processing step. It also performs a deeper check of hardware requirements exploiting the `hwOK/5` predicate (lines 25–28), knowing service requirements HWReqs, node capabilities HWCaps, the current hardware allocation AllocHW, and the cumulative allocation associated to the placement P built so far. This incrementally checks that the built placement does not exceed hardware capabilities of the target deployment nodes. The current allocation CurrHW (line 26) is summed up with the currently employed resources NewHW (line 27), collected via the `hardwareUsedOnN/3` predicate (line 29), to handle cases in which the hardware requirements of a service change triggered by Continuous Integration/Continuous Delivery (CI/CD) pipeline.

```
5   compatible(Ss,SNs) :- findCompatibles(Ss, Cs), sort(1, @>=, Cs, SNs).

6   findCompatibles([S|Ss], [(L,S,SCompatibles)|Rest]):-
7     findCompatibles(Ss, Rest),
8     findall((HWCaps, M), lightNodeOK(S, M, HWCaps), Compatibles),
9     sort(1, @>=, Compatibles, SCompatibles), length(SCompatibles,L).
10  findCompatibles([],[]).

11  servicePlacement([(_,S,Cs)|Ss], HW, NewHW, P, NewP) :-
12    member((_,N),Cs), nodeOK(S,N,P,HW),
13    servicePlacement(Ss, HW, NewHW, [on(S,N)|P], NewP).
14  servicePlacement([], _, NewHW, P, P) :- hwAllocation(P, NewHW).

15  lightNodeOK(S,N,HD) :-
16    service(S, SWReqs, HWReqs, DataIds, _),
17    node(N, SWCaps, HWCaps, SecCaps, _), HWCaps=(_, _,HD),
18    subset(SWReqs,SWCaps),
19    getSecReqs(DataIds, SecReqs), subset(SecReqs, SecCaps),
20    checkHW(HWReqs,HWCaps).

21  nodeOK(S, N, P, AllocHW):-
22    service(S, _, HWReqs, _, _),
23    node(N, _, HWCaps, _, _),
24    hwOK(HWReqs, HWCaps, N, P, AllocHW).

25  hwOK(HWReqs, HWCaps, N, P, AllocHW) :-
26    findall(HW, member((N,HW),AllocHW), HWs), sumHW(HWs, CurrHW),
27    findall(HW, hardwareUsedOnN(N,P,HW), HWonN), sumHW(HWonN, NewHW),
28    checkHW(HWReqs, HWCaps, CurrHW, NewHW).

29  hardwareUsedOnN(N,P,HW) :- service(S,_,HW,_,_), member(on(S,N), P).
```

Fig. 4. Pre-processing and service placement.

If service S can be placed on node N, the placement P is updated with the pair on(S,N) (line 13). Once a complete placement P has been fully determined, the associated hardware allocation is computed by predicate hwAllocation/2 (line 14) and returned to the caller (Fig. 4).

Routing. As mentioned above, once an eligible service placement as been determined by servicePlacement/5, DAPlacer relies on predicate findRoutes/7 predicate[4] to determine an associated eligible routing of data flows. DAPlacer handles both determining routings between services and between a service and an IoT device.

---

[4] Code of findRoutes/7 predicate is not shown. It is available at https://github.com/di-unipi-socc/daplacer/blob/main/daplacer.pl.

To do so, predicate `findRoutes/7` first collects interactions among all pre-viously deployed services, and within sensors and actuators. Each interaction is characterized by a maximum end-to-end latency and a set of data flowing through it at different transmission rates. For each interaction, DAPlacer defines a route (i.e. a list of nodes) over the infrastructure, that must traverse the net-work supporting latency and bandwidth requirements at each hop. Precisely, given two nodes, DAPlacer determines if they are connected directly or through any acyclic path, checking that the total latency does not exceed the maximum tolerated one, and all the links have enough available bandwidth to allow data flowing, considering also the bandwidth allocated so far.

If a traversable path is found, it is saved as a list of the traversed nodes, annotating the source and destination services with the maximum bandwidth required along the entire route (i.e. `((S1,S2),BW,R)`).

Example. To determine an eligible deployment and data routing for the applica-tion of Sect. 2 over the infrastructure described in Sect. 3.1 the following query can be run:

```
:- daplacer(museuMonitor, Placement, Routes).
```

Figure 5 shows the first eligible output placement returned by the query, along with SDN traffic routings. As shown, the three computing services `dataStorage`, `interface` and `controller` have been respectively placed onto `cloud`, `ISP` and `Fire & Police` nodes. The table in the lower right corner of the figure summarises all found routes and their characteristics. For instance, the dotted line from `dataStorage` to `controller` defines a path that starts from `cloud` node, passing through `ISP`, and finally to `Fire & Police` node.   ◇

Due to the NP-hard nature of the considered problem [4], in the worst-case, DAPlacer explores the whole search space to determine an eligible placement and routing (if any), incurring in exp-time complexity. Given an application with S services and a Cloud-IoT infrastructure with N nodes, determining an eligible placement incurs in worst-case $O(N^S)$ time complexity. Similarly, given a Cloud-IoT infrastructure with an average node degree of K and a network diameter of D, determining eligible routings shows a $O(K^D)$. Hence, the combination of the two steps above shows a worst-case complexity of $O(N^S \times K^D)$.

3.3 Continuous Reasoning

To tame the exp-time complexity of the considered problem for prompter decision-making at runtime, DAPlacer exploits *continuous reasoning* [7]. Once a deployment has been enacted according to a found placement and routing, continuous reasoning tries to reduce the size of the considered placement prob-lem instances at runtime, by focussing on re-placing those services and data routings that cannot currently meet their requirements. This can happen for two reasons:

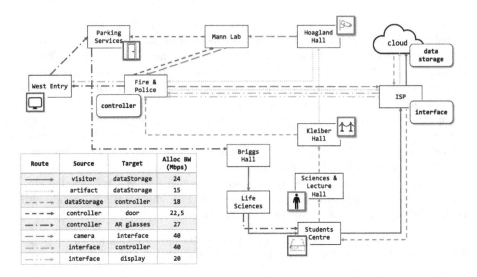

Fig. 5. Example output placement and routing.

- due to changes in the monitored[5] Cloud-IoT infrastructure (e.g. node crash or overloading, link QoS degradation) that prevent meeting application requirements, or
- due to changes in the declared application (e.g. service removal/addition, requirements update, changes in the data types handled) that require (un)deploying services, or migrating existing ones.

When possible, after identifying the deployment portion affected by the changes above, continuous reasoning attempts to determine a new placement and data routing only for such a portion.

To do so, predicate daplacer/3 (Fig. 6) determines an eligible placement NewP and the associated data routing NewRs for application App. Such a predicate handles the following three cases:

1. *First deployment.* In case a deployment of App does not exist, the first clause of daplacer/3 triggers (lines 30–34) and exploits predicate placement/8 (line 33) with initially empty resource allocations Alloc, placement P and routes Rs (line 32). If an eligible placement NewP and routing NewRs are found, they are asserted into the knowledge base of DAPlacer (line 34).
2. *Partial re-deployment.* In case a deployment of App already exists, the second clause of daplacer/3 triggers (lines 35–42) and exploits predicate newServices/2 (line 36) to determine the list NewSs of newly added services and predicate reasoningStep/8 (line 38) to determine the list SsToMove of services that need to be migrated and the partial placement TmpP and routing TmpRs that still have

---

[5] Monitoring tools for Cloud-IoT infrastructure exists such as FogMon [10] or those surveyed in [35].

their requirements satisfied. In this step, services are previously sorted with
sortByMigrationCost/2 (line 37), so that services with lower migration cost are
tried to migrate first. Indeed, as services are considered sequentially, migrating one might solve problems (e.g. node/link overloading) for its successors
and, therefore, avoid migrating them. Then, new services and services to be
migrated are appended into a single list (line 39), and predicate placement/8 is
exploited to complete the partial placement TmpP and routing TmpRs into NewP
and NewRs, respectively (line 40). Last, the previous placement is retracted
from the knowledge base of DAPlacer (line 41), and the new one is asserted
(line 42).

3. *Full redeployment.* In case a deployment of App already exists but the previous
   step fails, the third clause of DAPlacer (lines 43–47) looks for a complete new
   placement and routing for App, relying again on placement/8 (line 45). If one
   is found, the previous placement is retracted from the knowledge base of
   DAPlacer (line 46), and the new one is asserted (line 47).

Predicate reasoningStep/8 (lines 48–58) is the core of the continuous reasoning strategy implemented by DAPlacer. By recursively scanning the current placement SPrevP, it determines services that have been removed from an application
through the CI/CD pipeline (lines 48–50), services that have their requirements
satisfied on their current deployment node (lines 51–55), and – by exclusion –
services that need to be migrated (lines 56–57). Predicates nodeOK/4 (line 53) and
serviceRoutesOK/8 (line 54) check whether the (possibly updated) service requirements of S are currently satisfied by node N, and that traffic routes involving S
still feature suitable QoS. While performing the check, serviceRoutesOK/8 also
updates bandwidth allocation NewBW in case application requirements have been
changed in the application declaration through the CI/CD pipeline. The cut
operator(!) after the call to reasoningStep/8 (line 38) ensures the current placement is scanned only once.

As services to be placed can be determined with a poly-time scan of the
current application placement, assuming that only m out of S services need
to be replaced, the time complexity of completing a partial placement is in the
worst-case $O(N^m \times K^D) < O(N^S \times K^D)$. Hence, from an asymptotic complexity
analysis continuous reasoning can tame the complexity of the placement and
routing problems at runtime.

4   Scalability Assessment

In this section, we provide an experimental assessment[6] comparing exhaustive
and continuous reasoning approaches implemented by DAPlacer.

---

[6] All experiments were run on a machine featuring macOS Monterey 12.3, and
equipped with 16 GB of RAM and a 2,5 GHz Intel Core i7 quad-core processor.
Experiments code is accessible at: https://github.com/di-unipi-socc/daplacer/tree/
main/experiment.

```
30  daplacer(App, NewP, NewRs) :-
31    \+ deployment(App, _, _, _), application(App, Ss),
32    Alloc=([],[]), Rs=[], P=[], PrevBW=[],
33    placement(Ss, Alloc, PrevBW, Rs, P, NewAlloc, NewRs, NewP),
34    assert(deployment(App, NewP, NewRs, NewAlloc)).
35  daplacer(App, NewP, NewRs) :-
36    deployment(App, PrevP, PrevRs, PrevAll), newServices(PrevP, NewSs),
37    sortByMigrationCost(PrevP, SPrevP),
38    reasoningStep(SPrevP, PrevAll, PrevRs, SsToMove, TmpBW, TmpRs, TmpP),!,
39    append(NewSs, SsToMove, SsToPlace),
40    placement(SsToPlace, PrevAll, TmpBW, TmpRs, TmpP, NewAlloc, NewRs, NewP),
41    retract(deployment(App, _, _, _)),
42    assert(deployment(App, NewP, NewRs, NewAlloc)).
43  daplacer(App, NewP, NewRs) :-
44    deployment(App,_,_,Alloc), application(App, Ss), Rs=[], P=[], PrevBW=[],
45    placement(Ss, Alloc, PrevBW, Rs, P, NewAlloc, NewRs, NewP),
46    retract(deployment(App,_,_)),
47    assert(deployment(App, NewP, NewRs, NewAlloc)).

48  reasoningStep([on(S,_)|P], (HW,BW), Rs, Ss, NewBW, NewRs, NewP) :-
49    reasoningStep(P, (HW,BW), Rs, Ss, NewBW, NewRs, NewP),
50    \+ service(S, _, _, _, _).
51  reasoningStep([on(S,N)|P], (HW,BW), Rs, Ss, NewBW, NewRs, [on(S,N)|NewP]) :-
52    reasoningStep(P, (HW,BW), Rs, Ss, TmpBW, TmpRs, NewP),
53    nodeOK(S, N, NewP, HW),
54    serviceRoutesOK(S, N, NewP, BW, Rs, TmpBW, Tmp2Routes, NewBW),
55    append(TmpRs, Tmp2Routes, NewRs).
56  reasoningStep([on(S,_)|P], (HW,BW), Rs, [S|Ss], NewBW, NewRs, NewP) :-
57    reasoningStep(P, (HW,BW), Rs, Ss, NewBW, NewRs, NewP).
58  reasoningStep([],_,_,[],[],[],[]).
```

Fig. 6. Code of `daplacer/3` main predicate and the continuous reasoning step.

We consider the `museuMonitor` application of Sect. 2 to be placed onto random infrastructures built as per the Barabási-Albert model [2] at infrastructure varying sizes of 2^i nodes with $i \in [4, 9]$ and a node degree equal to i. We run discrete event simulations over 600 epochs[7] that vary infrastructure conditions according to a given probability (i.e. variation rate). At each epoch node hardware and link latency and bandwidth change[8] according to their set variation rate so to simulate a life-like monitoring and evolution of infrastructure resources. Considered

---

[7] Experimental results are aggregated over 10 repetitions of the described 600 epoch simulations.

[8] For each selected node, its hardware availability is changed by considering its initially available RAM and HDD resources and picking a value in the range $[1, 1.1 \times$ RAM$]$ and $[1, 1.2 \times$ HDD$]$, respectively. Analogously, the bandwidth of selected links is picked anew in the range $[1, 1.1 \times$ BW$]$, where BW is the initial bandwidth featured by the link. Similarly, the latency of selected links is changed within $[$LAT$/2, 1.5 \times$ LAT$]$, where LAT is the initial link latency.

variation rates are 10%, 20%, 40%, and 50%. For instance, a 50% variation rate corresponds to changing approximately a half of the nodes and links at each epoch. Besides, we consider a lifelike series of six application CI/CD commits that change application requirements and topology and that are enforced every 100 epochs throughout the simulation. Detailedly:

1. deploying the original museuMonitor application,
2. adding two interacting services, localisator and locStorage, which take care of processing and storing visitorStats data,
3. removing one service, by assuming that locStorage and localisator are merged into a single service managing and storing all visitorStats data,
4. increasing hardware requirements of the localisator service,
5. removing the e2e interaction between dataStorage and the visitor sensor, linking the latter to localisator, and localisator to interface and controller services, by adding new service-to-service interactions,
6. decreasing required maximum latency and increasing data rate for visitorStats data type.

Such a commit history covers and tests all CI/CD triggered changes that DAPlacer can handle, i.e. service addition/removal, service requirements updated, end-to-end QoS requirements update/addition/removal.

Figure 7 and Fig. 8 show the execution times and the number of Prolog inferences of the exhaustive and continuous reasoning strategy implemented by DAPlacer at varying infrastructure sizes and simulation rates. Note that the behaviour of the exhaustive search strategy of Fig. 7 reflects the exp-time complexity of finding a solution to the placement and routing problem both in execution times (Fig. 7(a)) and in the number of inferences (Fig. 7(b)), which increase as the infrastructure size and variation rate increase. Execution times settle between 0.04 and 0.08 s, while inferences settle between 80000 and 220000 approximately. Such a complexity is naturally experienced at first deployment, when a placement and routing for an application are to be found for the first time.

When exploiting continuous reasoning for runtime decision-making however, results substantially improve. Figure 8a and 8b show a more gradual increase in execution times and inferences as infrastructure sizes and variation rates increase. In comparison with the exhaustive strategy, continuous reasoning brings an average 21× speed-up on the execution times and of 13× on number of inferences. Indeed, execution times settle between 0.005 and 0.03 s, while inferences settle between a few 1000 s and 100000 approximately. It is worth noting that speed-ups are always positive, despite slightly decreasing as infrastructure sizes and variation rates increase.

These results illustrate the fact that – on average – continuous reasoning effectively reduces the size of the problem instance to be solved only to those services in need of attention, and manages to determine an alternative replacement for them. Summing up, the experimental assessment shows that DAPlacer can boost the runtime decision-making, achieving considerable average (inferences and time) speed-ups, which can – for instance – increase the number

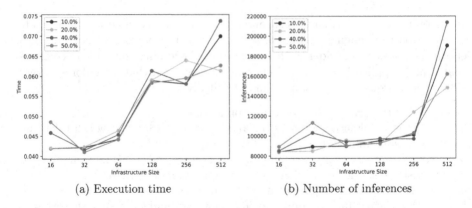

(a) Execution time   (b) Number of inferences

Fig. 7. Exhaustive search results.

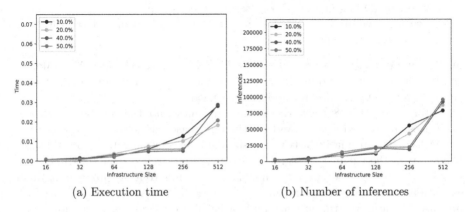

(a) Execution time   (b) Number of inferences

Fig. 8. Continuous reasoning results.

of considered placement requests and reduce management times for latency-sensitive applications (e.g. AR/VR, gaming, e-surgery). Simulations also confirm that DAPlacer can successfully handle both infrastructure and CI/CD application changes, even in large-scale Cloud-IoT infrastructures subject to high variation rates, confirming asymptotic considerations.

5 Related Work

Much literature has focussed on the placement of application services to physical servers in Cloud datacentres [28], only a few of which (e.g. [15,41]) employing a declarative approach. However, managing applications over the Cloud-IoT continuum introduces new challenges, mainly due to infrastructure scale and heterogeneity, need for QoS-awareness, dynamicity and support to interactions with the IoT, rarely considered in Cloud-only scenarios. Next, we briefly summarise the state of the art in the field of Cloud-IoT multi-service application placement and management, referring to recent surveys [5,22,37] for further details.

Among the first proposals investigating the peculiarities of Cloud-IoT application placement, [14] proposed a simple search algorithm to determine an eligible deployment of (multi-service) applications to tree-like Cloud-IoT infrastructures, open-sourced in the iFogSim Java prototype. Building on top of iFogSim, various works tried to optimise different metrics, e.g. service delivery deadlines [21], load-balancing [40], or client-server distances [13].

In our previous work [4], we proved NP-hardness of the placement problem, and we devised a backtracking strategy to determine context-, QoS- and cost-aware placements of multiservice applications to Cloud-IoT infrastructures, also employing continuous reasoning [7], and considering Osmotic service adaptation [8]. We have also exploited logic programming to assess the security and trust levels of application placements [9], and to determine the placement and network routing of Virtual Network Function chains in Cloud-IoT scenarios [12]. Still with a declarative approach, [6] and [27] devised an approach to service coordination based on *aggregate computing*, aiming at managing opportunistic resources via a hybrid centralised/decentralised solution by relying on a self-organising peer-to-peer architecture to handle churn and mobility. On a similar line, we proposed a declarative fully decentralised solution to write and enforce QoS-aware application and infrastructure management policies [11]. Last, proposals exist for simulating application placements and management policies in Cloud-IoT scenarios [23], e.g. YAFS [19], EdgeCloudSim [34], and iFogSim [14] itself. None of the works surveyed above considers, however, data characteristics to determine eligible application placements and traffic routings as we do in DAPlacer. Indeed, as stated in [31], most existing works in application placement in Cloud-IoT settings do not consider data-awareness.

To the best of our knowledge, only [24] and [25] propose some modelling of data storage services, IoT sources and destinations to determine *data flows* across the infrastructure. More in detail [24] and [25] model the placement problem as a *Generalized Assignment Problem* (GAP). A *divide and conquer* approach is used to tame the exp-time complexity of the problem, i.e. partitioning the infrastructure so as to solve sub-problems. Similarly, [18] exploits centrality indices to determine the closest and most balanced distance to data sources in order to obtain a target bandwidth distribution and an overall better network usage. Nor [24] or [25] however consider security, data rates and runtime data binding, nor exploit continuous reasoning to speed-up decision-making.

Finally, with a complementary architectural perspective, [38] provides a configurable and adaptive framework to process big data streams and minimize cloud fees, using microservices paradigm and mobile processing. In [1,17] they provide tools and techniques to improve software architectures, driven by QoS requirements.

6   Concluding Remarks

In this article, we presented a novel declarative model and methodology to determine data-aware eligible placements of multi-service applications over Cloud-IoT infrastructures and SDN routings of associated data flows. The model considers hardware, software, security, IoT application requirements and the corresponding infrastructure capabilities. It is among the first proposals to feature data-awareness, in that it accounts for data volume (i.e. data size), variety (i.e. different data types) and velocity (i.e. different transmission rates) to compute bandwidth and latency constraints on data flows to be routed across services.

Our methodology features both an exhaustive search strategy and a continuous reasoning engine to speed-up the search of suitable placements and routings at runtime. Continuous reasoning handles partial re-placement of services (and re-routing of traffic flows), limiting decision-making to those services (and routes) in need for attention either due to infrastructure changes or CI/CD modifications of the application requirements and topology. The DAPlacer prototype written in Prolog open-sources the proposed methodology.

DAPlacer is *declarative*, thus concise ($\simeq$ 170 lines of code) and easier to understand, update and maintain in contrast with procedural solutions. Additionally, it offers a high degree of flexibility and extensibility, which well suits the ever-changing needs of Cloud-IoT scenarios. Experimental results over a lifelike use case have shown that continuous reasoning boosts execution times of the exhaustive strategy to determine eligible placements and routing by 7× on average, across varying infrastructure sizes and infrastructure variation rates.

In our future work, we intend to:

- define a *cost model* (e.g. based on energy consumption and/or operational costs) to find and assess the optimality of alternative candidate placements and routings, also considering data replication on multiple nodes,
- allow for changing data bindings at runtime and to adaptively decide on which version of a service (and data flow) to place based on target resources, in the spirit of Osmotic computing [8,39],
- implement heuristic or meta-heuristic search strategies to speed-up finding an eligible solution, also including the possibility of relaxing soft constraints defined on the application, and
- run DAPlacer in real testbed settings over real applications and Cloud-IoT resources to measure and assess its results.

References

1. Aleti, A., Bjornander, S., Grunske, L., Meedeniya, I.: ArcheOpterix: an extendable tool for architecture optimization of AADL models. In: ICSE MOMPES (2009)
2. Barabási, A.L., Pósfai, M.: Network Science. Cambridge University Press, Cambridge (2016)
3. Bellavista, P., Berrocal, J., Corradi, A., Das, S.K., Foschini, L., Zanni, A.: A survey on fog computing for the internet of things. Pervasive Mob. Comput. **52**, 71–99 (2019)
4. Brogi, A., Forti, S.: QoS-aware deployment of IoT applications through the fog. IEEE Internet Things J. **4**(5), 1185–1192 (2017)
5. Brogi, A., Forti, S., Guerrero, C., Lera, I.: How to place your apps in the fog - state of the art and open challenges. Softw. Pract. Exp. **50**(5), 719–740 (2020)

6. Casadei, R., Viroli, M.: Coordinating computation at the edge: a decentralized, self-organizing, spatial approach. In: FMEC 2019 (2019)
7. Forti, S., Bisicchia, G., Brogi, A.: Declarative continuous reasoning in the cloud-IoT continuum. J. Logic Comput. **32**(2), 206–232 (2022)
8. Forti, S., Brogi, A.: Declarative osmotic application placement. In: Advanced Information Systems Engineering Workshops, vol. 423 (2021)
9. Forti, S., Ferrari, G.L., Brogi, A.: Secure cloud-edge deployments, with trust. Future Gener. Comput. Syst. **102**, 775–788 (2020)
10. Forti, S., Gaglianese, M., Brogi, A.: Lightweight self-organising distributed monitoring of Fog infrastructures. Future Gener. Comput. Syst. **114**, 605–618 (2021)
11. Forti, S., Lera, I., Guerrero, C., Brogi, A.: Osmotic management of distributed complex systems: a declarative decentralised approach. J. Softw. Evol. Process (2021)
12. Forti, S., Paganelli, F., Brogi, A.: Probabilistic QoS-aware placement of VNF chains at the edge. Theory Pract. Logic Program. **22**(1), 1–36 (2021)
13. Guerrero, C., Lera, I., Juiz, C.: A lightweight decentralized service placement policy for performance optimization in fog computing. J. Ambient. Intell. Humaniz. Comput. **10**(6), 2435–2452 (2018). https://doi.org/10.1007/s12652-018-0914-0
14. Gupta, H., Vahid Dastjerdi, A., Ghosh, S.K., Buyya, R.: iFogSim: a toolkit for modeling and simulation of resource management techniques in the internet of things, edge and fog computing environments. Soft. Pract. Exp. **47**(9), 1275–1296 (2017)
15. Kadioglu, S., Colena, M., Sebbah, S.: Heterogeneous resource allocation in cloud management. In: NCA 2016 (2016)
16. Khan, N., et al.: Big data: Survey, technologies, opportunities, and challenges. Sci. World J. (2014)
17. Koziolek, A., Koziolek, H., Reussner, R.: PerOpteryx: automated application of tactics in multi-objective software architecture optimization (2011)
18. Lera, I., Guerrero, C., Juiz, C.: Comparing centrality indices for network usage optimization of data placement policies in fog devices. In: 2018 Third International Conference on Fog and Mobile Edge Computing (FMEC) (2018)
19. Lera, I., Guerrero, C., Juiz, C.: YAFS: a simulator for IoT scenarios in fog computing. IEEE Access **7**, 91745–91758 (2019)
20. Lloyd, J.W.: Foundations of Logic Programming. Springer, Heidelberg (1987). https://doi.org/10.1007/978-3-642-83189-8
21. Mahmud, R., Ramamohanarao, K., Buyya, R.: Latency-aware application module management for fog computing environments. ACM Trans. Internet Technol. **19**(1), 1–21 (2018)
22. Mahmud, R., Ramamohanarao, K., Buyya, R.: Application management in fog computing environments: a taxonomy, review and future directions. ACM Comput. Surv. **53**(4), 1–43 (2020)
23. Margariti, S.V., Dimakopoulos, V.V., Tsoumanis, G.: Modeling and simulation tools for fog computing-a comprehensive survey from a cost perspective. Future Internet **12**(5), 89 (2020)
24. NAAS, M.I., Lemarchand, L., Boukhobza, J., Raipin, P.: A graph partitioning-based heuristic for runtime IoT data placement strategies in a fog infrastructure. In: Proceedings of the 33rd Annual ACM Symposium on Applied Computing (2018)
25. Naas, M.I., Parvedy, P.R., Boukhobza, J., Lemarchand, L.: iFogStor: an IoT data placement strategy for fog infrastructure. In: 2017 IEEE 1st International Conference on Fog and Edge Computing (ICFEC) (2017)

26. Ning, Z., Kong, X., Xia, F., Hou, W., Wang, X.: Green and sustainable cloud of things: enabling collaborative edge computing. IEEE Commun. Mag. **57**(1), 72–78 (2019)
27. Pianini, D., Casadei, R., Viroli, M., Natali, A.: Partitioned integration and coordination via the self-organising coordination regions pattern. Future Gener. Comput. Syst. **114**, 44–68 (2021)
28. Pietri, I., Sakellariou, R.: Mapping virtual machines onto physical machines in cloud computing: a survey. ACM Comput. Surv. **49**(3), 1–30 (2016)
29. Qiu, T., Chi, J., Zhou, X., Ning, Z., Atiquzzaman, M., Wu, D.O.: Edge computing in industrial internet of things: architecture, advances and challenges. IEEE Commun. Surv. Tutorials **22**(4), 2462–2488 (2020)
30. Rak, J.: Resilience of future internet communications. In: Rak, J. (ed.) Resilient Routing in Communication Networks. CCN, pp. 45–83. Springer, Cham (2015). https://doi.org/10.1007/978-3-319-22333-9_3
31. Salaht, F.A., Desprez, F., Lebre, A.: An overview of service placement problem in fog and edge computing. ACM Comput. Surv. **53**(3), 1–35 (2020)
32. Samizadeh Nikoui, T., Rahmani, A., Tabarsaied, H.: Data Management in Fog Computing: Principles and Paradigms. Wiley, Hoboken (2019)
33. Sándor, H., Genge, B., Sebestyén-Pál, G.: Resilience in the internet of things: the software defined networking approach. In: 2015 IEEE International Conference on Intelligent Computer Communication and Processing (ICCP) (2015)
34. Sonmez, C., Ozgovde, A., Ersoy, C.: EdgeCloudSim: an environment for performance evaluation of edge computing systems. Trans. Emerg. Telecommun. Technol. **29**, e3493 (2018)
35. Taherizadeh, S., Jones, A.C., Taylor, I., Zhao, Z., Stankovski, V.: Monitoring self-adaptive applications within edge computing frameworks: a state-of-the-art review. J. Syst. Softw. **136**, 19–38 (2018)
36. Tortonesi, M., Govoni, M., Morelli, A., Riberto, G., Stefanelli, C., Suri, N.: Taming the IoT data deluge: an innovative information-centric service model for fog computing applications. Future Gener. Comput. Syst. **93**, 888–902 (2019)
37. Vaquero, L.M., Cuadrado, F., Elkhatib, Y., Bernal-Bernabe, J., Srirama, S.N., Zhani, M.F.: Research challenges in nextgen service orchestration. Future Gener. Comput. Syst. **90**, 20–38 (2019)
38. Verginadis, Y., Alshabani, I., Mentzas, G., Stojanovic, N.: Prestocloud: proactive cloud resources management at the edge for efficient real-time big data processing. In: CLOSER (2017)
39. Villari, M., Fazio, M., Dustdar, S., Rana, O., Ranjan, R.: Osmotic computing: a new paradigm for edge/cloud integration. IEEE Cloud Comput. **3**(6), 76–83 (2016)
40. Wang, S., Zafer, M., Leung, K.K.: Online placement of multi-component applications in edge computing environments. IEEE Access **5**, 2514–2533 (2017)
41. Yin, Q., Schüpbach, A., Cappos, J., Baumann, A., Roscoe, T.: Rhizoma: a runtime for self-deploying, self-managing overlays. In: Middleware 2009 (2009)
42. Yousefpour, A., et al.: All one needs to know about fog computing and related edge computing paradigms: a complete survey. J. Syst. Archit. **98**, 289–330 (2019)
43. Zikria, Y.B., Ali, R., Afzal, M.K., Kim, S.W.: Next-generation internet of things (IoT): opportunities, challenges, and solutions. Sensors **21**(4), 1174 (2021)

Quantum Computing

Optimizing the Prioritization of Compiled Quantum Circuits by Machine Learning Approaches

Marie Salm$^{(\boxtimes)}$ ⓘ, Johanna Barzen ⓘ, Frank Leymann ⓘ, and Philipp Wundrack ⓘ

Institute of Architecture of Application Systems, University of Stuttgart, Universitätsstraße 38, Stuttgart, Germany
{salm,barzen,leymann,wundrack}@iaas.uni-stuttgart.de

Abstract. The performance of current quantum computers is limited by high error rates and few qubits. Nevertheless, more and more quantum computers are available in the cloud. Selecting a suitable quantum computer to execute a specific quantum circuit and receive precise results can be difficult. At the same time, it is crucial to choose an available quantum computer that offers the hardware characteristics required by the circuit to retrieve precise results, depending on the quantum computer's last re-calibration and the quantum compiler that maps the circuit to the hardware. Furthermore, cloud providers regulate hardware access, so waiting times must be considered. To support the choice of a quantum computer, we introduced an automated framework in previous work. It enables the user to analyze and prioritize the compiled circuits of a given input circuit for different quantum computers based on their requirements. In this work, we extend the framework by automating the prioritization of compiled circuits targeting short waiting times and precise executions based on previous results. We present our framework's prototype and case study to demonstrate and evaluate the practical feasibility.

Keywords: Quantum computing · NISQ · Decision support · MCDA · Machine learning · NISQ analyzer

1 Introduction

Quantum computers need a few more years until the *Noisy Intermediate-Scale Quantum (NISQ)* era is over and they can solve complex real-world problems [35]. Nevertheless, cloud providers constantly provide more and more quantum computers from different vendors [22,24]. Thus, a diversity of quantum computers is available. But choosing a quantum computer for a given quantum circuit that offers the required hardware characteristics, i.e., enough qubits and low error rates, is crucial to receive precise execution results, i.e., results that

© The Author(s), under exclusive license to Springer Nature Switzerland AG 2022
J. Barzen et al. (Eds.): SummerSOC 2022, CCIS 1603, pp. 161–181, 2022.
https://doi.org/10.1007/978-3-031-18304-1_9

were not excessively disturbed by appearing errors [39–41]. The selection of a suitable quantum computer is also affected by regular calibrations that modify the error rates and decoherence times [41,46,53]. Furthermore, compiling a circuit to the hardware characteristics of a selected quantum computer is necessary to execute it [23]. This can cause changes in the required number of gates and qubits as, e.g., SWAP gates are introduced, leading to more errors [40,41]. Existing quantum compilers used for compilation vary in the resulting compiled circuits, as the mapping is known to be NP-hard [11,42]. Passing a circuit to different compilers is often impossible without further translation effort as the *Software Development Kits (SDKs)*, in which the compilers are embedded, differ in their supported programming languages [42]. In addition, the number of users who want to run their circuits on the available quantum computers is increasing. Cloud providers, thus, manage the access, e.g., by queues, resulting in long waiting times until a circuit is executed, especially for quantum computers with many qubits [22,48].

To assist the user's choice of a suitable quantum computer, we introduced a framework in previous work [41] that compiles a circuit for different quantum computers with multiple compilers and analyzes and prioritizes the compiled circuits based on the user's requirements. We analyzed several quantum SDKs and vendors to identify metrics targeting the common need for precise execution results within short waiting times. The metrics describe properties of compiled circuits and quantum computers, e.g., the *number of operations*, *average T1*, and *waiting time* [22,41,48,53]. To prioritize the compiled circuits based on the identified metrics, we used well-known *Multi-Criteria Decision Analysis (MCDA) methods* [41,51]. MCDA methods use *weights* to determine the importance of individual metrics representing the user's requirements [51]. In the first approach, we manually defined initial weight sets targeting precise results and short waiting times to support the user in setting weights [41]. We examined the metric values of quantum computers and compilation results of three circuits and compared them with the associated results. However, more circuits have to be considered to assess the quality of future executions, and manual examination is error-prone. Thus, the first research question we want to answer in this work is the following:

> **RQ 1**: *How can the determination of metric weights be automated to prioritize compiled quantum circuits of an input circuit and associated quantum computers targeting precise results of their future executions?*

We present an extension of the framework from [41] that *(i) learns metric weights* based on previous execution results of associated compiled circuit and quantum computer metric values using machine learning. It also enables the user to *(ii) select between predefined preferences* regarding precise results and short waiting times or to *define their own weights*. Furthermore, the framework enables the *(iii) application of automated sensitivity analyzes* on calculated rankings to prove their stability by automatically adapting the weights [16,25]. With the automated approach to determine metric weights with the focus on precise execution results, our second research question rises:

> **RQ 2**: *Which quantum computer and quantum circuit metrics influence the execution results of compiled quantum circuits the most?*

We present a case study that *(i) compares ranking performances* of different supported machine learning algorithms and MCDA methods to answer this question. We, then, *(ii) examine the learned metric weights* of the best-performing machine learning and MCDA combinations. Finally, we *(iii) apply sensitivity analyzes* to detect metric weights that influence the calculated rankings the most.

The structure of the paper is as follows: Sect. 2 introduces the fundamentals about MCDA and machine learning algorithms to learn weights. Section 3 presents the approach of our extended framework. Section 4 shows the framework's system architecture and the prototypical implementation. Section 5 demonstrates the case study, and Sect. 6 discusses actual limitations. In Sect. 7, related work is shown. Finally, we conclude the paper and present future work in Sect. 8.

2   Fundamentals

This section presents the fundamentals about MCDA methods and different machine learning algorithms to learn weights based on given data.

2.1   MCDA Methods

When several alternatives exist, MCDA methods assist the decision-maker in choosing an alternative according to respective requirements by, e.g., calculating a ranking [41,51]. These methods are, e.g., applied in e-commerce [6] and sustainable energy [50]. The properties of alternatives used to compare their performances regarding the requirements are called *criteria* and serve as input for an MCDA method [41,51]. The importance of individual requirements is represented by weights that regulate the influence of each criterion. The stability, i.e., the susceptibility of the resulting ranking's order is usually evaluated with a sensitivity analysis [16,25]. The analysis enables the decision-maker to observe to what extent the orders change, and which metrics influence the ranking the most [16,25]. One approach to analyzing the sensitivity of a ranking is by repeatedly changing initial weights and their application with the selected MCDA method [25].

In our approach, an alternative is a compiled circuit together with the related quantum computer, and the criteria are the metrics defined in previous work [41] (see Fig. 4 for an overview). A common goal regarding the usage of quantum computers could be a soon as possible execution that can contradict the desire of precise execution results [16,41]. As the set of existing MCDA methods is difficult to oversee and each has advantages and disadvantages [51], we used the *MCDA Method Selection Tool* [51,52] in previous work [41] to select suitable methods for our framework. A detailed explanation of how we chose an initial set of MCDA methods is described in [41]. We consider the selected methods *Technique for Order Preference by Similarity to Ideal Solution (TOPSIS)* [21] and *Preference Ranking Organization METHod for Enrichment of Evaluations II (PROMETHEE II)* [9] also for the expansion of our framework to learn weights, as both return precise ranking scores. The precise scores enable a more accurate determination of the weights. A description of both methods is presented in [41]. Further MCDA methods can be added to our framework.

2.2   Learning Weights Based on Historical Data

Besides choosing a suitable MCDA method, especially the precise selection of weights for given criteria is crucial to obtain a meaningful ranking of alternatives considering the decision-maker's requirements [29]. Ranking compiled quantum circuits and their related quantum computers based on the waiting time only requires maximum normalized weight of 1 for the metric *weighting time* and minimum weight of 0 for the others [41]. However, ranking regarding the objective of precise execution results depends on the properties of the compiled circuits and the related quantum computers and, thus, involves all other metrics collected in [41]. Interviewing experts to determine the weights of these metrics is imprecise [49]. Instead, metric values and associated histogram intersection values of previously executed compiled circuits should be considered [41]. A histogram intersection value represents the precision of the measurement results of a quantum computer and shows the effects of occurred errors. Therefore, a compiled circuit is executed on a simulator parallel to the execution on a quantum computer, and their execution results, commonly presented as histograms, are superimposed [45]. The dependencies between histogram intersection and metric values can automatically be revealed via machine learning, serving as expert's knowledge for actually compiled circuits [41]. Several weighting methods for MCDA methods based on prior data exist [26,29,30]. As a first attempt, we choose the two heuristic optimizers *genetic algorithm* [20] and *evolution strategy* [13], and the deterministic optimizer *Constrained Optimization BY Linear Approximations (COBYLA)* [34] as weight learning methods [8,10]. All three methods enable the encapsulation of MCDA methods as they do not require specific preliminaries, e.g., being derivable, besides returning ranking scores [8,10,19]. However, further weighting methods can be added to our plug-in-based framework.

Genetic Algorithm simulates the optimization process of evolution [13]. It is known to be robust, more resistant to local minima, and requires fewer prerequisites than classical optimizers such as gradient-based approaches [10,19]. However, genetic algorithms can be slow and may not deliver the best solutions [10].

One possible procedure is as follows: Random parents, i.e., solution candidates, are determined that build the first population [31]. The fitness of each parent to solve the given problem is calculated [19]. The fittest parents generate children, i.e., a new *generation*. *Crossover* between parents and *mutation* is applied to create children [31]. New generations are created until a satisfying solution is found.

Evolution Strategy is also an evolutionary optimization method [13]. It can be faster in finding suitable solutions than a genetic algorithm but can be stuck in local minima [10]. Thereby, the general procedure of evolution strategy can roughly be described as follows [13]: The aim is, e.g., to find the global minimum. An initial set of parents is randomly defined, building the first population. Then, Gaussian noise is added to each parent, generating its child. The fitness of each parent and child is calculated. The new population consists of the fittest parents and children. This procedure is repeated until a satisfying solution exists.

COBYLA is a gradient-free optimization algorithm [34]. It is designed to find the local minimum or maximum; however, it can perform better in certain cases than a genetic algorithm [8,32,34]. COBYLA linearly approximates the objective function based on the interpolation of function points [33]. The gradients of the approximated objective function are calculated, and a new function point is determined to evaluate the objective function that has to be optimized [8,54]. The process is repeated until a satisfactory solution is found.

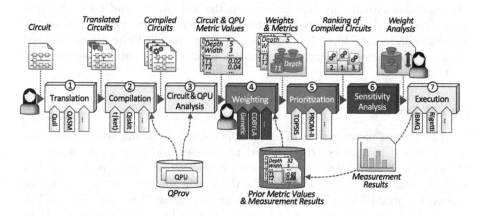

Fig. 1. Automated translation, compilation, and prioritization of quantum circuits for available quantum computers using Machine Learning (extending [41]). Light components are from prior work, middle grey are extended, and dark are new.

3   Learning to Prioritize Compiled Quantum Circuits

In this section, we address **RQ 1** by presenting an extension of our framework from [41] to automatically learn weights for prioritizing compiled quantum circuits for available quantum computers based on previous execution results. An overview of our approach is presented in Fig. 1, where components from previous work are light [39,41,42], extended components are middle grey, and new components are dark. Detailed descriptions of light components are given in [39,41,42].

3.1   Translation

As described in [39,41,42], SDKs of existing quantum compilers often provide different programming languages and gate sets to implement, compile, and execute quantum circuits. In the *(1) Translation* phase, the input circuit of the user is therefore automatically translated into the different formats of the SDKs of provided quantum compilers if required [41,42].

3.2   Compilation

In the *(2) Compilation* phase, all compilers supporting given vendors are selected to compile the translated circuits on all available quantum computers and simulators using their maximum optimization level [41,42,53].

3.3   Circuit and QPU Analysis

The compiled circuits are handed over to the *(3) Circuit and QPU Analysis* phase. The circuits and related quantum computers are analyzed based on the metrics collected in [39,41,53]. Additionally, the compiled circuits are filtered based on their executability on the target quantum computers, as described in [39,42].

3.4   Weighting

The determined metric values of executable compiled circuits and their associated quantum computers are presented to the user and serve as input for the *(4) Weighting* phase. The user can now choose one of the supported MCDA methods that should be used as basis for the weight learning process and will be applied for prioritization in the *(5) Prioritization* phase (Sect. 3.5). The MCDA method TOPSIS [21] is selected as default as it performed best in our case study (Sect. 5) combined with the weight learning method COBYLA [34]. The user can also decide between determining the weights of the individual metrics based on their unique requirements as in previous work [41] or selecting predefined preferences such that, e.g., the automated process to learn metric weights based on previous execution results is initiated. For the former, the user can assign 0 to 100 points to each metric, reflecting their importance based on the weighting method SMART [12]. To finally calculate the weights, the number of points of each metric is automatically divided by the sum of points of all other metrics [12,41]. For the latter, the user can choose a prioritization targeting precise execution results, short waiting times, or both in combination. For example, if the user desires a prioritization only targeting short waiting times, the metric *waiting time* gets maximum weight of 1, whereas the other metrics get 0 weight.

If the user desires a prioritization based on precise execution results, the user is also enabled to select between three different machine learning algorithms, presented in Sect. 2.2, determining the weights based on previous results: evolution strategy [13], genetic algorithm [20], or COBYLA [34]. COBYLA is automatically chosen as default, see Sect. 5. The selected algorithm accesses metric values and histogram intersection values of previously executed compiled circuits of different input circuits and associated quantum computer data, serving as *training data*. In general, the machine learning algorithm repeatedly executes the MCDA method with different weights on the historical metric values, and compares the normalized ranking scores with the normalized histogram intersection values until an optimized set of weights is found [3]. We defined the *objective function* describing the performance of the resulting rankings as the mean square error between the normalized scores of the MCDA method and the ordered histogram intersection values which should be minimized [18]. Finally, it returns the learned metric weights. The weights are presented to the user and can be adjusted.

The weights and the metric values of the compiled circuits to be prioritized are passed to the next phase. If the user wants a prioritization based on short waiting times and precise execution results, both weight sets are passed.

3.5   Prioritization

In the *(5) Prioritization* phase, the chosen MCDA method is now applied to prioritize the recent compiled circuits based on determined weights, as presented in [41]. If the user requested a prioritization combining short waiting times and precise execution results, the chosen MCDA method is applied twice with both weight sets. Then, the well-known Borda count is used to merge the two calculated rankings [6,50]: Given n compiled circuits to be ranked. For each of the two previously calculated rankings, the compiled circuit in the first ranking place gets $n - 1$ points, the one in the second place earns $n - 2$ points, and so forth. The circuit in the last place gets 0 points. Now, the assigned points in both rankings are summed up for each compiled circuit. The descending number of points builds the ranking of compiled circuits and their target quantum computers. Finally, the resulting ranking with metric values is presented to the user.

3.6   Sensitivity Analysis

In the *(6) Sensitivity Analysis* phase, the user can optionally prove the stability of the ranking regarding each of the previously applied weights [16]. We use the method of Li et al. [25] as the weights of the supported MCDA methods have to be normalized between 0 and 1 to serve as input [7,16]. Now, assume the sensitivity of the ranking based on changes of weight ω_k of a given metric have to be examined. For n metrics n weights exist, and let $1 \leq k \leq n$ [25]:

$$\omega_k' = \frac{\gamma_k \omega_k}{\omega_1 + \omega_2 + ... + \gamma_k \omega_k + ... + \omega_n} \tag{1}$$

$$\omega_j' = \frac{\omega_j}{\omega_1 + \omega_2 + ... + \gamma_k \omega_k + ... + \omega_n} \quad \text{with } j = 1, ..., k-1, k+1, ..., n \tag{2}$$

where γ_k defines by which factor ω_k should be changed [25]. For normalization, $\gamma_k \omega_k$ is divided by the sum of all weights, resulting in ω_k', see Eq. (1). Also, all other ω_j therefore have to be divided by the sum of all weights, resulting in ω_j', see Eq. (2). The normalized weights are handed over to the MCDA method returning a ranking that is automatically compared with the initial ranking. This procedure is independently repeated for each metric weight to examine their individual influence on the ranking [25]. We apply this method using different γ_k within a user-defined range, building the prerequisite to be able to answer **RQ 2**. Each ω_k is step-wise increased until the initial ranking changes or an upper bound is reached, and step-wise decreased until the initial ranking changes or a lower bound is reached. All other ω_j are respectively adapted. The user defines the size of the steps and the lower and upper bound. We start with $\gamma_k = 1.01$ and $\gamma_k = 0.99$ to step-wise in- and decrease ω_k as these showed to be valid starting values by the case study (Sect. 5), where we recognized no ranking changes for smaller values. Regarding increase, the greater the γ_k that changes the initial ranking, the less sensitive the ranking is to ω_k. For decrease, the smaller the γ_k that changes the initial ranking, the less sensitive the ranking is to ω_k. If a change in the ranking is detected, it is shown to the user. If Borda count was applied in the previous phase (Sect. 3.5) to fulfill the requirement for precise and fast executions, the weights regarding precise execution results are changed. Then, Borda count is applied to merge each resulting ranking with the previously calculated waiting time ranking, as presented in Sect. 3.5. Finally, the user views detected Borda count rankings that deviate from the initial merged ranking.

3.7   Execution

In the *Execution* phase, the user chooses which of the prioritized compiled circuits should be executed, as described in previous work [39,41,42]. Parallel to the execution on a quantum computer, a compiled circuit is executed on an available simulator if the simulator provides enough computing resources [41]. If the execution results of both backends are available, histogram intersection is applied. Besides the metric values, the measurement values and the histogram intersection value are presented to the user and stored for learning of weights with the supported machine learning algorithms. Finally, the user can prioritize the compiled circuits again using another machine learning algorithm, weight set, or MCDA method, as described in the *(4) Weighting* phase (Sect. 3.4).

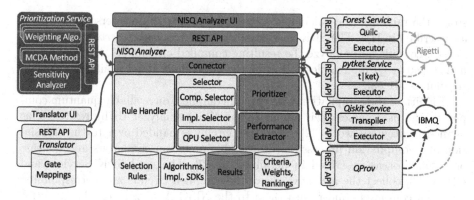

Fig. 2. System architecture to learn weights and prioritize compiled quantum circuits. Extending [41].

4 System Architecture and Prototype

In this section, we present the overall architecture and prototypical implementation of our weight learning and prioritization approach, presented in Sect. 3.

4.1 System Architecture: Behavioral View

Figure 2 gives an overview of our system architecture, which extends previous work [39,41,42]. We, therefore, added additional components to the *NISQ Analyzer* [39] to enable the learning of weights for prioritizing compiled quantum circuits. New components in Fig. 2 are dark, adapted components are middle grey, and components from previous work are light grey [39,41,42]. With its *Translator UI* on the left of Fig. 2, the *Translator* translates the user's input circuit into the formats required by the integrated quantum compilers and their SDKs [42]. The *Prioritization Service* offers weight learning with several supported *Weighting Algorithms* explained in Sect. 2.2. Furthermore, it prioritizes compiled quantum circuits for different quantum computers via various *MCDA Methods* and calculates the Borda count if needed, as described in Sect. 3.5. The *Sensitivity Analyzer* enables sensitivity analyzes on resulting rankings. The Prioritization Service offers an HTTP REST API to be called by the NISQ Analyzer. For this purpose, we expanded the *Connector* of the NISQ Analyzer in the middle of Fig. 2. Furthermore, we extended the *NISQ Analyzer UI* and the HTTP REST API of the NISQ Analyzer to enable the selection between different weighting methods and analyzing resulting rankings, as described in Sect. 3. Besides collecting and extracting metric values, we adapted the *Performance Extractor* from [41] to prepare all stored metric values and measurement results of prior executions for the Weighting Algorithms. Besides the circuit metric values, also the related quantum computer metric values are stored in the *Results* repository as analysis results. The *Prioritizer* [41] invokes the Prioritization Service to learn weights, prioritize compiled circuits, and analyze rankings. It further stores the rankings and calculates corresponding histogram intersection values, as described in [41]. The SDK Services *Forest Service*, *pytket Service*, and *Qiskit Service* compile and analyze the resulting compiled circuits [41,42]. The provenance system *QProv* enables collecting the latest data about available quantum computers [41,53].

To initiate the compilation with several compilers on available quantum computers, the user passes their circuit to the NISQ Analyzer UI by reference, as defined in previous work [42]. Then, the circuit is handed over to the translation and compilation process on all available quantum computers and at least one simulator as described in detail in [41,42]. The used SDK Services and QProv [53] collect the metric values of the compiled circuits and corresponding quantum computers and return them to the NISQ Analyzer [41]. The *Selector* filters executable compiled circuits, stores them with their related circuit and quantum computer metric values, and presents them to the user [39,41].

The user can now initiate the prioritization of the executable compiled circuits by either determining individual metric weights based on SMART [12,41] or choosing the predefined preferences short waiting times, precise execution results, or both. Furthermore, the user is able to select an MCDA Method [41], and, in case of preferring precise execution results, to select one of the supported Weighting Algorithms. The Prioritizer therefore calls the Performance Extractor to prepare all previously executed compilation results, related metric values, and histogram intersection results, which are, then, send to the selected Weighting Algorithm of the Prioritization Service via the Connector. Furthermore, the name of the selected MCDA Method is transferred. The Weighting Algorithm repeatedly calls the chosen MCDA Method to optimize weights, as described in Sect. 3.4. The Prioritization Service, eventually, returns the learned weights to the Prioritizer to store and present them to the user for optional adjustments.

Now, the Prioritizer calls the Performance Extractor to prepare the metric values and stored weights (SMART-based or learned) of the compiled circuits to be ranked and sends them with the Connector to the selected MCDA Method of the Prioritization Service. Thereby, the Prioritizer also informs the Prioritization Service whether Borda count for including waiting time should be applied and attaches another weight set only targeting the *waiting time* metric. The Prioritization Service therefore calls the selected MCDA Method again, with the waiting time weight set and applies Borda count on this and the ranking based on weights targeting precise execution results. The ranking based on defined weights and, if desired, the Borda count ranking are returned to the Prioritizer and are stored. Finally, the requested ranking is presented to the user via the NISQ Analyzer UI.

The user can optionally analyze the sensitivity of the ranking by defining the boundaries and the step sizes for γ, as described in Sect. 3.6. Therefore, the Prioritizer invokes the Performance Extractor again to extract recent metric values and weights, and uses the Connector to send the data and the name of the previously applied MCDA Method to the Sensitivity Analyzer in the Prioritization Service. If Borda count was previously applied, the *waiting time* weight set is again attached. The Sensitivity Analyzer repeatedly invokes the corresponding MCDA Method with the metric values and γ-changed weights for the analyzes. For Borda count, the ranking based on *waiting time* is calculated and merged with the γ-shifted rankings based on learned weights. The resulting analysis data is returned to the NISQ Analyzer and presented via its UI.

With the presented ranking and sensitivity analysis, the user is shown the importance of individual metric values based on the defined preferences and can execute compiled circuits, as presented in previous work [39]. Therefore, the Executor of the SDK Service that previously compiled the circuit is called [41]. As described in [41], also the compiled circuit of a simulator is executed. As soon as both execution results are returned to the NISQ Analyzer, the Prioritizer applies the histogram intersection and stores the result as well as the measurement results for later learning. The results are finally presented to the user. The presented framework is plug-in based such that further MCDA Methods, Weighting Algorithms, formats, metrics, and SDK Services can be integrated.

4.2 Prototype

The Translator, the SDK Services, and the Prioritization Service are implemented in Python using the framework Flask. The Translator UI and the NISQ Analyzer UI are implemented in TypeScript with the framework Angular. Java and Spring Boot are used for the NISQ Analyzer and QProv. The implementation details about the existing components are presented in [39,41,42]. Thereby, the overall implementation of our framework is available open-source[1] [47].

In previous work, we integrated the project Decision Deck [37] to invoke several web services via SOAP, enabling the application of MCDA methods on our data [41]. However, with the new approach to learning weights, the supported machine learning algorithms have to invoke the MCDA methods frequently. The sequential execution via SOAP to call the web services builds a response time problem. Thus, we decided to integrate the MCDA methods locally in the Prioritization Service, where the machine learning algorithms are implemented. We, therefore, used the Python library *pymcdm*[2], offering the application of several MCDA methods. The implementation of the genetic algorithm as a Weighting Algorithm is based on the work of Hassan and Hamada [19]. The implementation of evolution strategy is based on Fogel [13]. For the support of COBYLA, we used the Python library SciPy[3]. The logic of the Sensitivity Analyzer is implemented based on [25].

5   Case Study

This section presents the case study of our framework proposed in Sect. 3. First, we evaluate the ranking performance of each MCDA and weighting method

---

[1] https://youtu.be/luSWN5SRxNg.

[2] https://pypi.org/project/pymcdm/.

[3] https://docs.scipy.org/doc/scipy/reference/optimize.minimize-cobyla.html.

combination targeting prospects of precise execution results. Then, we examine the learned weights of the two best-performing combinations to analyze which metrics influence the execution results the most, answering **RQ 2**. Finally, we present a sensitivity analysis of both of them to investigate the sensitivity of learned weights. An example of a ranking targeting a precise and fast execution for a sample input circuit using the Borda count can be seen in [47].

For the evaluation, we compiled different randomized circuits[4] in addition to the three algorithmic circuits from [41] with the t|ket⟩ compiler [43] and Qiskit Transpiler [2]. To generate randomized circuits, we used the provided function of Qiskit[5] that creates random Clifford Gate sequences whose execution results are the initial state if there have been no errors [27]. Thus, the execution on the simulator is not necessary to obtain the exact measurement result for histogram intersection, which enables a decoupling to quantum simulation limits. We generated random circuits of widths between three and five qubits and depths between 11 and 355 containing single- and two-qubit gates. As compilation targets the free accessible IBMQ 5-qubit quantum computers *ibmq_lima*, *ibmq_quito*, *ibmq_belem*, and *ibmq_bogota*, as well as the *ibmq_qasm_simulator* for histogram intersection, were considered. Our training and test data to learn weights comprises of 228 compiled and executed circuits of 52 input circuits with 8192 shots each. Our sample data can be viewed here [47]. To evaluate the similarity of the target ranking based on the histogram intersection values and a calculated ranking of compilation results, we apply the known *Spearman rank correlation coefficient* [38,44]. As TOPSIS and PROMETHEE II return a total ordering, we apply the following formula to measure the ranking performances [1,38]:

$$\rho = 1 - \frac{6\sum_{i=1}^{n}(R_{X_i} - R_{Y_i})^2}{n(n^2 - 1)} \tag{3}$$

where the both rankings to be compared have n elements [1]. R_{X_i} is the rank of compiled circuit X_i, e.g., in the target ranking based on the histogram intersection values, and R_{Y_i} is the rank of the compiled circuit Y_i, e.g., in the calculated ranking of a MCDA-weighting method combination. If $\rho = 1$ of Eq. (3), the compared rankings are identical. For $\rho = 0$, the rankings do not correlate, and with $\rho = -1$, the rankings are the exact opposite of each other.

We randomly split the sets of circuits to be ranked in 70% training and 30% test data for each MCDA-weighting method combination serving as input for learning which is a common approach [26]. We repeat this procedure 100 times.

5.1 Performance of MCDA-Weighting Method Combinations

In Fig. 3, the average Spearman rank correlation coefficient of all test data over all learning procedures for each MCDA-weighting method combination is

---

[4] https://github.com/UST-QuAntiL/nisq-analyzer-content/tree/paper/optimizing-prioritization/benchmarking.

[5] https://qiskit.org/textbook/ch-quantum-hardware/randomized-benchmarking.html.

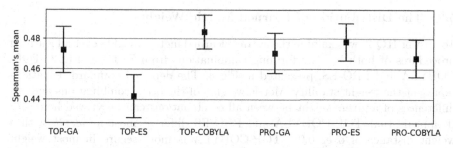

Fig. 3. Mean of Spearman rank correlation coefficient for all MCDA-weighting method combinations with standard errors estimating the average standard deviations.

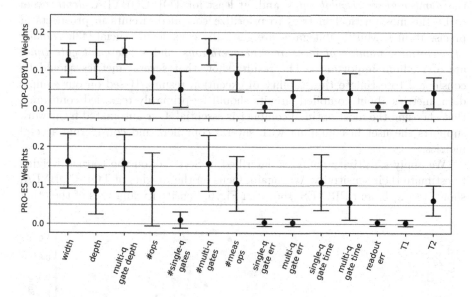

Fig. 4. Average metric weights of TOP-COBYLA (top) and PRO-ES (bottom) with standard deviations representing the weight stability.

presented. The standard errors represent the average standard deviations. Regarding TOPSIS, COBYLA (TOP-COBYLA) calculates with a coefficient of over 0.48 the best overall rankings on average. In combination with evolution strategy (TOP-ES), the worst rankings overall are returned. In contrast, evolution strategy combined with PROMETHEE II (PRO-ES) produces the second best rankings. PROMETHEE II and the genetic algorithm (PRO-GA), PROMETHEE II and COBYLA (PRO-COBYLA), and TOPSIS and genetic algorithm (TOP-GA) present similar performances. All combinations have a similar error range. In general, PROMEHTEE II appears to perform better in our approach.

5.2   The Distribution of Learned Metric Weights

To answer **RQ 2**, we examine the average learned metric weights over all learning procedures of both best performing combinations from Sect. 5.1, Fig. 3, TOP-COBYLA and PRO-ES, presented in Fig. 4. The depicted standard deviations represent the weight stability. Metric weights of the other combinations and the differences of a given weight between all combinations can be viewed here [47]. It appears that TOP-COBYLA and PRO-ES differ at most for *depth* with a weight distance of over 0.05. TOP-COBYLA is more secure in most weight values in terms of standard deviations compared to PRO-ES. In general, *width*, *multi-qubit gate depth*, i.e., the maximum sequence of multi-qubit gates, and the *number of multi-qubit gates*, and, at least for TOP-COBYLA, *depth*, seem to be the most critical metrics to prioritize compiled circuits in prospects of precise results. Multi-qubit gates are generally considered crucial [43]. *Number of operations*, *number of measurement operations*, and *single-qubit gate times* are of medium importance. The results show that several metrics should be considered to estimate the stability of execution results. Based on our sample data, metrics about compiled circuits should be primarily regarded confirming that choosing the most optimal compiler is essential. Our automated framework supports the user in compiling with several compilers and considering several metrics.

We apply sensitivity analyzes described in Sect. 3.6, on the learned weights to estimate their sensitivity. We, again, focus on the weights of TOP-COBYLA, shown in Fig. 5, and PRO-ES, shown in Fig. 6. Sensitivity analyzes of the other

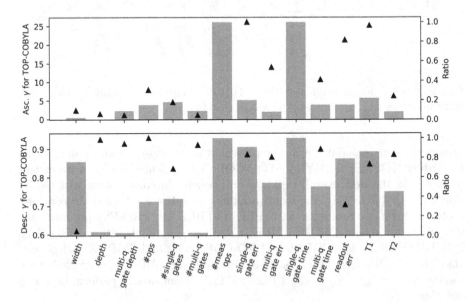

Fig. 5. Sensitivity Analysis on average metric weights of TOP-COBYLA with increasing (top) and decreasing (bottom) γ (triangles) and ratios (bars).

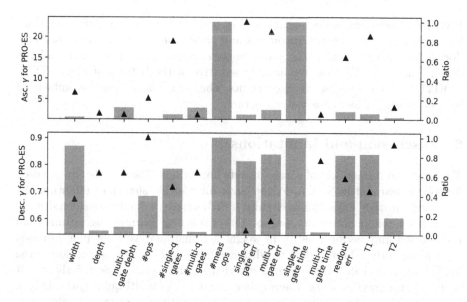

Fig. 6. Sensitivity Analysis on average metric weights of PRO-ES with increasing (top) and decreasing (bottom) γ (triangles) and ratios (bars).

combinations can be viewed here [47]. We set the lower bound for γ to 0.99^{500} such that the normalized weight comes close to 0, resulting in a minor influence of the metric on the ranking compared to the others. The upper bound is set to 1.01^{500} such that the normalized weight comes close to 1, resulting in a major influence of the considered metric compared to the others. We set the step size to 0.01. Thus, the respective weight is multiplicatively in- and decreased by 1% in each step, allowing a fine granular coverage inside the bounds. Figure 5 and Fig. 6 present the mean values of γ for which, on average, a changed ranking was detected for the 100 weight sets of all 100 learning procedures with TOP-COBYLA and PRO-ES. The lower γ is when increasing a metric weight (Fig. 5/Fig. 6 (top)), the more sensitive the metric is. Reversed for a γ when decreasing a weight (Fig. 5/Fig. 6 (bottom)), the lower γ, the more insensitive is the respective metric. A bar in Fig. 5/Fig. 6 represents the frequency ratio a γ was found that changed the initial ranking regarding the related metric overall 100 weight sets. With a ratio equal to 0, a value for γ was found in all 100 weight sets for the given weight. With a ratio equal to 1, no change was detected within the bounds. It appears that the metrics with high weights in Fig. 4, such as *multi-qubit gate depth* and *number of multi-qubit gates*, are more sensitive and have an appropriately low ratio. Even minor adjustments in their weights and the opposite adjustments of the other weights change the rankings. The *depth* and *multi-qubit gate error* of PRO-ES in Fig. 6 are more insensitive regarding a decreasing γ, and *number of single-qubit gates* regarding an increasing γ, as their average weights are smaller compared to TOP-COBYLA in Fig. 5. *Multi-qubit gate depth* and *number of multi-qubit gates* are more insensitive with

PRO-ES considering a decreasing γ (Fig. 6 (bottom)). The weight adaptions for *number of measurement operations* and *single-qubit gate time* have not produced any changes within the given bounds. *Single-qubit gate error* and the decoherence time *T1* seem remarkably sensitive at the bottom of Fig. 5 (TOP-COBYLA), even with low average weights. The detection of a ranking influenced by a decreasing γ for these metrics is rare.

6   Discussion and Limitations

The proposed framework, of course, has its limitations. The sample circuits used for weight learning in Sect. 5 do not cover all possible shapes of quantum circuits, e.g., further algorithmic circuits. Furthermore, we only considered gate-based five-qubit quantum computers. Other machine learning algorithms than the selected may perform better in weight learning; however, our plug-in-based system supports adding other weighting methods. Also, the set of supported MCDA methods can be extended. Nevertheless, the results of Sect. 5 show that especially the metrics about the number and depth of multi-qubit gates, known for their high error rates, have to be considered with respect to, e.g., the qubit connectivity of the quantum computer when targeting precise execution results, which is consistent with other work [43]. We do not consider monetary metrics, as we currently access free-of-charge quantum computers. However, further metrics and SDK Services can be added to our framework.

7   Related Work

MCDA methods are applied in several fields such as e-commerce [6], sports [29], and sustainable energy [50], as stated in previous work [41]. In [6], a framework is presented that compromises the rankings of multiple MCDA methods using the Copeland method. They present a sensitivity analysis of the resulting rankings to evaluate their approach and compared the different rankings. An weighting method is used that determines weights by considering actual metric values. Thus, no learning of weights based on previous results is shown. Other weighting methods are presented by several approaches that calculate weights based on experts' knowledge, metric values of alternatives to be ranked, or both in combination [38,49,50]. However, the approaches do not consider historical data as a basis to learn weights. The framework proposed in [14] combines several weighting methods to a single method. They evaluate it using TOPSIS and PROMETHEE II. Nevertheless, this work does not provide a prototype that enables a dynamical selection between several MCDA and weighting methods.

Several approaches train weights based on available data sets in the context of MCDA. Olson [29] analyzes the ranking performance of TOPSIS with different weighting approaches such as linear regression. The weights based on regression were trained and applied on a test data set. The work presents that accurate weights are important for precise ranking results. Luu et al. [26] propose combining multiple linear regression to define weights with TOPSIS for ranking. In [4], the combination of logical regression for determining weights and PROMETHEE for ranking is presented. The work of Mojtahedi and Oo [28] proposes to determine weights with bootstrap resampling based on small data sets in the context of flood risk analysis. The weights are then used with TOPSIS. Orak et al. [30] present an approach that uses an artificial neuronal network to define weights and pass them as input for TOPSIS. However, these approaches only considered single MCDA methods and their focus was not the implementation of an automated plug-in-based framework offering several MCDA methods and weighting algorithms.

Regarding the area of quantum computing, approaches exist that automatically select or recommend quantum computers based, e.g., on their availability. For example, Ravi et al. [36] present a scheduling framework for executions on quantum computers. They use a prediction model for the scheduling that considers quantum computer fidelities and waiting times. However, as described in [41], the user cannot define individual requirements. The work of Garcia-Alonso et al. [15] introduces a Quantum API Gateway that recommends quantum computers based on the number of qubits, estimated costs, and estimated waiting time. Also, Grossi et al. [17] propose a framework that enables the scheduling of execution jobs for quantum computers based on available qubits and the size of the queues, as discussed in [41]. However, both approaches do not consider further technical properties about compiled circuits and quantum computers regarding precise results and do not enable the user to define their requirements.

8 Conclusion and Future Work

We extended the framework from previous work [41] that prioritizes compiled circuits of a quantum circuit for several quantum computers by (i) learning preferences based on previous circuit executions using three different machine learning algorithms. The user can thereby (ii) select between defining own or predefined preferences regarding short waiting times and precise execution results, answering **RQ 1**. Furthermore, (iii) sensitivity analyzes can be applied to calculated rankings of compiled circuits. To answer **RQ 2**, we presented a case study where we (i) compared the ranking performances of the different MCDA-weighting method combinations, (ii) examined the metric weights of the best-performing combinations, and (iii) applied sensitivity analyzes on the learned weights. As expected, the case study showed that especially the *number* and *depth of multi-qubit gates* influence the execution results. Nevertheless, both metrics have to be considered jointly with, e.g., the *width* and *depth* to estimate the quality of execution results in advance. The case study also confirmed that the comparison of different quantum compilers is crucial as their compilation results have major impact on the executions on quantum computers [42].

In the future, we want to use further circuits and quantum computers to consider if the learned weights change. We also plan to support additional MCDA methods and weighting methods to examine their ranking performances. Furthermore, we want to support monetary metrics as they are crucial for accessing quantum computers on a fee-base. Finally, an integration of the NISQ Analyzer into QHAna [5] is intended to support a proper selection of quantum computers when comparing classical algorithms with their quantum counterparts.

Acknowledgements. This work was partially funded by the BMWK project *PlanQK* (01MK20005N).

References

1. Dodge, Y.: Spearman rank correlation coefficient. In: Dodge, Y. (ed.) The Concise Encyclopedia of Statistics, pp. 502–505. Springer, New York (2008). https://doi.org/10.1007/978-0-387-32833-1_379
2. Aleksandrowicz, G., et al.: Qiskit: An Open-source Framework for Quantum Computing (2019). https://doi.org/10.5281/zenodo.2562111
3. Alpaydin, E.: Machine Learning: The New AI. MIT Press, Cambridge (2016)
4. Balugani, E., Lolli, F., Butturi, M.A., Ishizaka, A., Sellitto, M.A.: Logistic regression for criteria weight elicitation in PROMETHEE-based ranking methods. In: Ahram, T., Karwowski, W., Vergnano, A., Leali, F., Taiar, R. (eds.) IHSI 2020. AISC, vol. 1131, pp. 474–479. Springer, Cham (2020). https://doi.org/10.1007/978-3-030-39512-4_74
5. Barzen, J.: From Digital Humanities to Quantum Humanities: Potentials and Applications (2022, to appear). https://doi.org/10.48550/ARXIV.2103.11825
6. Bączkiewicz, A., Kizielewicz, B., Shekhovtsov, A., Wątróbski, J., Sałabun, W.: Methodical aspects of MCDM based E-commerce recommender system. J. Theor. Appl. Electron. Commer. Res. **16**(6), 2192–2229 (2021). https://doi.org/10.3390/jtaer16060122
7. Bilbao-Terol, A., Arenas-Parra, M., Cañal-Fernández, V., Antomil-Ibias, J.: Using TOPSIS for assessing the sustainability of government bond funds. Omega **49**, 1–17 (2014). https://doi.org/10.1016/j.omega.2014.04.005
8. Bös, J.: Numerical optimization of the thickness distribution of three-dimensional structures with respect to their structural acoustic properties. Struct. Multidiscip. Optim. **32**(1), 12–30 (2006). https://doi.org/10.1007/s00158-005-0560-y
9. Brans, J.-P., Mareschal, B.: Promethee methods. In: Figueira, J., Greco, S., Ehrgott, M. (eds.) Multiple Criteria Decision Analysis: State of the Art Surveys. ISORMS, vol. 78, pp. 163–186. Springer, New York (2005). https://doi.org/10.1007/0-387-23081-5_5
10. Choi, K., Jang, D.H., Kang, S.I., Lee, J.H., Chung, T.K., Kim, H.S.: Hybrid algorithm combing genetic algorithm with evolution strategy for antenna design. IEEE Trans. Magn. **52**(3), 1–4 (2016). https://doi.org/10.1109/TMAG.2015.2486043
11. Cowtan, A., Dilkes, S., Duncan, R., Krajenbrink, A., Simmons, W., Sivarajah, S.: On the qubit routing problem. In: 14th Conference on the Theory of Quantum Computation, Communication and Cryptography (TQC 2019). Leibniz International Proceedings in Informatics (LIPIcs), vol. 135, pp. 5:1–5:32. Schloss Dagstuhl-Leibniz-Zentrum fuer Informatik (2019). https://doi.org/10.4230/LIPIcs.TQC.2019.5
12. Edwards, W.: How to use multiattribute utility measurement for social decision-making. IEEE Trans. Syst. Man Cybern. **7**(5), 326–340 (1977). https://doi.org/10.1109/TSMC.1977.4309720

13. Fogel, D.: An introduction to simulated evolutionary optimization. IEEE Trans. Neural Networks **5**(1), 3–14 (1994). https://doi.org/10.1109/72.265956
14. Gao, R., Nam, H.O., Ko, W.I., Jang, H.: National options for a sustainable nuclear energy system: MCDM evaluation using an improved integrated weighting approach. Energies **10**(12) (2017). https://doi.org/10.3390/en10122017
15. Garcia-Alonso, J., Rojo, J., Valencia, D., Moguel, E., Berrocal, J., Murillo, J.M.: Quantum software as a service through a quantum API gateway. IEEE Internet Comput. **26**(1), 34–41 (2022). https://doi.org/10.1109/MIC.2021.3132688
16. Geldermann, J., Lerche, N.: Leitfaden zur Anwendung von Methoden der multikriteriellen Entscheidungsunterstützung. Promethee, Methode (2014)
17. Grossi, M., et al.: A serverless cloud integration for quantum computing (2021)
18. Guo, M., Zhang, Q., Liao, X., Chen, F.Y., Zeng, D.D.: A hybrid machine learning framework for analyzing human decision-making through learning preferences. Omega **101**, 102263 (2021). https://doi.org/10.1016/j.omega.2020.102263
19. Hassan, M., Hamada, M.: Genetic algorithm approaches for improving prediction accuracy of multi-criteria recommender systems. Int. J. Comput. Intell. Syst. **11**, 146–162 (2018). https://doi.org/10.2991/ijcis.11.1.12
20. Holland, J.H.: Genetic algorithms and the optimal allocation of trials. SIAM J. Comput. **2**(2), 88–105 (1973). https://doi.org/10.1137/0202009
21. Hwang, C.L., Yoon, K.: Methods for multiple attribute decision making. In: Hwang, C.-L., Yoon, K. (eds.) Multiple Attribute Decision Making, pp. 58–191. Springer, Heidelberg (1981). https://doi.org/10.1007/978-3-642-48318-9_3
22. LaRose, R.: Overview and comparison of gate level quantum software platforms. Quantum **3**, 130 (2019). https://doi.org/10.22331/q-2019-03-25-130
23. Leymann, F., Barzen, J.: The bitter truth about gate-based quantum algorithms in the NISQ era. Quantum Sci. Technol. **5**(4), 1–28 (2020). https://doi.org/10.1088/2058-9565/abae7d
24. Leymann, F., Barzen, J., Falkenthal, M., Vietz, D., Weder, B., Wild, K.: Quantum in the cloud: application potentials and research opportunities. In: Proceedings of the 10th International Conference on Cloud Computing and Services Science (CLOSER 2020), pp. 9–24. SciTePress (2020)
25. Li, P., Qian, H., Wu, J., Chen, J.: Sensitivity analysis of TOPSIS method in water quality assessment: I. Sensitivity to the parameter weights. Environ. Monit. Assess. **185**(3), 2453–2461 (2013). https://doi.org/10.1007/s10661-012-2723-9
26. Luu, C., von Meding, J., Mojtahedi, M.: Analyzing Vietnam's national disaster loss database for flood risk assessment using multiple linear regression-topsis. Int. J. Disaster Risk Reduct. **40**, 101153 (2019). https://doi.org/10.1016/j.ijdrr.2019.101153
27. Magesan, E., et al.: Efficient measurement of quantum gate error by interleaved randomized benchmarking. Phys. Rev. Lett. **109**, 080505 (2012). https://doi.org/10.1103/PhysRevLett.109.080505
28. Mojtahedi, S., Oo, B.: Coastal buildings and infrastructure flood risk analysis using multi-attribute decision-making. J. Flood Risk Manag. **9**(1), 87–96 (2016). https://doi.org/10.1111/jfr3.12120
29. Olson, D.: Comparison of weights in topsis models. Math. Comput. Model. **40**(7), 721–727 (2004). https://doi.org/10.1016/j.mcm.2004.10.003
30. Orak, S., Arapoğlu, R.A., Sofuoğlu, M.A.: Development of an ANN-based decision-making method for determining optimum parameters in turning operation. Soft. Comput. **22**(18), 6157–6170 (2017). https://doi.org/10.1007/s00500-017-2682-8
31. Pathak, S. (ed.): Intelligent Manufacturing. MFMT, Springer, Cham (2021). https://doi.org/10.1007/978-3-030-50312-3

32. Pellow-Jarman, A., Sinayskiy, I., Pillay, A., Petruccione, F.: A comparison of various classical optimizers for a variational quantum linear solver. Quantum Inf. Process. **20**(6), 1–14 (2021). https://doi.org/10.1007/s11128-021-03140-x

33. Powell, M.: A view of algorithms for optimization without derivatives. Math. TODAY **43** (2007)

34. Powell, M.J.D.: A direct search optimization method that models the objective and constraint functions by linear interpolation. In: Gomez, S., Hennart, J.P. (eds.) Advances in Optimization and Numerical Analysis, pp. 51–67. Springer, Dordrecht (1994). https://doi.org/10.1007/978-94-015-8330-5_4

35. Preskill, J.: Quantum computing in the NISQ era and beyond. Quantum **2**, 79 (2018). https://doi.org/10.22331/q-2018-08-06-79

36. Ravi, G.S., Smith, K.N., Murali, P., Chong, F.T.: Adaptive job and resource management for the growing quantum cloud (2021)

37. Ros, J.C.: Introduction to Decision Deck-Diviz: Examples User Guide. Departament d'Enginyeria Informàtica i Matemàtiques (2011)

38. Sałabun, W., Wątróbski, J., Shekhovtsov, A.: Are MCDA methods benchmarkable? A comparative study of TOPSIS, VIKOR, COPRAS, and PROMETHEE II methods. Symmetry **12**(9) (2020). https://doi.org/10.3390/sym12091549

39. Salm, M., Barzen, J., Breitenbücher, U., Leymann, F., Weder, B., Wild, K.: The NISQ analyzer: automating the selection of quantum computers for quantum algorithms. In: Dustdar, S. (ed.) SummerSOC 2020. CCIS, vol. 1310, pp. 66–85. Springer, Cham (2020). https://doi.org/10.1007/978-3-030-64846-6_5

40. Salm, M., Barzen, J., Leymann, F., Weder, B.: About a criterion of successfully executing a circuit in the NISQ era: what $wd \ll 1/\epsilon_{eff}$ really means. In: Proceedings of the 1st ACM SIGSOFT International Workshop on Architectures and Paradigms for Engineering Quantum Software (APEQS 2020), pp. 10–13. ACM (2020). https://doi.org/10.1145/3412451.3428498

41. Salm, M., Barzen, J., Leymann, F., Weder, B.: Prioritization of compiled quantum circuits for different quantum computers. In: Proceedings of the 2022 IEEE International Conference on Software Analysis, Evolution and Reengineering (SANER 2022), pp. 1258–1265. IEEE (2022). https://doi.org/10.1109/SANER53432.2022.00150

42. Salm, M., Barzen, J., Leymann, F., Weder, B., Wild, K.: Automating the comparison of quantum compilers for quantum circuits. In: Barzen, J. (ed.) SummerSOC 2021. CCIS, vol. 1429, pp. 64–80. Springer, Cham (2021). https://doi.org/10.1007/978-3-030-87568-8_4

43. Sivarajah, S., Dilkes, S., Cowtan, A., Simmons, W., Edgington, A., Duncan, R.: t|ket⟩: a retargetable compiler for NISQ devices. Quantum Sci. Technol. **6**, 014003 (2020). https://doi.org/10.1088/2058-9565/ab8e92

44. Spearman, C.: The proof and measurement of association between two things. In: Studies in Individual Differences: The Search for Intelligence, pp. 45–58 (1961). https://doi.org/10.1037/11491-005

45. Swain, M.J., Ballard, D.H.: Color indexing. Int. J. Comput. Vision **7**(1), 11–32 (1991). https://doi.org/10.1007/BF00130487

46. Tannu, S.S., Qureshi, M.K.: Not all qubits are created equal: a case for variability-aware policies for nisq-era quantum computers. In: Proceedings of the Twenty-Fourth International Conference on Architectural Support for Programming Languages and Operating Systems, ASPLOS 2019, pp. 987–999. ACM (2019). https://doi.org/10.1145/3297858.3304007

47. University of Stuttgart: NISQ Analyzer Content Repository (2022). https://github. com/UST-QuAntiL/nisq-analyzer-content/tree/paper/optimizing-prioritization/ prioritization-based-on-learned-weights
48. Vietz, D., Barzen, J., Leymann, F., Wild, K.: On decision support for quantum application developers: categorization, comparison, and analysis of existing technologies. In: Paszynski, M., Kranzlmüller, D., Krzhizhanovskaya, V.V., Dongarra, J.J., Sloot, P.M.A. (eds.) ICCS 2021. LNCS, vol. 12747, pp. 127–141. Springer, Cham (2021). https://doi.org/10.1007/978-3-030-77980-1_10
49. Wang, J.J., Jing, Y.Y., Zhang, C.F., Zhang, X.T., Shi, G.H.: Integrated evaluation of distributed triple-generation systems using improved grey incidence approach. Energy **33**(9), 1427–1437 (2008). https://doi.org/10.1016/j.energy.2008.04.008
50. Wang, J.J., Jing, Y.Y., Zhang, C.F., Zhao, J.H.: Review on multi-criteria decision analysis aid in sustainable energy decision-making. Renew. Sustain. Energy Rev. **13**(9), 2263–2278 (2009). https://doi.org/10.1016/j.rser.2009.06.021
51. Wątróbski, J., Jankowski, J., Ziemba, P., Karczmarczyk, A., Zioło, M.: Generalised framework for multi-criteria method selection. Omega **86**, 107–124 (2019). https:// doi.org/10.1016/j.omega.2018.07.004
52. Wątróbski, J., Jankowski, J., Ziemba, P., Karczmarczyk, A., Zioło, M.: MCDA Method Selection Tool (2021). http://mcda.it
53. Weder, B., Barzen, J., Leymann, F., Salm, M., Wild, K.: QProv: a provenance system for quantum computing. IET Quantum Commun. **2**(4), 171–181 (2021). https://doi.org/10.1049/qtc2.12012
54. Wundrack, P.: Quantenunterstütztes Clustering mit hybriden neuronalen Netzen. Master's thesis (2021). http://dx.doi.org/10.18419/opus-11422

Author Index

Printed in the United States
by Baker & Taylor Publisher Services

Printed in the United States
by Baker & Taylor Publisher Services